Philoponus

*On Aristotle
Categories 6–15*

Ancient Commentators on Aristotle

GENERAL EDITORS: Richard Sorabji, Honorary Fellow, Wolfson College, University of Oxford, and Emeritus Professor, King's College London, UK; and Michael Griffin, Assistant Professor, Departments of Philosophy and Classics, University of British Columbia, Canada.

This prestigious series translates the extant ancient Greek philosophical commentaries on Aristotle. Written mostly between 200 and 600 AD, the works represent the classroom teaching of the Aristotelian and Neoplatonic schools in a crucial period during which pagan and Christian thought were reacting to each other. The translation in each volume is accompanied by an introduction, comprehensive commentary notes, bibliography, glossary of translated terms and a subject index. Making these key philosophical works accessible to the modern scholar, this series fills an important gap in the history of European thought.

A webpage for the Ancient Commentators Project is maintained at ancientcommentators.org.uk and readers are encouraged to consult the site for details about the series as well as for addenda and corrigenda to published volumes.

Philoponus

*On Aristotle
Categories 6–15*

Translated by
Michael Share

BLOOMSBURY ACADEMIC
LONDON • NEW YORK • OXFORD • NEW DELHI • SYDNEY

BLOOMSBURY ACADEMIC
Bloomsbury Publishing Plc
50 Bedford Square, London, WC1B 3DP, UK
1385 Broadway, New York, NY 10018, USA
29 Earlsfort Terrace, Dublin 2, Ireland

BLOOMSBURY, BLOOMSBURY ACADEMIC and the Diana logo are trademarks of
Bloomsbury Publishing Plc

First published in Great Britain 2020
This paperback edition published in 2022

Copyright © Michael Share, 2020

Michael Share has asserted his right under the Copyright, Designs and Patents Act, 1988, to be identified as Author of this work.

For legal purposes the Acknowledgements below constitute an extension of this copyright page.

All rights reserved. No part of this publication may be reproduced or transmitted in any form or by any means, electronic or mechanical, including photocopying, recording, or any information storage or retrieval system, without prior permission in writing from the publishers.

Bloomsbury Publishing Plc does not have any control over, or responsibility for, any third-party websites referred to or in this book. All internet addresses given in this book were correct at the time of going to press. The author and publisher regret any inconvenience caused if addresses have changed or sites have ceased to exist, but can accept no responsibility for any such changes.

A catalogue record for this book is available from the British Library.

Library of Congress Cataloging-in-Publication Data
Names: Philoponus, John, active 6th century, author. | Share, Michael John, translator.
Title: Philoponus on Aristotle Categories 6–15 / translated by Michael Share.
Other titles: Ancient commentators on Aristotle.
Description: London : Bloomsbury Academic, 2019. | Series: Ancient commentators on Aristotle
Identifiers: LCCN 2019011798| ISBN 9781350112674 (hb) | ISBN 9781350113145 (epub)
Subjects: LCSH: Aristotle. Categoriae—Early works to 1800. | Categories (Philosophy)—Early works to 1800.
Classification: LCC B438 .P453 2019 | DDC 160—dc23 LC record available at
https://lccn.loc.gov/2019011798

ISBN:	HB:	978-1-3501-1267-4
	PB:	978-1-3501-9316-1
	ePDF:	978-1-3501-1313-8
	eBook:	978-1-3501-1314-5

Series: Ancient Commentators on Aristotle

Typeset by RefineCatch Limited, Bungay, Suffolk

To find out more about our authors and books visit www.bloomsbury.com and sign up for our newsletters.

Acknowledgements

The present translations have been made possible by generous and imaginative funding from the following sources: the National Endowment for the Humanities, Divison of Research Programs, an independent federal agency of the USA; the Leverhulme Trust; the British Academy; the Jowett Copyright Trustees; the Royal Society (UK); Centro Internazionale A. Beltrame di Storia dello Spazio e del Tempo (Padua); Mario Mignucci; Liverpool University; the Leventis Foundation; the Arts and Humanities Research Council; Gresham College; the Esmée Fairbairn Charitable Trust; the Henry Brown Trust; Mr and Mrs N. Egon; the Netherlands Organisation for Scientific Research (NOW/GW); the Ashdown Trust; the Lorne Thyssen Research Fund for Ancient World Topics at Wolfson College, Oxford; Dr Victoria Solomonides, the Cultural Attaché of the Greek Embassy in London; and the Social Sciences and Humanities Research Council of Canada. The editors wish to thank John Dillon, Paolo Fait, Sebastian Gertz, Andrew Smith, Sten Ebbesen for their comments; Dawn Sellars for preparing the volume for press; and Alice Wright, Publisher at Bloomsbury Academic, for her diligence in seeing each volume of the series to press.

Contents

Conventions	vi
Abbreviations	vii
Introduction	1
Departures from Busse's Text	25
Translation	27
Notes	137
English–Greek Glossary	183
Greek–English Index	191
Subject Index	213

Conventions

[...] Square brackets enclose words or phrases that have been added to the translation for purposes of clarity.

(...) Round brackets, besides being used for ordinary parentheses contain transliterated Greek words.

Abbreviations

Ackrill	J.L. Ackrill (tr.), *Aristotle's Categories and De Interpretatione*, Oxford: Clarendon Press, 1963.
Ammonius (or Amm.)	Ammonius *in Cat.*
Busse	A. Busse, *Philoponi (olim Ammonii) in Aristotelis Categorias Commentarium*, CAG 13.1, Berlin: Reimer, 1898.
CAG	*Commentaria in Aristotelem Graeca*, 23 vols, Berlin: Reimer, 1882–1909.
Cohen and Matthews	S. Marc Cohen and Gareth B. Matthews, *Ammonius, On Aristotle's Categories*, London: Duckworth, 1991.
Heath	Thomas L. Heath, *The Thirteen Books of Euclid's Elements: Translated from the Text of Heiberg*, 2nd edn, Cambridge: Cambridge University Press, 1926.
LSJ	H.G. Liddell and R. Scott (comps), *A Greek-English Lexicon*, rev. H. Jones; with a New Supplement, 9th edn, Oxford: Clarendon Press, 1996.
Lampe	G.W.H. Lampe (ed.), *A Patristic Greek Lexicon*, Oxford: Clarendon Press, 1961.
Philoponus (or Philop.)	Philoponus *in Cat.*
Sirkel, Tweedale and Harris	Riin Sirkel, Martin Tweedale, and John Harris, *Philoponus, On Aristotle Categories 1–5*; with Daniel King, *Philoponus, A Treatise Concerning the Whole and the Parts*, London: Bloomsbury, 2015.
TLG	*Thesaurus Linguae Graecae.*

Introduction

Four of Philoponus' seven Aristotelian commentaries are described in their titles as his notes from Ammonius' seminars.[1] The present work is not one of these,[2] but it so happens that we have an anonymously recorded set of notes from Ammonius' lectures on the *Categories* from which much in Philoponus' commentary appears to be taken, at times word for word.[3] The closeness of the two commentaries has long been appreciated,[4] but it was not until 2001, when Concetta Luna made a detailed comparison of twenty-one pages of Philoponus with the corresponding part of Ammonius, that anyone looked very closely at the relationship between them.[5] Luna concluded from the nature of the parallels between the two commentaries that Philoponus' commentary is an amplified version of the anonymously recorded commentary in the written form in which we have it and further demonstrated that the amplifications are numerous, in fact thirteen substantial ones in the twenty-one pages she examined.[6] In principle some or all of the additions to the anonymous commentary could have been made by Ammonius himself, but, as Richard Sorabji argues,[7] it is much more likely that they were made by Philoponus.

An examination of the part of Philoponus translated in the present volume reinforces Luna's findings. On the one hand there is, as anticipated, a considerable amount of verbal agreement between the two commentaries and I have identified about eighty pairs of passages showing such agreement.[8] Very few of them are word for word the same throughout but all show significant agreement. Most of these passages are quite short, the longest being twenty-seven lines in length and only five of them ten or more, and their average length is about four lines. The total number of lines involved is 329, which amounts to about 9 per cent of Philoponus and about 24 per cent of Ammonius.[9] And the dependence of Philoponus on Ammonius goes beyond this. It was of course difficult to establish clear-cut criteria for determining just what constituted 'significant verbal agreement' and there were many near misses. In fact I identified forty-five of these. And, apart from verbal agreement, the general approach, the choice of topics and issues for comment, and the interpretations adopted in Philoponus are often clearly influenced by Ammonius. On the other hand Philoponus' amplifications are very considerable. The much greater length of his commentary is enough to make this clear. The part of Philoponus translated here covers 122 *CAG* pages and the corresponding part of Ammonius only fifty-one. Moreover, Philoponus has about three more lines per page on average, so Ammonius is actually equivalent to only about forty-six pages of Ammonius. Some of this additional bulk can be explained by Philoponus' greater wordiness. Ammonius is normally very economical in his explanations whereas Philoponus will often add extra detail and multiply examples. However, much of it consists of what is essentially new material. In fact I have identified a large number of such additions or major expansions, which I shall now list.[10]

1. He gives additional reasons for Aristotle's treating quantity second after substance (83,6–84,4).
2. He adds a long excursus on line, surface, and body (84,9–86,10). (But he omits Ammonius' report that 'some people' say that there are really only three species of quality at the corresponding point.)
3. He adds the argument that place and time are not continuous quantities in their own right (86,12–87,20).
4. He adds an alternative explanation for Aristotle's not counting motion as a species of the continuous (87,25–32).
5. He adds a stone as an example of a thing with internal parts with relative position (88,22–4).
6. Unlike Ammonius (or Aristotle himself), he includes speech among things that exhibit natural order (89,7–9).
7. He adds a statement that inner language is, if anything, a quality of the soul (90,5–7).
8. He adds comments on the common boundary at which the parts of the body meet (91,4–15).
9. He adds an explanation of why quantity can't be defined and a description of how Aristotle looks for its distinctive feature as a substitute (93,17–28).
10. He greatly expands on the statement that large and small and many and few are relatives (94,10–31).
11. He adds a lengthy discussion of why there are no indefinite quantities (95,9–96,22).
12. He adds a lengthy excursus on (i) the correct use of large and small, long and short, and many and few, and (ii) whether Aristotle uses many and few consistently (98,4–99,15).

13. He expands Ammonius' six lines on the non-occurrence of up and down in nature by a further twenty-one lines (99,26–100,15).
14. He adds the point that quantities are receptive of contraries and counters some supposed exceptions to the rule that quantities have no contraries (101,9–19).
15. He adds a paragraph on the possibility of calling the category 'the relative' in the singular (103,5–17).
16. He adds additional examples. And he seems to understand the interpretation of relatives reported by Ammonius differently from Ammonius himself (103,18–31).
17. He expands Ammonius' account of Protagorean relativism, adding extra examples and referring to Aristotle's refutation of it as well as to Plato's (103,31–104,25).
18. He adds that relatives have no being of their own but occur in other categories and that they have been likened to suckers or to mutually supporting logs (104,28–36).
19. He adds a paragraph on the verbal expression of relationship, which Ammonius only deals with later (105,19–29).
20. He adds an analysis of the difference between positions and items in the category 'being positioned' (107,7–18).
21. He criticizes Aristotle for saying that virtue and vice and knowledge and ignorance are relatives. They would be relatives under the first definition of relatives, but under it items in the nine categories of accidents would all be relative to substances (108,31–109,26).
22. He claims that the statement that the equal and the unequal admit of degrees is either a mistake on Aristotle's part or an interpolation (110,15–111,8).
23. He has a defence of the practice of coining a name for the correlate of a relative that lacks a named correlate (113,13–114,3).
24. He criticizes Aristotle for using head and rudder as examples of relatives (114,7–29).
25. He adds an explanation based on the premiss that relations have no separate existence but occur in the other categories (116,21–7).
26. He adds the example of Thales and the lunar eclipse (118,7–25).
27. He has extra examples and discussion (119,2–25).
28. He adds (doubtfully relevant) geometrical information (120,9–24).
29. He expands Ammonius' four lines of explanation to twenty (121,20–122,9).

30. He adds the examples of Thales and the lunar eclipse (again) and of the squaring of the circle and proposes a solution to a well-known legal puzzle (123,20–124,14).
31. Contrary to Aristotle and Ammonius, he argues that the first definition of relatives makes the parts of primary substances as well as those of secondary substances relatives (125,30–126,15).
32. He says that Aristotle uses *reductio ad absurdum* to discredit the first definition of relatives and provides a lengthy example of such an argument (126,18–129,5).
33. Unlike Ammonius, he is firmly of the opinion that the first definition of relatives makes a head a relative and believes that this is the belief of Aristotle (129,13–20).
34. He says that Aristotle includes the *definiendum* in the definition and explains why he does so (130,22–31).
35. He adds an additional interpretation (131,20–29).
36. Unlike Ammonius, he recapitulates the reasons (adding an additional one) why quality had a claim to come before relatives and the explanation of why it hasn't (133,9–21).
37. In explaining 'state' (*hexis*), he cites the usage of cognate words (134,29–135,1).
38. He again cites the usage of a cognate word (135,14–19).
39. He adds an explanation of the terms 'perfective' and 'harmful' (135,20–30).
40. He argues that one subdivision of Ammonius' division is unnecessary (135,30–136,22).
41. He adds an extra step to Ammonius' division of quality and assigns one of the two new subdivisions generated to the category being-affected rather than to quality (137,2–7).
42. He adds an explanation of how it is that pallor and the like can be said to have 'gone deep' (137,12–18).
43. He gives a rather different account of 'figure' and 'shape' with some different examples and a different puzzle (137,19–31).
44. He provides a diagram of the division of quality (138).
45. He adds an explanation for the order of the four species of quality (138–139,22).
46. He adds excursuses on types of knowledge and types of virtue (140,23–142,3).
47. He replaces Ammonius' much shorter and quite different discussion of capacity and incapacity with one largely concerned with the difference

between rational and non-rational and human and divine capacities (144,26–147,2).
48. He adds a reference to essential, or substantive, colour (150,7–9).
49. He adds a note on the point, the line, the surface, and the solid as bearers of qualification (152,5–19).
50. Ammonius remarks that the porosity Aristotle describes as positional is artificial and that he defines porous and dense differently in the *Physics*. Philoponus expands Ammonius' account of artificial porosity, giving extra examples (152,24–153,24), and adds a page on natural, or qualitative, porosity as described in the *Physics* (153,25–154,28) and a rebuttal of the suggestion that straightness and crookedness may also be positional rather than qualitative (154,29–156,4).
51. He adds that qualified things may be named homonymously as well as paronymously (157,16–20).
52. He adds that contrariety is particularly associated with quality, even when it is present in other categories (157,25–30).
53. Ammonius argues (briefly) that justice admits of more and less. Philoponus argues that *no* quality as such does, although qualified entities can partake more or less of a quality (158,26–159,24).
54. He adds the argument that for things that are qualified in the same way to be described as more or less so qualified the qualification must admit of the same definition but only loosely (160,6–161,3).
55. He adds the claim that Aristotle's distinctive feature of quality is unsatisfactorily expressed and tweaks it to make it more accurate (161,11–27).
56. He adds a division to show that there are only four categories in the strict sense and that the other six are combinations of them (163,8–16).
57. He adds an argument designed to show that there must be exactly six species of place (164,25–165,17).
58. He adds a scholium on (i) why acting and being-affected are not included under the relatives, (ii) the justification for the section title, and (iii) the concomitants of acting and being-affected (165,22–167,9).
59. He adds a scholium on a remark of Aristotle's that some had cited as evidence that he only acknowledges conceptual genera (167,12–17).
60. Unlike Ammonius, he recapitulates the tripartite division of the *Categories* that was given in the introductory section of the commentary (167,22–168,3).
61. He adds an argument for the authenticity of the third and final part of the *Categories* (168,3–9).

62. Ammonius simply says that privation and state don't change into one another. Philoponus says that state can change to privation and that there is even a sense (described in the *Physics*), in which privation can change to state (168,27–169,2).
63. He adds a rebuttal of the view that contraries are in fact relatives, even though contrariety itself *is* a relative (170,21–9).
64. He adds a scholium on the kind of good that is opposed to bad (170,31–171,15).
65. He gives an account of Aristotle's procedure that has no equivalent in Ammonius (172,1–11).
66. He inserts an extra scholium which includes an account of two senses of per se based on a passage in Aristotle's *Posterior Analytics* (173,3–19).
67. He adds a scholium with examples of per se and accidental contraries (173,22–174,7).
68. He uses lengthier (and different) arguments to show that being deprived or having a state are different from a privation and a state (175,19–176,15).
69. He provides a summary of Aristotle's argument while Ammonius doesn't (177,17–24).
70. He expands Ammonius' three lines on whether blindness can be referred to as the blindness of sight to three *CAG* pages (178,5–180,27).
71. He adds a scholium on 12b21-2 (180,28–181,4).
72. He adds a scholium on 13a22-3 in which he argues that Aristotle is talking about the conventionally good man rather than the perfectly good one (184,3–9).
73. He adds the comment that there may have been cases where the blind recovered their sight by divine intervention (184,17–18).
74. He adds a method, taken from the *Isagoge*, for calculating the possible conjunctions of a given number of terms (184,22–185,2).
75. He adds an amplification of Aristotle's statement that things said without combination, including things opposed in other ways than as affirmation and negation, are neither true nor false, going into the grammatical requirements for true and false statements (185,2–23).
76. He expands Ammonius' ten lines to forty-five and widens the discussion to include (as Aristotle does) state and privation and relatives (186,9–187,24).
77. He adds explanations of how two things can be opposed to one and of how good and bad things are opposed as symmetry and asymmetry and bad things as excess and defect (188,4–17).

78. He adds two possible explanations of the statement in the lemma (189,5–9).
79. He expands on Aristotle's statement that contraries belong to things the same in either genus or species, understanding it differently from Ammonius and giving extra examples, and offers two explanations of why Aristotle didn't add 'or in number' (189,16–190,5).
80. He adds a discussion of the sense in which good and bad can be called genera and argues that, contrary to what Aristotle says, they are not really contraries at all but possession and privation (190,13–191,5).
81. Ammonius has one line on the 'prior in order', Philoponus twenty-one. He elaborates on each of Aristotle's examples and then argues that in the case of writing letters are in fact prior to syllables, words, and sentences in nature as well as in order (192,20–193,27).
82. He argues that Aristotle means the fifth sense of the prior to replace the fourth (193,29–194,3.8–10).
83. He adds the example of father and son (194,13–16).
84. He adds extra examples of co-ordinate species (196,26–8).
85. Ammonius merely says that Aristotle has a section on motion because he has mentioned it earlier. Philoponus says that we need to ask why he talks about it since it is really a subject for the natural scientist (197,12–16; cf. 198,15–20). He then rejects the answer of certain earlier writers (197,16–198,1) and goes on to agree with Ammonius that it is because he has mentioned it earlier, but, unlike Ammonius, gives a summary of the earlier passage (198,1–15).
86. He derives the six species of motion from a different division (198,26–199,9) then goes on to outline a different schema, taken from the *Physics*, in which generation and destruction are not motions. In the *Categories*, he says, Aristotle is talking as a logician and to beginners rather than as a natural scientist (199,10–24).
87. He adds a scholium on the difference between the motions other than qualitative change (199,28–200,9) and one with a general statement about the difference between qualitative change and the other motions (200,13–21).
88. He adds the argument that although both qualitative change and local motion, for the most part at least, accompany each of the other motions, neither of them is identical with any of them (201,3–202,7).
89. He has two scholia on rest as the contrary of motion in general and on the opposition of particular motions to one another, and two on the category 'having', but Ammonius has left off and has no equivalent (203,27–205,28).

As we saw, Sorabji found thirteen additions in Luna's twenty-one pages. In my 122 pages there are eighty-nine, a somewhat higher but not altogether different level of addition. What was the origin of this additional material? Philoponus was an original thinker and we would expect at least some of it to be Philoponus' own work and, as we shall see, this indeed seems to be the case. But an obvious question is whether some of it is taken from or inspired by the works of other thinkers, in particular other commentaries on the *Categories*.

The extant ancient commentaries on the *Categories*, apart from those of Ammonius and Philoponus himself, are Porphyry's brief question and answer commentary and those of Dexippus, Boethius, Simplicius, Olympiodorus, and David.[11] Of these only Porphyry and Dexippus are earlier than Philoponus and Dexippus doesn't extend to the part of the *Categories* we are concerned with. This on the face of it thwarts any search for Philoponus' possible sources before it gets off the ground. However, the results of an earlier study by Luna[12] of the treatment of *Categories* 1a-15 in all of the extant commentaries show that it should be worth looking at the commentaries that post-date Philoponus as well as at Porphyry.

Largely on the basis of the strong thematic similarities between the commentaries, which normally pose and answer the same questions, both philosophical and exegetical, at the same points, Luna concluded that they were all operating within a single, unitary tradition that predated all of them. And largely on the basis of Simplicius' revelation of his sources, she further concluded that this common tradition went back to Porphyry's, now lost, longer commentary on the *Categories*, either directly or via Iamblichus', also lost, commentary, which was in large part based on it. However, although the similarities between the commentaries were strong they were far from total and a number of questions and themes appeared in some commentaries but not in others. Analysing these differences, Luna found that there was a bipartition of the tradition, with Porphyry's shorter commentary, Dexippus (rather ambiguously), Boethius, and Simplicius in one group and Ammonius, Philoponus, Olympiodorus, and David in another. To account for this bipartition, she hypothesized that Ammonius had access to the common tradition through the teaching of his master Proclus, who probably favoured Iamblichus over Porphyry and who doubtless added something of his own, and that Philoponus and Olympiodorus drew on Ammonius, and David on Olympiodorus. Further, and importantly for present purposes, she found no sign that Simplicius, who doesn't mention any recent work among his sources, had any knowledge of the commentaries of Ammonius or Philoponus.

Luna's analysis seems plausible and I have seen no reason why it shouldn't, with two provisos, apply to the relationships between the commentaries on the part of the *Categories* that concern us here. The first is that the commentators show rather more individuality, both in the formulation of questions and answers and, even more, in expression, phrasing, and choice of examples, than it seems to suggest. The second is that, contrary to what Luna appears to believe, David knew Philoponus' commentary, explicitly rejecting one of its arguments and seemingly drawing directly on it on at least two other occasions, and so may well have been influenced by it in other less obvious cases.[13]

Now it turns out that there are parallels in one or more of the other commentaries on the *Categories* to fifty-three of the eighty-nine (i.e. more than half) of the passages of Philoponus under consideration. (In looking for such parallels, I have interpreted 'parallel' very liberally, so that it sometimes means little more than a shared topic or question with a very different treatment or answer. This approach seems legitimate because even such a tenuous similarity may point to an influence, even though it may admittedly also be entirely coincidental.) In the light of Luna's findings, the following conclusions seem warranted. (1) A parallel in Porphyry's short commentary may point to Porphyry's long commentary being the ultimate inspiration of the passage in Philoponus. (2) A parallel in Simplicius may point to either Porphyry's long commentary or to Iamblichus' commentary. (3) A parallel in either Olympiodorus or David may similarly point to either Porphyry or Iamblichus as the ultimate source, but may also, perhaps especially in the case of David, be the result of acquaintance with Philoponus. (I say 'may' throughout because in any given case it is always possible that Philoponus has addressed the same question or issue independently of the common tradition.)

Of the parallels I have identified, nine are in Porphyry (one in him alone), thirty-three in Simplicius (seven in him alone), thirty in Olympiodorus (two in him alone), and forty-one in David (seven in him alone).[14] Clearly a parallel in Porphyry or Simplicius will be better evidence for a possible common source than one in Olympiodorus or David, so it is also worth mentioning that there are eleven cases where there are parallels in both Olympiodorus and David but not in the other two commentators.

Here is a list of the more interesting parallels. (In each case I repeat an item from my earlier list of Philiponus' additions to Ammonius followed by a brief description of the parallel(s) in the other commentaries.)

4. He adds an alternative explanation for Aristotle's not counting motion as a species of the continuous (87,25-32).

The alternative explanation is that motions or changes are not quantities or to be assigned to any other category but routes to the categories, or, if they are to be assigned to the categories, to be distributed among a number of them. For the idea that motions are either routes to the categories or belong under a number of different categories Philoponus refers back to *in Cat.* 48,14-27 and the two passages taken together go beyond anything in Ammonius and are close at a number of points to Simplicius *in Cat.* 66,16-29 and Dexippus *in Cat.* 34,5-17. David 188,7-15 also shows some similarities.

6. Unlike Ammonius (or Aristotle himself), he includes speech among things that exhibit natural order (89,7-9).

Porphyry, qualifiedly, (104,25-30), Simplicius (138,3-4), Olympiodorus (89,14-22), and David (195,3-4) all do too. (Olympiodorus and David both interpret *logoi* as speeches.)

7. He adds a statement that inner language is, if anything, a quality of the soul (90,5-7).

Simplicius (124,21-2) attributes this view to Porphyry, although Porphyry in his short commentary (101,26-7) calls it 'either an activity or an affection', which Simplicius (124,20-21) says is Iamblichus' position.

13. He expands Ammonius' six lines on the non-occurrence of up and down in nature by a further twenty-one lines (99,26-100,15).

Simplicius, Olympiodorus, and David all have long discussions of the lemma with little detail in common with Philoponus. However both Simplicius (149,1-10) and David (199,1 ff.) have, like Philoponus, something to say about the claims of the ends of a diameter of the cosmos to represent 'up' and 'down' and, again like Philoponus, bring the location of fire and the other elements into the discussion.

15. He adds a paragraph on the possibility of calling the category 'the relative' in the singular (103,5-17).

Simplicius 159,23-161,11 shows that this issue goes back a long way. Philoponus' position is perhaps closest to the one Simplicius attributes to Iamblichus (160,10-34). Olympiodorus (97,28-37) and David (205,32-206,9) have similar discussions but are not very close.

Introduction   11

23. He has a defence of the practice of coining a name for the correlate of a relative that lacks a named correlate (113,13–114,3).

Simplicius (186,25–187,9), Olympiodorus (105,16–35), and David (211,17–33) also have defences of the practice. None of them is very close to Philoponus but Simplicius does, like Philoponus, invoke the practice of geometers and musicians.

26. He adds the example of Thales and the lunar eclipse (118,7–25).

Porphyry (120,18–22), Simplicius (191,6), Olympiodorus (109,1–2), and David (214,3–4) all cite Thales at this point, but, unlike Philoponus, who goes into the science, only very briefly. Also, Olympiodorus and David have Thales initiating astronomy rather than explaining eclipses.

30. He adds the examples of Thales and the lunar eclipse (again) and of the squaring of the circle and proposes a solution to a well-known legal puzzle (123,20–124,14).

Simplicius (194,12–13) also mentions Thales a second time. (The other commentators don't.)

34. He says that Aristotle includes the *definiendum* in the definition and explains why he does so (130,22–31).

cf. Porphyry 123,31 ff. (not close), Simplicius 201,34 ff. (especially 202,25–203,2, which is fairly close), and David 217,4–9 (a similar explanation).

45. He adds an explanation for the order of the four species of quality (138–139,22).

Simplicius deals with the question of order at 243,28–244,17, 259,14–20, and 261,20–22. Except for the reason offered for figure and shape coming last, the reasons he gives for Aristotle's order are not close to those Philoponus gives. Olympiodorus (117,17–25) and David (224,13–20) both have brief comments. David is quite different throughout, but Olympiodorus justifies the positions of the first and fourth of the four types of quality similarly.

51. He adds that qualified things may be named homonymously as well as paronymously (157,16–20).

Simplicius (264,8–10) makes the same point but with different examples. Olympiodorus (127,13–21) and David (235,2–5) also identify homonymously

12   Introduction

named qualities, though both explain their occurrence differently and provide different examples.

52. He adds that contrariety is particularly associated with quality, even when it is present in other categories (157,25–30).

Simplicius (280,13–15) makes the same claim in similar terms, as do Olympiodorus (127,28–38) and David (235,25–236,2), but with further elaboration.

53. Ammonius argues (briefly) that justice admits of more and less. Philoponus argues that *no* quality as such does, although qualified entities can partake more or less of a quality (158,26–159,24).

Porphyry (137,15–138,32) and Simplicius (284,12–285,8) both list four views on the issue, the one that Porphyry places third (and attributes to Aristotle) and Simplicius second being closest to Philoponus'. Olympiodorus (128,17–40) attributes a position like Philoponus' to 'some people'. He initially combats it but goes on to claim that Aristotle at times holds it, at times not, and that it is from one point of view correct, from another not. David (237,13–18) mentions the view that it is only qualified things that admit of more and less as 'an opinion'. Like Philoponus, he uses the simile of people standing nearer or further away from a fire to illustrate the relationship of qualified things to the qualities themselves.

58. He adds a scholium on (i) why acting and being-affected are not included under the relatives, (ii) the justification for the section title, and (iii) the concomitants of acting and being-affected (165,22–167,9).

With (i) cf. Simplicius 63,9–15 and 299,1–27 (neither very close), with (ii) Simplicius 301,27 ff. (the name of the category rather than the title is in question, but there are similarities), with (iii) Simplicius 296,12–297,11, where all the same ingredients are present. Olympiodorus (131,25–132,5) takes the same view as Philoponus on (i) but his arguments are different. (He has nothing on (ii) or (iii).) David covers (i) at 239,34–240,13, (ii) at 240,19–23, and (iii) at 240,23–30. He is nowhere very close to Philoponus in detail, but some of his arguments on (i) are similar to Philoponus'.

62. Ammonius simply says that privation and state don't change into one another. Philoponus says that state can change to privation and that there is even a sense (described in the *Physics*), in which privation can change to state (168,27–169,2).

Simplicius considers the possibility of a switch from privation to state at 401,3 ff., citing the same *Physics* passage at 401,14.

63. He adds a rebuttal of the view that contraries are in fact relatives, even though contrariety itself *is* a relative (170,21-9).

cf. Simplicius 384,14 ff., especially 385,10 ff., where the view opposed by Philoponus is attributed to Nicostratus and refuted in the same way.

72. He adds a scholium on 13a22-3 in which he argues that Aristotle is talking about the conventionally good man rather than the perfectly good one (184,3-9).

Simplicius (401,24-402,4) treats the same themes at greater length but includes the same arguments.

77. He adds explanations of how two things can be opposed to one and of how good and bad things are opposed as symmetry and asymmetry and bad things as excess and defect (188,4-17).

cf. Simplicius 410,3-24. Simplicius' argument is more complex but at bottom much the same. Olympiodorus (141,32-142,2) and David (249,2-13) both address the same issue, the former quite differently, but the latter very similarly.

79. He expands on Aristotle's statement that contraries belong to things the same in either genus or species, understanding it differently from Ammonius and giving extra examples, and offers two explanations of why Aristotle didn't add 'or in number' (189,16-190,5).

Simplicius' rather longer discussion (413,18-414,19) covers much the same ground and shows many similarities. Olympiodorus (142,12-16) is quite different and has nothing on Aristotle's failure to add 'in number'.

80. He adds a discussion of the sense in which good and bad can be called genera and argues that, contrary to what Aristotle says, they are not really contraries at all but possession and privation (190,13-191,5).

Simplicius 414,26-418,18 shows that Aristotle's statement that some contraries, such as good and bad, are not in a genus but genera themselves was much discussed. The issue was whether this would somehow put them outside the ten categories. Philoponus in effect offers two solutions. The first has them pervade all ten categories (which doesn't really seem to solve the problem), while the second sidesteps the issue by arguing that good and bad are not contraries at all but possession and privation. The first solution has some similarity to one that Simplicius attributes to 'the students of Porphyry' at 414,33 ff., the second, interestingly, is put forward by Simplicius as his own at 416,21ff., which would seem to suggest that Philoponus didn't find it in an earlier commentary. Olympiodorus (142,29–143,3) and more so David (249,28–250,27) cover much of the same ground but with many differences of detail.

85. Ammonius merely says that Aristotle has a section on motion because he has mentioned it earlier. Philoponus says that we need to ask why he talks about it since it is really a subject for the natural scientist (197,12-16; cf. 198,15-20). He then rejects the answer of certain earlier writers (197,16-198,1) and goes on to agree with Ammonius that it is because he has mentioned it earlier, but, unlike Ammonius, gives a summary of the earlier passage (198,1-15).

Simplicius (427,11-28) explains why Aristotle deals with a science topic in the *Categories* in the same way as Philoponus, mentioning the same earlier views at 427,12-15. David (253,15-26) also explains the appearance of a science topic in the same way but doesn't mention earlier views.

86. He derives the six species of motion from a different division (198,26-199,9) then goes on to outline a different scheme, taken from the *Physics*, in which generation and destruction are not motions. In the *Categories*, he says, Aristotle is talking as a logician and to beginners rather than as a natural scientist (199,10-24).

Simplicius (427,29-428,2), Olympiodorus (146,3-16) and David (253,28-33) all give divisions that are rather different from those of either Ammonius or Philoponus. Simplicius goes on to say (428,3-13) that Nicostratus makes the differing treatments of generation and destruction in the two works a criticism of Aristotle and defends him against such criticism on the ground that the *Categories* is written for beginners.

From one point of view, these results are disappointing. Taken individually, none of the parallels is close enough to Philoponus either verbally or in content to guarantee a common source. However, it seems to me that the same questions and topics, and even enough similarities of solution and treatment, crop up often enough to suggest that Ammonius' commentary wasn't Philoponus' only access to what Luna calls the common tradition.[15] This certainly doesn't seem to have been through either Porphyry or Iamblichus. In fact neither Ammonius nor Philoponus show any signs of direct knowledge of their commentaries. Both refer directly only to Porphyry's *Isagoge* and although Philoponus does have one reference to Iamblichus (Ammonius has none), he shows no signs of direct acquaintance with his commentary, displaying no hint of any knowledge of his use of pseudo-Archytas or of his 'intellective theory' for instance. As we have seen, Luna suggests that Ammonius' access to earlier scholarship on the *Categories* may have been through the teaching of his master Proclus. If this was the case, perhaps his rather brief commentary was a subset of his notes from those classes intended for beginning students and Philoponus had access to the longer version in its written form. In fact there is something else that may point in this direction. After comparing the somewhat different versions of the ten-point introduction to the philosophy of Aristotle prefixed to the commentaries on the *Categories* of each of the Alexandrian commentators and of Simplicius, Ilsetraut Hadot concluded that all five commentators had independent access to Proclus' *Sunanagnôsis*, or '*Commentary on a Text Under the Direction of a Master*', the ultimate source of such introductions.[16] If this text, which was probably brought to Alexandria by Ammonius, was passed down over several generations of teachers at the school, a written version of Proclus' commentary on the *Categories* could also have been.

I identified no parallels in other commentaries on the *Categories* for thirty-six of the passages in my list of Philoponus' additions to Ammonius.[17] A few of these are actually recapitulations of, or inspired by, material elsewhere in Philoponus' commentary, often in its turn taken from Ammonius. Passage number 60, for example, is a brief summary of 13,6–32 in the introductory material that precedes the commentary proper and 13,6–32 is itself based on Ammonius 14,2–15,2.[18] Many of the remainder are the kind of paraphrase, expansion (of Aristotle or Ammonius), or explanatory comment that Philoponus in all probability contributed himself after a consideration of the text.[19]

More interesting are a number of cases where Philoponus includes material of marginal interest at best to commentary on the *Categories*. In passages 2 and 28 he provides lengthy and doubtfully relevant geometrical information. In 32 he provides an example of a *reductio* argument involving issues irrelevant to the *Categories* and extending over the best part of three *CAG* pages.[20] In 26 he unnecessarily goes into the causes of lunar eclipses, in 46 into kinds of knowledge and kinds of virtue. There are other, less striking cases, but these are perhaps the best examples. One gets the impression that Philoponus, who tends to be wordy in his other works, felt that Ammonius' rather sparse comments needed a bit of padding. Most of the material involved may well have come from the fund of knowledge acquired in his earlier, pre-philosophical, education.

Much in the commentary reflects Philoponus' personal interests. He was educated as a *grammatikos*, a grammarian or, perhaps better, a philologist, before turning to philosophy and seems to have continued to identify himself as a *grammatikos*.[21] His philological interests are on display in a number of passages. 12, 39, 70, 75, and 81 are all concerned, in part at least, with issues of linguistic usage or grammar.[22] In 37 and 38 in explaining the term *hexis* ('state') he cites the usage of cognate words. In 61, defending the authenticity of the third part of the *Categories*, he appeals, unlike any other commentator, to grammatical considerations. Of these passages, 70 is particularly interesting. At the end of a long scholium largely concerned with linguistic usage, he adduces a number of etymologies, one of which he attributes to Herodian. Herodian was a philologist of the second century CE and, in his role as a *grammatikos*, Philoponus actually produced a kind of epitome, which still survives, of Herodian's most important work *Peri katholikês prosôidias* ('On prosody in general').[23] Simplicius probably knew something of his work on Herodian, since he disparagingly states that 'he came to us [i.e. to philosophy] from Menander and Herodian and such people'.[24] In later life Philoponus wrote controversial works defending Christian cosmological and theological positions and eventually became a Christian theologian. There are already hints of where he was heading in the earlier commentaries on Aristotle, including the present one. In passage 73 he observes that there may have been occasions when the blind recovered their sight through divine intervention and he may well, as Busse apparently thought,[25] have Christ's miracles in mind. The example of a *reductio* argument in passage 32 expatiates at length on the immortality of the soul, the *post mortem* punishment of sins, and the providential governance of the cosmos in a manner that would probably have been acceptable to both pagans and Christians. In the course of a discussion of the capacity of rational beings to choose to act or refrain from acting (passage 47) he finds occasion to discuss the relationship between divine will and divine power in a manner quite reminiscent of certain arguments in his later *Against Proclus on the Eternity of the World*. Again, what he says would probably have been quite acceptable to Christians. In passage 64 he distinguishes accidental good, or the good in us, from the good that is above being and belongs to the essence of the divinity. This of course calls to mind the Good of the Neoplatonists, but I don't think that the language here either would have been unacceptable to the Christians. All in all, I have the impression that in choosing his words he always has an eye to both camps.[26] In his later works Philoponus shows an interest in identifying argument forms and this is already evident here. At 126,18 he identifies Aristotle's argument as a *reductio ad absurdum* and, as we have seen, goes on to provide his own, lengthy, example of such an argument. At 131,3 he tells us that Aristotle is drawing a corollary and shapes the same material to illustrate the drawing of one.[27] Other examples of his identification of argument types are listed under 'argument types' in the subject index.

In other, probably later, Aristotelian commentaries, especially the one on the *Physics*, and in his polemical works Philoponus criticizes Neoplatonic cosmology and aspects of Aristotle's physics freely, at times even aggressively. In commenting on the *Categories* there would have been few occasions for such criticism, but, even though this was probably one of his earliest philosophical works, Philoponus already shows a readiness to criticize or correct Aristotle when he thinks it warranted. In contrast, his master Ammonius, who seems to have been of a more pacific temperament and who was committed to the Neoplatonic project of harmonizing Aristotle and Plato, rarely, if ever, does. I have noted the following criticisms or corrections of Aristotle in the present commentary. In passages 21 and 24 Philoponus accuses Aristotle of making careless errors brought about by his desire to denigrate the definition of relatives offered at *Categories* 6a36-7, a definition which Philoponus, following Ammonius, believed to be pre-Aristotelian and rejected by Aristotle. In the former case Aristotle has, he says, wrongly described virtue and vice and knowledge and ignorance as pairs of relatives, in the latter wrongly used head and rudder as examples of relatives when they are in fact parts of substances. In passage 22 he claims that Aristotle's statement that the equal and the unequal admit of degrees is either a careless error on his part or an interpolation. In passage 55 he finds the distinctive feature that Aristotle assigns to quality unsatisfactory and suggests a modification of it. In passage 80 he claims that, contrary to what Aristotle says, good and bad are not contraries but instances of possession and privation. In passage 81 Aristotle gives letters, syllables, and words as one example of things that exhibit one type of the prior, the prior in order. Philoponus believes that this is not the whole story and that they are also prior by nature. There is also one case where Philoponus makes what appears to be an implicit criticism of Ammonius, although he is not named. In the course of giving a division of quality which closely follows a similar division in Ammonius, at a certain point Philoponus argues that further division of one particular subdivision would be inappropriate. It would, he implies, involve unnecessary repetition and risk over-complexity. This seems to be directed at Ammonius who does subdivide at this point. (For this see passage 40).

Our comparison of the part of Philoponus translated in this volume (approximately two thirds of the commentary) with the corresponding part of

Ammonius has shown that although Philoponus contains a significant amount taken more or less verbatim from Ammonius (about 9 per cent of its text) and is influenced by Ammonius in other ways too, the bulk of the material it contains was either generated by Philoponus himself or taken from other sources. In later works Philoponus comes to disagree, at times aggressively, with aspects of the pagan theology and cosmology of his master Ammonius and other Neoplatonists and with aspects of Aristotle's *Physics*. At the time he wrote the present commentary he may not as yet have formulated such disagreements, or if he had, not yet felt free to express them, and he would have found relatively little to object to in the *Categories* anyway. There are however already signs of his independence of mind. Not only does he introduce material representative of his own interests or of a kind not normally found in a commentary on the *Categories*, but on occasion shows a willingness to criticize or correct Aristotle. Considered in conjunction with its scribal title and its probable relative earliness, these features of *in Cat.* rather set it apart from Philoponus' other Aristotelian commentaries and raise some interesting questions.

First, we know from references in some of Philoponus' other commentaries that he attended at least some of Ammonius' classes.[28] The *Categories* was the first Aristotelian work taught in the standard Neoplatonic curriculum and we would expect it to have been among them. Why then was he dependent on someone else's notes for his knowledge of Ammonius' teaching? Didn't he take any notes himself, or only inadequate ones? Or had he somehow missed the seminars on the *Categories* after all? Or was he perhaps the anonymous note-taker himself?

Second, although only a fairly small proportion of the material in the commentary is taken directly from Ammonius, his influence on it is nevertheless substantial. Why then isn't he credited in the scribal title as he is in the titles of nearly all of Philoponus' other Aristotelian commentaries? Was it because in the commentaries in which Ammonius is acknowledged the proportion of material taken from Ammonius was much higher than it is in *in Cat.*? If so, that would be something to be taken into account in any attempt to decide how much in the other commentaries is Ammonius and how much Philoponus.[29]

Third, what implications, if any, do our findings have for the status of the commentary? If, as has been suggested, it is, along with other commentaries, a record of Ammonius' seminars that was commissioned, or at least sanctioned, by Ammonius,[30] is it at all likely that something containing so little Ammonius and so much else would have been found satisfactory by Ammonius? If, on the other hand, it is a text that Philoponus prepared to support his own teaching of the *Categories* in Ammonius' school,[31] is it plausible that a course two to three times as long as the one given by Ammonius would have been acceptable?[32] The nature of *in Cat.* also seems to create particular difficulties for Verrycken's hypothesis as to the circumstances under which Philoponus' commentaries were produced. Verrycken holds that they were composed neither as official records of Ammonius' seminars nor to support or record Philoponus' own teaching.[33] This might make sense in the case of the other commentaries if they were in fact Philoponus' notes from seminars he had attended along with his reflections on what he had heard, but it is hard to see what his reason for producing *in Cat.* in its present form would have been.

Notes

1 The four are those on the *Prior Analytics*, the *Posterior Analytics*, *De Anima*, and *De Generatione et Corruptione*. Of these, the last three are also said to include reflections, perhaps critical reflections, of Philoponus' own. On this last point, see Richard Sorabji, 'Dating of Philoponus' Commentaries on Aristotle and of his Divergence from his Teacher Ammonius', in his (ed.), *Aristotle Re-Interpreted: New Findings on Seven Hundred Years of the Ancient Commentators*, London: Bloomsbury Academic, 2016, 368–70.

2 The other two with no mention of Ammonius in the title are those on the *Physics* and the *Meteorology*. However there is a complication. The titles preceding each of the four surviving books of the *Physics* commentary in the *CAG* edition were formulated by Vitelli, the *CAG* editor, and he reports that Trincavelli, the editor of the *editio princeps*, prints a title that makes the *Physics* commentary too one of those consisting of notes from Ammonius' seminars together with Philoponus' own reflections (*CAG*, 16, preface, v). The small part of the title that Vitelli says is still legible in the manuscript he believes was used by Trincavelli is compatible with at least part of this and Sorabji reports ('Dating of Philoponus' Commentaries', 368) that Golitsis will be taking Trincavelli's title seriously in a forthcoming publication. This would mean that, apart from *in Meteor.*, which is generally agreed to be late and which may not include material taken from Ammonius, *in Cat.* would be the only one of Philoponus' Aristotelian commentaries whose scribal title does not state that it is based on Ammonius' seminars.

3 Of course we would not expect this to be an entirely accurate report of Ammonius (unless, which seems unlikely, Ammonius delivered his lectures at a pace that allowed verbatim transcription) and, moreover, Sorabji identifies what looks likely to be a deliberate (and misguided) departure from Ammonius (Sorabji, 'Dating of Philoponus' Commentaries', 381). Nevertheless, I shall, for convenience, refer to this commentary as Ammonius *in Cat.*, or simply as Ammonius.

4 Already by Busse, the editor of both commentaries for the *CAG* series (*CAG*, 4, pt. 4, preface, v-vi).
5 C. Luna, *Commentaire sur les Catégories d'Aristote. Chapitres 2-4*, Paris: Les Belles Lettres, 2001. I have not been able to see Luna's publication and have been dependent on Sorabji, 'Dating of Philoponus' Commentaries' for knowledge of her results.
6 These are listed by Sorabji ('Dating of Philoponus' Commentaries', 382).
7 Sorabji, 'Dating of Philoponus' Commentaries', 382.
8 The pairs of passages are these: Philop. 83,19-20 : Amm. 54,10-12; Philop. 88,28-30 and 89,1-2 : Amm. 59,11-13; Philop. 89,2-7 : Amm. 59,15-19; Philop. 89,2-7 : Amm. 59,15-19; Philop. 89,10-17 : Amm. 59,21-60,8; Philop. 92,11-93,13 : Amm. 60,14-61,5; Philop. 93,15-17 : Amm. 61,7-9; Philop. 94,5-7 : Amm. 62,2-4; Philop. 97,32-98,1 : Amm. 64,16-18; Philop. 101,3-4 : Amm. 65,10-11; Philop. 101,22-6 : Amm. 65,12-17; Philop. 101,29 : Amm. 65,22; Philop. 102,3-6 : Amm. 65,23-6; Philop. 104,25-8 : Amm. 67,7-10; Philop. 105,1-11 : Amm. 67,16-25; Philop. 106,2 : Amm. 67,28; Philop. 106,5-6 : Amm. 68,2-3; Philop. 106,14-17 : Amm. 68,9-12; Philop. 106,18-24 : Amm. 68,14-19; Philop. 107,4-6 : Amm. 68,23-5; Philop. 108,10-12 : Amm. 69,24-6; Philop. 108,15-30 : Amm. 69,26-70,8; Philop. 109,26-31 : Amm. 70,10-14; Philop. 110,7-12 : Amm. 70,17-21; Philop. 111,15-18 : Amm. 70,25-71,1; Philop. 111,19-22 : Amm. 71,1-5; Philop. 111,25-6 : Amm. 71,5-6; Philop. 112,5-10 : Amm. 71,11-17; Philop. 112,12-18 : Amm. 71,19-24; Philop. 112,20-2 : Amm. 71,24-7; Philop. 112,23-5 : Amm. 71,29-72,3; Philop. 114,7-8 : Amm. 72,25-6; Philop. 116,18-21 : Amm. 73,18-21; Philop. 117,20-118,7 : Amm. 74,12-23; Philop. 118,26-9 : Amm. 74,23-5; Philop. 118,32-119,2 : Amm. 74,27-75,1; Philop. 120,3-6 : Amm. 75,6-9; Philop. 121,13-16 : Amm. 75,21-4; Philop. 122,24-123,3 : Amm. 76,10-22; Philop. 129,10-13 : Amm. 77,22-6; Philop. 131,7-9 : Amm. 78,29-31; Philop. 132,9-10 : Amm. 79,10-11; Philop. 132,23 : Amm. 79,25; Philop. 134,8-10 : Amm. 81,3-7; Philop. 139,32-140,4 : Amm. 80,24-9; Philop. 140,12-15 : Amm. 84,13-16; Philop. 143,3-6 : Amm. 84,7-8; Philop. 147,9-12 : Amm. 86,2-5; Philop. 149,11-25 : Amm. 86,13-25; Philop. 150,3-4 : Amm. 87,2-3; Philop. 150,6-7 : Amm. 87,5-6; Philop. 150,11-12 : Amm. 87,8-9; Philop. 150,15-16 : Amm. 87,11-12; Philop. 151,3-5 : Amm. 87,14-16; Philop. 151,8-10 : Amm. 87,18-20; Philop. 151,13-19 : Amm. 87,22-88,4; Philop. 156,7-11 : Amm. 88,19-23; Philop. 156,17-21 : Amm. 88,25-89,1; Philop. 158,8-10 : Amm. 89,18-21; Philop. 158,14-19 : Amm. 89,23-90,1; Philop. 162,7-10 : Amm. 91,10-13; Philop. 164,6-15 : Amm. 92,12-22; Philop. 164,18-25 : Amm. 93,1-4; Philop. 168,9-15 : Amm. 93,12-17; Philop. 169,6-8 : Amm. 94,4-5; Philop. 170,5-7 : Amm. 94,17-18; Philop. 170,8-9 : Amm. 94,19-20; Philop. 170,12 : Amm. 94,21-2; Philop. 170,13-15 : Amm. 94,27-9; Philop. 171,18-24 : Amm. 95,2-7; Philop. 171,28-172,1 : Amm. 95,9-10; Philop. 172,13-21 : Amm. 95,11-19; Philop. 174,9-10 : Amm. 95,21-2; Philop. 174,13-14 : Amm. 95,24-5; Philop. 175,5-6 : Amm. 96,8-9; Philop. 175,6-7 :

Amm. 96,15; Philop. 177,3-5 : Amm. 97,11-13; Philop. 177,30-178,1 : Amm. 97,24-5; Philop. 182,7-9 : Amm. 99,5-7; Philop. 182,13-15 : Amm. 99,7-8; Philop. 194,28-195,3 : Amm. 104,8-12.

9 Ammonius has 1,361 *CAG* lines, Philoponus 3,614. Because we are primarily interested in the amount of Ammonius in Philoponus, the 329 lines are lines of Ammonius rather than of Philoponus.

10 I have adopted the format that Sorabji ('Dating of Philoponus' Commentaries', 382) used when listing the additions Luna identified in the part of Philoponus she examined. Perhaps at this point it is worth mentioning another way in which Philoponus doesn't always follow Ammonius, his somewhat different choice of lemmas. Ammonius has 131 lemmas, Philoponus 147. They have eighty-five in common, but Ammonius has forty-six that are not used by Philoponus and Philoponus sixty-two that are not used by Ammonius.

11 If its editors are right, we also have a small portion of Porphyry's longer commentary on the *Categories* (Riccardo Chiaradonna, Marwan Rashed, David Sedley, with Natalie Tchernetska, 'A rediscovered *Categories* commentary', *Oxford Studies in Ancient Philosophy*, 44, 2013, 129-94; reprinted (but without the Greek text in the original) as 'A Rediscovered *Categories* Commentary: Porphyry (?) with fragments of Boethus', in Richard Sorabji (ed.), *Aristotle Re-Interpreted: New Findings on Seven Hundred Years of the Ancient Commentators*, London: Bloomsbury Academic, 2016, 231-62), but the part that is preserved only comments on *Categories* 1a20-b24, so it is not relevant here. The Latin commentary of Boethius, which is approximately contemporary with Philoponus' commentary, clearly depends on Greek sources, but I don't take it into account in what follows. Again for convenience, I shall refer to the commentary attributed to Elias in *CAG*, 18, pt. 1 and now generally reassigned to David, as 'David' in this introduction rather than as 'David (Elias)', as I do in the notes to the translation.

12 C. Luna, 'Les rapports entre les commentaires néoplatoniciens au premier chapitre des *Catégories*', in *Simplicius, Commentaire sur les Catégories d'Aristote*, fasc. 3, Leiden: Brill, 1990, 127-46.

13 He disagrees with Philoponus at 246,14 ff. and the passages taken from Philoponus are at 250,19-27 (= Philop. 190,28-191,5) and 231,30-232,18 (= Philop. 150,1-151,10). The *CAG* editor of David (or Elias as he has it) indexed the first two under 'Philoponus' in his index of proper names but didn't pick up the last. (Actually, I wouldn't be surprised if the two borrowed passages were interpolations, but the reference would remain.)

14 With parallels in Porphyry 6, 7, 13, 20, 22, 26, 31, 34, 53 (alone 31); in Simplicius 4, 6, 7, 13, 15, 16, 21, 22, 23, 24, 26, 30, 34, 45, 51, 52, 53, 58, 61, 62, 63, 72, 74, 77, 78, 79, 80, 81, 83, 84, 85, 86, 88 (alone 21, 24, 30, 61, 63, 72, 78); in Olympiodorus 1, 6, 10, 12, 13, 15, 16, 17, 20, 23, 25, 26, 29, 45, 50, 51, 52, 53, 58, 59, 62, 70, 71, 75, 76, 77, 79, 80, 86, 89

(alone 12, 59); in David 1, 4, 6, 8, 10, 13, 15, 16, 17, 20, 23, 25, 26, 29, 34, 45, 48, 50, 51, 52, 53, 54, 57, 58, 62, 70, 71, 74, 75, 76, 77, 80, 81, 82, 83, 84, 85, 86, 87, 88, 89 (alone 8, 48, 54, 57, 82, 87, 88); in both Olympiodorus and Elias but in neither Porphyry nor Simplicius 1, 10, 17, 25, 29, 50, 70, 71, 75, 76, 89.

15 Luna, 'Les rapports entre les commentaires néoplatoniciens au premier chapitre des *Catégories*', 127. To single out a few examples, I think it unlikely that the parallels listed for passages 6, 15, 26 (especially taken together with 30), 53, 63, 77, and 86 are all coincidental.

16 I. Hadot, 'Conclusion. (A) Les rapports entre les commentaires', in *Simplicius, Commentaire sur les Catégories*, fasc. 1, Leiden: Brill, 1990, 169–77.

17 In the list these were passage numbers 2, 3, 5, 9, 11, 14, 18, 19, 27, 28, 32, 33, 35, 36, 37, 38, 39, 40, 41, 42, 43, 44, 46, 47, 49, 51, 55, 56, 60, 64, 65, 66, 67, 68, 69, and 73.

18 Other passages in this category are 9, 19, 35, 36, and 55. The passages to which they are related are cited in notes ad loc.

19 In this group I would include 3, 5, 11, 14, 39, 40, 41, 42, 43, 44, 49, 56, 65, 67, 68, 69, and 73. (Although I don't include them, many of the passages with parallels, especially with parallels only in Olympiodorus and/or David, doubtless belong here.)

20 He gives a much briefer version of the same example at *in An. Pr.* 38,3–8, which could perhaps be added to the two references back to *in Cat.* in that work identified by Sorabji ('Dating of Philoponus' Commentaries', 383–4).

21 The author statements to *in Meteor.* and to the first books of *in An. Pr.* and *in GC* all identify him as a *grammatikos* and three passages in Simplicius' *in Cael.* (49,10–11; 71,8; 119,7) seem to be telling us that this was also so in the case of his *Contra Aristotelem*.

22 To these add 165,25 ff., where he distinguishes between the connotations of the infinitive and finite forms of a verb.

23 This work, most recently edited as Georgios A. Xenis (ed.), *Iohannes Alexandrinus. Praecepta Tonica*, Berlin: de Gruyter, 2015, is largely concerned with the correct accentuation of Greek words.

24 Simplicius, *in Cael.* 26,22. The Menander in question is presumably the dramatist. The only grammarian called Menander mentioned by Kaster is a certain Menander of Kassopa of the first century BCE of whom all that is known is that he refused payment after giving a lecture at Delphi. (Robert A. Kaster, *Guardians of Language: The Grammarian and Society in Late Antiquity*, Berkeley: University of California Press, [1988] 1997, 123, n. 129).

25 *CAG* 4, pt.4, preface, v.

26 Verrycken finds a number of examples of 'the philosophy of the early Philoponus' (*sc*. Neoplatonism) in *in Cat.*, (Koenraad Verrycken, 'John Philoponus', in Lloyd Gerson (ed.), *The Cambridge History of Philosophy in Late Antiquity*, Cambridge: Cambridge University Press, 2010, vol. 2, 738–45). I agree that the later Philoponus

would have reformulated at least some of these passages, but it also seems to me that most, if not all, of them could, as it happens, have been read in a way that would have been acceptable to Christians.

27 Actually he is dependent on Ammonius here and the material used in his example of a *reductio* argument is an expansion of the material he takes from Ammonius.
28 See the passages referred to by Sorabji, 'Dating of Philoponus' Commentaries', 371 and 378, and Koenraad Verrycken, 'The Development of Philoponus' Thought and its Chronology', in Richard Sorabi (ed.), *Aristotle Transformed: The Ancient Commentators and Their Influence*, London: Duckworth, 1990, 261, n. 181. The scribal titles of many of the commentaries also suggest this of course.
29 For some attempts to answer this question in the case of particular commentaries, see Sorabji, 'Dating of Philoponus' Commentaries', 371–2.
30 A possibility entertained at least in the case of the commentaries on Aristotle's logical works by Sorabji ('Dating of Philoponus' Commentaries', 391).
31 For this see, for example, Pantelis Golitsis, *Les commentaires de Simplicius et de Jean Philopon à la Physique d'Aristote: tradition et innovation*, Berlin: de Gruyter, 2008, 24.
32 However *in Cat.* is a good deal shorter than most of Philoponus' other commentaries, both those that announce themselves as a record of Ammonius' classes, and *in Phys.*, which may, at least in part, represent Philoponus' own teaching. In fact, if the no longer extant commentary on the last four books of the *Physics* was as lengthy as that on the first four books, *in Phys.* would have been more than seven times as long as *in Cat.* (the equivalent of about 196 lessons (*praxeis*) of the length of those into which *in DA* 3, which may or may not be by Philoponus, is divided). This suggests that Philoponus' commentary was not in itself over-long, but it still remains a question as to whether something so much longer that Ammonius' own course would have been acceptable.
33 Verrycken, 'The Development of Philoponus' Thought', 238.

Departures from Busse's Text

The following list records all departures from the text printed in A. Busse, *Philoponi (olim Ammonii) in Aristotelis Categorias Commentarium*, CAG 13.1, Berlin: Reimer, 1898. Emendations for which Busse is acknowledged are based on suggestions he makes in his critical apparatus but does not adopt in his text.

88,22	Correcting *mora*, which is clearly a misprint, to *moria*.
94,16	Omitting *ti* (Busse).
95,24	Punctuating with a full stop rather than a comma after *ontos*.
96,16	Changing *hoti* to *eti*.
103,6	Changing *ta peri tôn pros ti* to *ta pros ti*.
103,7	Changing *peri tou pros ti* to *to pros ti*.
105,7	Correcting *aithêton*, which is clearly a misprint, to *aisthêton*.
109,26	Adding *en* before *tôi*.
112,9	Punctuating with a full stop rather than a comma after *pros ti*.
113,20	Changing *autous* to *auta*.
119,19	Changing *ê mê tote* to *mêpote*.
122,18	Punctuating with a question mark rather than a comma after *legô* and a full stop rather than a comma after *phêsin*.
122,20	Punctuating with a full stop rather than a question mark after *stoikheiôn*.
125,14–15	Transposing *merikon* and *meros* (Busse).
125,19	Changing *suzugia* to *ousia*.
132,17	Punctuating with a comma rather than a full stop after *eidenai*.
145,19	Changing *tis* to *ti*.
145,27	Correcting the second *hê*, which is clearly a misprint, to *ê*.
146,18	Repositioning the *to* after *autos* to follow *touto* (Busse).
154,4	Punctuating with a full stop rather than a question mark after *esti*.
156,23	Adding *allôs* after *ê hopôsoun*.
164,19	Correcting *anakekelisthai*, which is clearly a misprint, to *anakeklisthai*.

165,4	Changing *hôrismenôs* to *hôrismenê*.
168,26	Adding *kai* before *askheta*.
172,3	Deleting *eidôn* and accenting *diaphorôn* with a circumflex on the final syllable.
172,7	Deleting *eidôn* and accenting *diaphorôn* with a circumflex on the final syllable.
174,3	Changing *hina* to *ean* and adding *noson* before *pasan* (Busse).
174,9	Changing *rhêtheiê* to *heuretheiê*.
175,4	Changing *en tôi khronôi* to *ton khronon* (Busse).
176,1	Changing *ê dia* to *kai*.
178,14	Changing *ei gar hê* to *hê gar* (Busse).
179,23	Deleting *onomaseien* (Busse).
180,21	Changing *hêmôn to eidenai* to *hêmas tou theasasthai* (Busse).
180,22	Changing *epikheirêsis* to *epekhei*.
180,23	Changing *tuphos* to *tuphlos*.
181,15	Adding *deixai* after *gar* (Busse).
188,13	Transposing *huperbolê* and *endeia*.
190,27	Changing *khrômati* to *khrôma*.
191,13	Deleting *anôthen te kai katôthen*.
191,24	Changing *kuriôtata* to *kuriôtaton*.
195,13	Changing *ephthên* to *ephthê*.
195,17	Changing *kuriôtata* to *kuriôtaton*.
196,2	Changing *elegomen* to *elegeto*.
196,9	Deleting *to loipon*.
201,14	Adding *amelei* before *tois* (Busse).
201,32	Adding *dêlon* before *hoti* (Busse).
202,7–8	Repositioning the *kai* following *epipherei* to before *phêsi*.

Philoponus

*On Aristotle
Categories 6–15*

Translation

On Quantity

4b20 Of quantity some is discrete and some continuous.

We have already given[1] the reason why substance is placed before all the [other] categories, and for a number of reasons quantity occupies second place among the categories. First, because he mentioned[2] quantity in the section (*logos*)[3] on substance [in the passage] where he said that it is not peculiar to substance that there is nothing that is contrary to it since [this] is [a characteristic] of quantity as well. So, in order not to leave us long in ignorance of the nature of quantity, he fittingly gives an account of it immediately after substance. Second, because quantity also occupies second place in the nature of things. For prime matter, which is, as has often been stated,[4] incorporeal and formless and shapeless, first acquires extension [and] receives the three dimensions and becomes the three-dimensional, which Aristotle calls[5] the second substratum, and then receives the qualities and creates the elements. (And so qualification (*poion*)[6] occupies third place among existing things (*onta*) – and relatives fourth; for relatives are a kind of relationship between [things in] other categories, while place and time and the rest are derived from these[7] [*sc.* from substance, quantity, and quality].) The third reason is that since substance was divided into first and second and first and second are [instances] of number and number [an instance] of quantity, quantity has with reason been placed after substance. And, besides, the very act of asking which of the categories should be placed earlier (*proteros*) or later (*deuteros*) involves quantity. [And], again, the definition of body uses number – *sc.* the *three*-dimensional[8] – and body is a substance and number [is an instance] of quantity. And so on all counts [it is] with good reason [that] Aristotle puts the section on quantity second.[9]

He divides quantity into the continuous and the discrete. Continuous quantity is that which has parts that are united and naturally joined (*sumphuein*) to one another, discrete the opposite, I mean that which has parts that are separate from one another. He says that there are five species of the continuous – line, surface, body, place, time – and two of the discrete – number and language[10] (*logos*).[11] For the sake of those not initiated into geometry one should make a few brief remarks about these.[12]

One should be aware, then, that by body the geometers mean that which has the three dimensions length, breadth [and] depth. Body [must be] either finite or infinite. That it is not infinite has been shown by the philosopher [*sc.* Aristotle] in the physics course.[13] So, if it has been shown that nothing can be infinite, all body must be finite. [Now] what is finite is bounded by limits. Therefore limit is different from what is bounded, since [otherwise] it would be[14] necessary to call both limits or both bounded. For if the one is a limit and the other bounded and limit is the same as what is bounded and not something else, language[15] (*to eirêmenon*), would have to follow. For, just as Socrates and his likeness, being different things, are not [one and] the same – if they were one and the same, either both would be likenesses of Socrates or both would be Socrates – just so is it with limit and the bounded: since it is agreed that they are different things (for that which bounds is one thing, the bounded another), they are of necessity not one and the same.

Now, if body has three dimensions, then its limit will not have three. So it will have either two or one. But it is impossible for it to have [just] one. It [would] not bound body as a whole, and limit must externally delimit the whole of that which is bounded. Therefore a body's limit must externally surround the whole of it, not touching its interior (*bathos*). And if this is the case, the body's limit will only have length and breadth – and so will have one less [dimension] than body so as not to be the same as body –[16] which is precisely [the nature of] surface, which bounds and circumscribes body in length and breadth. But, since this [*sc.* surface] is not infinite either, its limit too must, by the argument used in the case of body, have one less dimension than it does. So, since the latter [*sc.* surface] is seen with (*kata*) both length and breadth,[17] the former [*sc.* its limit] will only have one dimension, that of length. And this is the line, which, as its definition has it, is a length without breadth.[18] And, since a line too, one supposes, is also limited, its limit must by the same argument also have one less dimension than it. So, since it is seen in connexion with length alone, its limit will be entirely dimensionless, in other words a point – for which reason, in defining it, the geometer [*sc.* Euclid] says, 'a point is that which has no part'.[19]

The boundaries between illuminated and shadowed areas clearly show that the existence of a length without breadth is not a construct (*anaplasma*) of our intellect (*dianoia*) but also exists in the nature of things. For when the sun strikes, say, a wall and illuminates, let us say, part of it, the demarcation (*to diorizon*) between the illuminated and shadowed areas must be only a length without breadth. For if it has breadth, this is in every case (*pantôs*) either illuminated or shadowed, since there is nothing between these [two conditions]. But if it is illuminated, it will be counted with the illuminated [area], and if shadowed, with the shadowed. But by all accounts a line is clearly seen in between, which, extending in length alone, separates the shadowed part from the illuminated. For if these [two areas] are separated from one another, there must be something besides them that separates them, which, being neither illuminated nor shadowed, will not have breadth either. For if it has breadth it must be either illuminated or shadowed. But, being the boundary of both [*sc.* of light and shadow], it is neither of these. And so there is every necessity that the boundary of the illuminated and shadowed areas should be only a length without breadth, in other words, a line. Moreover common practice too in the nature of things (*phusikôs*) involves a notion of the line whenever we measure roads, for we only take the length without the breadth – and, further, a notion of surface when we measure areas, since we only calculate their length and breadth. And when we measure wells or walls or logs, we obtain a notion of the volume (*sôma*) by using depth along with length and breadth. So, again, if the line is not unbounded but is bounded, there is every necessity that its limit too should have one dimension fewer than it does. Since, then, a line is something that is extended in one dimension, its limit is something that is without extension, that is to say, a point. And hence they define it [*sc.* the point] as 'that which has no part'. We have in this way shown by means of analysis how these things [*sc.* body, surface, line, and point] form a series and we shall [now] show the same thing again by means of synthesis. The point by flowing creates the line, for it is the principle of the line, just as the 'now' is that of time and the movement of motion. For this reason Aristotle does well to say[20] that they – the point, the now, and the movement – are analogous to one another. For, in that they [too] are extensionless principles of what follows them, the now has the same relationship to time and the movement to motion as the point, which is the extensionless principle of the line, does to the line. And the line creates the surface by moving into the second dimension, and that creates body by moving into the third.[21]

Thus much to acquaint us with the precise nature of line, surface, and body.

[Now] that [line, surface, and body] are continuous is clear, for their parts are naturally joined and united with one another. Place and time, on the other hand, do not have continuity in their own right (*oikothen*). Hence Aristotle, after enumerating the first three – line, surface, body – added, as though making a new beginning, 'also, in addition to these, time and place', on the basis that the former have continuity in their own right, the latter not in their own right but for other reasons. For time is nothing other than a measure of motion, for we say that a day is '[the time it takes for] the return of the sun from rising-point back to rising-point'; and, again, that a month is 'when the moon returns to the same point that it started from', or rather, 'when after departing from the sun, it has come back to the same longitudinal (*kata mêkos*) point as it [*sc.* the sun]'; and, similarly, that the year is 'the sun's circuit in the zodiac'. And so time is [indeed] a measure of motion. And motion takes place in a magnitude, for Aristotle shows that no motion can take place through a void:[22] should anyone, he says, want motion to take place through a void, he would be unable to give a reason (*logos*) why spherical bodies fall faster than leaf-shaped (*petaloeidês*)[23] ones even when they have the same mass, and adds yet other proofs to this one. And so, since these three – magnitude, motion, time – form a series, however magnitude is, so too is motion, and however motion is, so too is time. If magnitude is continuous, the motion that takes place in it will also be continuous; and the motion being continuous, the time too is continuous. And, in the same way, if the magnitude is divided, the motion and the time will be divided as well. For example, if the motion takes place in a log, if its parts are divided, the motion will also take place in a divided manner, but if they are continuous, the motion will also be continuous. So if the heavenly sphere is continuous, the motion that takes place in it is also continuous, and time is continuous too; for time is nothing other than a measure of the motion that takes place in it [*sc.* the heavenly sphere]. And so the time does not have continuity in its own right but on account of the motion, and the motion [has it] on account of the body in which the motion also [takes place]. And so time too has continuity on account of body.

But nor does place have continuity in its own right. For place is, as we have already stated,[24] the limit of the container by (*kata*) which it contains what is contained. The wine jar, for example, is the place of the wine not with respect to the whole of itself but only with respect to its concave [inner] surface. So, whatever the characteristics of what is contained may be, the place will share them. So, since every body is continuous and is necessarily in place, place too will be continuous. And so place too[25] has continuity [only] on account of the body in it. For inasmuch as it is the limit of the container it is called surface, not place, and is continuous [in its own right], but inasmuch as it contains [it is called] place and has continuity from the very content in relation to which it is a place. And that every place *is* continuous is also clear from the following. If you [notionally] divide the wine jar and hypothesize nothing outside the wine, neither air nor any other body, you will find that the portion of the wine at (*kata*) the division appears not to be in a place, which is absurd (*atopos*)[26] because every body must be in a place (*topos*).[27] These, then, are the five species of the continuous.

But why doesn't he count motion (*kinêsis*)[28] among the species of the continuous? We reply that motion is a kind of indeterminate thing, for it is the path (*hodos*) from potentiality to actuality (*energeiâi*).[29] So for this reason he hasn't mentioned it – and also because he is addressing beginners, since the [full] account of it requires further instruction.[30] Or perhaps one should rather say that motion isn't even properly a quantity, since it is a kind of activity (*energeia*) of the thing that is moving. After all, how could I call qualitative change or increase or diminution a quantity? And so nor therefore is generation a quantity – or any motion [at all]. For not even local motion itself is a quantity but a kind of activity – and it has continuity on account of the subject in which (*peri ho*) it occurs and not on its own account. And so, as I also said earlier,[31] changes in general should be described as routes to the categories, not as categories, or[32] each should be placed (*anagein*) under a different [category], as was stated there.[33] Time, on the other hand, being the number and measure of motion, is a quantity in the strict sense, for number and measure both belong to quantity. So time is a quantity, even though it gets continuity from an external source (*heterôthen*).

There is a question as to how it is that body is reckoned among the species of quantity even though body is substance. I reply that there is, as we also stated earlier,[34] both a substantial (*ousiôdês*)[35] qualification and a substantial quantity. The heat in fire, for instance, is a substantial qualification and the three-dimensional in body a substantial quantity. So just as, should one view the heat in fire simply as a quality and not as fire, one will include it under quality, in exactly the same way, if we consider body simply in so far as it has length and breadth and depth, we shall see it as a kind of quantity and not as a substance.[36]

The species of the discrete are, as has been stated,[37] language and number, for language is both a quantity and a discrete quantity; a quantity, he says, because 'it is measured out by the short and the long syllable', a discrete one because each of the syllables has its own boundary (*perigraphê*) and we can voice one syllable and not voice another.[38] And number too is one of the things that are discrete, for each of its units also has its own boundary.

Having employed division and subdivision as [described] above, he divides quantity again in a different way,[39] saying that 'some quantities are composed (*sunistanai*) of internal (*en autois*) parts that have position relative to one another, while others are not [composed] of [parts] that have position'. Things that are said to be composed of internal parts with position relative to one another are those which are situated somewhere and can be pointed to (*deiktos*) and have parts[40] that all exist (*sunistanai*) at once, for instance a stone, since this has a position (in a wall, say) and can be pointed to (for it is subject to perception) and all of its parts exist at once. Things that [are composed of parts] that have position are body and surface and line and place, since these can all be pointed to and are situated somewhere and have parts all of which exist [at once]. Time and language, however, cannot be pointed to (they are not even subject to perception),[41] and do not have parts that exist at once:[42] the whole of time does not exist at once but just in the form of the 'now' (for its being exists in coming to be and immediately perishing), and nor does language exist all at once as a whole, since a syllable that has been uttered does not wait for (*hupomenein*) the one that is about to be uttered but the first one has already perished before the second is uttered. So how could something that doesn't last (*hupomenein*) have any position? But, one might rather say that these things have a kind of natural order because the 'now' comes before the future but the future does not come before the 'now'. (An order is a natural one when it isn't reversible (*anakamptein*), and an order that is relative to us is one that is arbitrarily (*adiaphorôs*) reversible, as when, starting with things on the right, we mention the thing on the right [end] first, but, should we wish to start again with the things on the left, mention the thing on the left [end] first.) Language too has natural order since the word (*logos*) pronounced 'Socrates' has a first syllable and [then] a second. And there is order in number too in that one is enumerated before two. And since number is twofold, one [kind], which enumerates, in the soul, the other in the things that are counted (just as a pint too is twofold, the one that measures and the one that is measured), the one in the soul clearly will not [consist] of parts with position (its parts do not have any position because it is intelligible), while the one in things that can be counted, for example in [a group of] ten horses, [does consist] of [parts] that have position because its parts are situated somewhere and have a position relative to one another. This is why he says as he does, 'but you would not in every case (*ou panu*)[43] find any position' and not 'in no event', knowing that one kind of number [does consist] of [parts] with position and another of [parts] not having position.

But it is worth examining what he has said (*ta eirêmena*) textually as well.

4b25 For there is no common boundary of the parts of a number at which its parts join together.

He doesn't even think it worth producing a proof that number is a quantity because anyone not wanting [to accept that] number is a quantity wouldn't think anything else was either. But he does prove that it is a *discrete* quantity. It doesn't, he says, have a common boundary at which its parts join together.[44] For example, if we separate the number ten into two groups of five, we shall find that each is discrete with its own boundary.[45] There is no unit joined to both parts and bestowing continuity upon them by means of itself. And the same goes for the number seven: the fourth unit doesn't join either one of the triads either to itself or [the two of them] to one another but [in this case] too [each part] is seen [to be contained] within its own boundary.

And so number is [indeed] a discrete quantity. But language too, he says, is a discrete quantity for the same reason; for it is not possible to observe the parts of language either, I mean the syllables, joined by way of a common boundary, but each of them is circumscribed.[46]

'I mean', he says, 'voiced (*meta phônês*) language', for since there is a kind of language that is spoken [aloud] and a kind that is internal (*endiathetos*) – the kind seen in the soul – for that reason he indicates that he is talking about language that is spoken [aloud].[47] Internal language isn't a quantity at all but, if anything, a quality of the soul, if indeed it is a condition or a state of the soul and [both] a condition and a state are, as we shall learn,[48] qualities.

> **5a1** The line, on the other hand, is continuous. For it is possible to find a common boundary at which its parts join together, a point; and in the case of a surface, a line.

That the line is continuous is as one would expect. Each of its parts joins with one another, having a common boundary, the point, and the point [itself] is without parts and without extension. So it is to be expected that its parts too are continuously and extensionlessly united, for the line is divided at a point, at which its parts also join. But one must understand the point, or the division, as potential and not actual. If you understand [it] as actual, the line as a whole will not be continuous.[49]

The parts of the surface too are joined by a common boundary, the line.[50] And so the surface too is continuous, for it is divided by the line. And if the line is length without breadth,[51] the surface being divided with respect to length, its parts will be extensionless with respect to breadth, since the line does not even have the extension of breadth.[52] (Line here is also to be understood as potential and not actual.)

> **5a3** For the parts of a plane join together at some common boundary.

Older [writers] call just any surface a plane, using the terms interchangeably,[53] for it is a matter of indifference to them whether they say surface or plane. More recent [writers], on the other hand, don't call every surface a plane but only one that is flat[54] (*apotetamenê*).[55] For they recognize (*eidenai*) surface as a genus and divide it into the plane, the cylindrical, the spherical, and such others as there may be.

91,1 **5a5** In the same way, in the case of body too, you could find a common boundary, a line or surface, at which the parts of the body join together.

[This is so] because the parts of the body join together at a common boundary, the surface, and, thanks to it, at the line too. For, since the surface divides bodies in the third dimension[56] (*kata bathos*) and is itself entirely extensionless with respect to depth (*kata bathos*), the parts of body also necessarily join together extensionlessly at the surface. (Here again we understand the division, or the surface, potentially.)[57] And, thanks to the surface, the parts of the body also join together at a line. For since, as we stated, the line creates the surface by flowing [into the second dimension],[58] the person who divides the body at a surface must start from a line and by, as it were, drawing it [down] create a surface, and cut the underlying [matter] by means of this.[59] And so, since it is the surface as a whole that cuts the body, it must also join the extremities of the body together at its [own] limit, I mean the line.[60]

5a6 Time and place are also of this kind. For present time joins to past time and future time. Again, place is one of the continuous [quantities], for the parts of body, which join together at some common boundary, occupy some place.

For if it has been proved that body has parts which are massed together (*sullambanein*) and continuous, and if every body in its entirety is in place, then the place that encompasses the body is continuous, since none of the parts of the body escapes being in place. Therefore it is thanks to the continuity of body that place too possesses continuity.[61]

5a15 Further, some [quantities] are composed of internal (*en autois*) parts that have position in relation to one another while others are not [composed] of [parts] that have position.

One should note that in the previous division he classes time with the continuous quantities – line, surface, body, place – but here with those not [composed] of [parts] that have position, since things [composed] of [parts] that have position are characterized by the following three features, (1) being situated somewhere, (2) being capable of being pointed to, and (3) having parts that coexist (i.e. existing all at once), not one of which is a property of time.[62]

Having counted number among the discrete [quantities] in the first division, he here seems in a sense [to count] it among those [composed] of [parts] that have position. But we have explained above[63] what [kind of] number his account is concerned with.[64]

5a38 Only those mentioned are properly called quantities, all the rest [only] derivatively (*kata sumbebêkos*), for it is looking to them that we also call the others quantities; for example, [an area of] white is described as large (*polus*)[65] because the surface [it covers] is large.

It is the job of the scholar (*epistêmôn*) not merely to investigate things that fall within his own field of knowledge but to look into and rule out things that seem to but in reality do not. Aristotle himself does this. For after enumerating the seven species of quantity, five of continuous quantity and two of discrete, he has not stopped there but asks whether anything else can also be included under quantity. Accordingly, since [an area of] white seems either large or small (*oligos*) and 'large' and 'small' belong to quantity, and since we moreover call an activity (*praxis*) long or short, he states that these are not properly quantities but [only] derivatively, for it is because they are *in* quantities that they too are called quantities. So since the white is on a surface and that [surface] is either large or small, we say that the [area of] white is large or small by transference from it[66] [*sc.* the surface]. And, similarly, an activity also has [the property of being] long (*makros*) or short (*brakhus*) only derivatively. So since the Trojan War, say, took place over a period of time, namely, over ten years, and we call that period of time 'long', on that account we also derivatively refer to the activity that took place over [that] long period of time as 'long'. And so those listed[67] are quantities in the strict sense whereas the others are called quantities derivatively because of them.

Motion too is said to be [of] long (*polus*) [duration] because the period of time over which it has taken place is long. For time is the measure of motion, since we call the time [it takes] for the return of the moon to its original position a month and the [corresponding period] for the sun a year.[68]

5b5 He will define [it] by the time, [saying] 'a year long' [or something similar].

For if someone is asked how long an activity is, he answers with a time, for instance, 'ten years'.

5b7 Whatever the size of the surface, he would say the white [area] is also that size.

For if we are asked the size of [an area of] white, we answer that it is two cubits or three cubits long, say, that being also the size of the surface bearing the white. So we are not [really] calling the [area of] white itself large (*polus*) or small (*oligos*) but the surface, for the white on a cubit-long surface can [it is true] be more white than that on a two cubit one, but then we don't say that [one] white is larger (*pleiôn*) than [the other] white but that one [lot of] white is more white than the other.

5b11 Further, there is no contrary to a quantity.

Having given us the division of quantity and having told us the nature of quantities in the strict sense and the nature of the derivative ones, he now wants to give us, as he did in the case of substance,[69] a distinctive feature (*idion*) of quantity.[70] For it wasn't possible to provide a definition of it [*sc*. quantity] for the reason stated earlier,[71] [namely,] that it is not possible to give a definition of the most generic genera because being is not predicated of the ten categories qua genus, as was shown in the *Isagoge*.[72] For if he were talking about some particular quantity, two cubits, for example, he would be able to reveal its nature by means of a definition, using quantity *tout court* as genus. But as the case stands he is dealing with quantity *tout court*, for which it would not have been possible to find a higher genus, by [the use of] which he could have given its definition.

Just as, in the case of substance,[73] he first stated what appeared to be its distinctive features and then, after finding fault with them, gave us its truly (*ontôs*) distinctive feature, so too does he proceed here, and after first finding fault with all of the [merely] apparent distinctive features of quantity, after that gives its truly distinctive feature. And first he says that it seems to be a distinctive feature of quantity that it has no contrary. For what could be contrary to a discrete quantity such as two cubits or three cubits?

5b14 Unless someone were to say that many (*polus*) is contrary to few (*oligos*) or large (*megas*) to small (*mikros*).

He fittingly examines the question (*logos*) with respect to these things here – [I mean] whether the large and small are contraries, or even [indeed] quantities. In the section on substance he merely mentioned them and, after conceding them to be contraries, moved on.[74] Now he shows that they are not quantities but relatives. And he again shows it in two ways:[75] by the objection that they are not quantities, and by the counter-objection that even should they be conceded to be quantities, they are not contraries.[76]

First, then, by the objection, as follows: 'none of these is a quantity, but rather [they are all] relatives, for nothing is said to be large or small in its own right but is compared to something else'.[77] For it is a distinctive feature of relatives that when one is affirmed the other is implied along with (*suneisagein*) it, and when one has been eliminated the other is also eliminated. For example, when [the existence of] a father has been affirmed [the existence of] the son[78] is in every case also implied, and if a father has been eliminated the son is also eliminated. Thus the many is not said to be many[79] in its own right but [only] as compared with the few, and the few, likewise, [only as compared] with the many. And so too with the small and the large: each has reference to the other and no [instance] of them has any defined nature in its own right. And this is clear from the following. 'A mountain is called small', he says, 'and a grain of millet large', and yet if each of these was being referred to in its own right and not as compared with another thing [of the same kind] in comparison with it, we would not call the mountain small and the millet grain large, for that would be ridiculous. In reality (*nun de*) we clearly call the mountain that is smaller than another mountain small – and [equally] clearly the grain of millet that is larger than another grain of millet large.[80] Thus we also say that there are few people in Athens, either comparing it with itself [on another occasion] or with another city, but that there are many in a village, even though they are fewer than those in Athens, clearly making the comparison with another village.[81]

And so either one must say that the category of quantity and the category of the relative are one and the same, or, if [these] categories are [to be] distinguished, these items [*sc.* many and few, large and small] are not to be placed under quantity but rather under the relatives.

> **5b26** Further, 'two cubits' and 'three cubits' and all such indicate a quantity, but 'large' or 'small' do not indicate a quantity but rather a relative.

For a quantity in the strict sense, he says, also indicates the magnitude [of the quantity] involved. This particular line, for instance, is both a quantity by its own nature and indicates how great [a quantity] is involved, since it is, let us say, three cubits or two cubits long. And so quantities in the strict sense also indicate how great a quantity they involve. The large and the small and the many and the few, on the other hand, do not possess any definite quantity, since each of them is indefinite, and consequently these are not quantities.[82]

So why, someone may perhaps ask, isn't there indefinite quantity?[83] After all, when I say that a number or a line or something of that sort is continuous, I am mentioning (*eipein*) a quantity even though I'm not also defining the magnitude [of the quantity] involved as I do when I specify (*legein*) 'three', or 'five', or 'three cubits long'. I reply that it is not even the case that the same indefiniteness is seen in these as [is found] in the small and large and the many and few. For genera are always more indefinite than their own species. At any rate, when I say 'animal', I don't define the subject in the same way as when I say 'man' or 'horse'. However, since 'animal' is not just a homonymous word but a substance that is present in common to a number of things, it is possible to define what is meant by the word 'animal' and to state that it is 'an animate, perceptive, substance' and that what is meant by 'animal' is some defined entity (*phusis*). The same goes for the entities under discussion. The word 'continuous', being more generic, is more indefinite than a definite quantity such as 'three cubits' (for this last is immediately[84] an individual, as Socrates too is an individual there[85]), and similarly the [word] 'number' more generic than 'three' and 'five', which are individual.[86] But[87] nevertheless, even in these [*sc.* the more generic items] there is something being definitely indicated. For a continuous thing is one whose parts join at some common boundary and a discrete thing is one not like this; and by 'line' I mean the magnitude extended in one [dimension], by 'surface', the one [extended] in two, by 'body', the three-dimensional. And each of these is determinate, being always the same, and does not take on a different nature as a result of (*pros*) a different relationship, as do large and small and many and few. For if, to take an example, somebody means by large something that overtops another thing and therefore calls Mount Olympus, say, large because it overtops Hymettus, he will nevertheless call this same [Olympus] small when comparing it to the earth as falling short of it [in size]. Therefore the thing described as large is not a defined quantity in the way that each of the previously mentioned quantities is not only a quantity but also defines the magnitude [of the quantity] involved, whether that it is, for example, extended in one dimension like a line, or that it is extended in two like a surface, or that it is seen in the unity of its parts like a continuous [quantity], or in their division and separation like a discrete [quantity]. And besides, the large and the small occur immediately in particular quantities, as in this particular line, in this particular body, in this particular surface, and likewise the many and the few in this particular number. And so each of these things occurs in individual quantities; for there isn't even any genus of large and small. So if one ought to compare individual things with individual things and not individual things with genera, and if the large and the small occur in individual quantities, and if individual quantities not only convey that they are quantities but the magnitude [of the quantity] each of them involves, as do three and five, then the large and the small are not quantity. This is why Aristotle used examples of this kind, saying 'further,[88] "two cubits" and "three cubits" and all such', that is, individual quantities with actual existence (*en huparxei*); for if the large and the small is quantity at all, it is certainly an individual [one], since there is not, as I said,[89] anything large *tout court*, but a thing we call large has actual existence (*en huparxei estin*) and is an individual magnitude. Therefore if every individual quantity also defines the magnitude [of the quantity] involved, and if the large and the small and the many and the few, while being individual, are indefinite entities (*tina*), then the large and the small are not quantities.

Thus, through the objection, he does not even concede that they are quantities, and, through the counter-objection, having conceded that they are quantities, he shows that they are not contraries.[90] The counter-objection begins as follows:

> 5b30 Further, whether one regards them as quantities or not, nothing is contrary to them. For how could anything be contrary to something that it is not possible to grasp in itself but which is referred to something else?

What he means is something like this. Contraries initially exist separately, having independent existence, and [only] then enter into mutual warfare.[91] For example, white and black, which were previously separate things (for they are qualities), subsequently entered into mutual strife. For relatives differ from contraries in this, in that contraries initially exist separately (for it is possible to speak of white without invoking black, or even for it not to exist at all even though white exists, or conversely for there to be black although there is no white) then war with one another, whereas relatives are born together and perish together; for by mentioning the father I have also implied the son, and if he is eliminated, the son disappears along with him. So since the large and the small and the many and the few do not exist separately and no instance of them could subsist on its own apart from its relationship to the other, it is clear that they are not contraries but relatives. For we said[92] that contraries first have their own separate existence and [only] then war with one another.[93]

> 5b33 Further, if the large and the small are to be contraries, the result will be that the same thing admits contraries at the same time and [things] are contrary to themselves.

By this he shows, by *reductio ad impossibile*, that they are not contraries. For he says that if the large and the small are contraries, the result will be that contraries are in the same thing at the same time. For the same thing will be both large and small, both many and few. For instance, a grain of millet is called small as compared to a bean but large as compared to a mustard seed, and you will describe the people in Athens as many as compared to those in the village but few as compared to those in the whole of Greece, and consequently these things will be receptive of contraries at the same time, which is impossible. Substance was said to be receptive of contraries, but not to admit contraries at the same time, for the same thing will never be at the same time both hot and cold, both white and black. But, he says, [things] will not only admit contraries, but will also be contrary to themselves – for the same thing is called both small and large and many and few – which is absurd, for nothing there is wars with itself.[94]

6a8 Therefore the large is not contrary to the small, nor the many to the few.

First he hypothesized that they are contraries and showed that they are not quantities, then he hypothesized that they are quantities and showed that they are not contraries, because the truth is that they are neither quantities nor contraries but relatives.[95] That they are not quantities he showed by way of the objection, that they are not contraries by way of the counter-objection. They are, then, as I said, cases of relatives that have their existence among quantities. Large (*megas*) and small (*mikros*) are properly said of the continuous, for we refer to body as large and small – and similarly as long (*makros*) and short (*brakhus*). And the same goes for surface. And we properly describe the remaining species of the continuous as large and small or long and short [as well]. On the other hand, [we use] many (*polus*) and few (*oligos*) of what is discrete and has no position, for time is described [in terms of] 'many' and 'few',[96] and likewise number. Hence, conducting (*gumnazein*)[97] the argument by means of examples, he has used large and small in the case of the mountain and the grain of millet, which are continuous things (for each is body) and many (*polus*) and (*oligos*) few in the case of number (I mean [the numbers] of the people in Athens and of those in the village), which are discrete, since number is a discrete quantity. However, we often incorrectly apply small and large to discrete things and many to continuous things. For example, we call a speech of Demosthenes small or large[98] because it focuses (*blepein*) on a single and continuous subject, and consequently we are accustomed to apply small and large to it too on account of the continuity and unity of its subject. Of course we would not call the nine public speeches of Demosthenes a long (*makros*) speech, because their subject is not single and continuous, nor the eleven against Philip either;[99] instead, we call them many. Moreover, we describe water as 'much' (*polus*) even though it is continuous, perhaps because it is readily divided. And we also often call a road 'long' (*polus*)[100] even though it is continuous, because it is divided into many stades[101] and is after a fashion divided by feet in the act of walking.

It is also quite appropriate to raise the question here as to how it is that a little earlier[102] he said that the many (*polus*) and few are quantities – in the passage where he said 'only those things are properly called quantities' that he had earlier taught [us] about, [namely,] the five species of the continuous, line, surface, body, time, and place, and the two of the discrete, language and number, 'and all the rest', he says, '[only] derivatively; for it is looking to the former', he says, 'that we

also call the others quantities; for example, [an area of] white is described as large (*polus*) because its surface is large' – how, then, having made these statements previously ([statements] by which he clearly indicated that the many (*polus*)[103] and the few are quantities), does he state in the present passage that the many 99,1
and the few do not belong to quantity but to the relatives? If it is correctly shown here that these do not belong to quantity, he has wrongly called them quantities earlier.

Well, what do we say to this? Something often stated[104] by us, [namely,] that the relatives have no separate nature but exist in the other categories. The many 5
and few, the large and the small, the double and the half and the like, are relatives that exist in quantity, not in qualification, just as whiter, sweeter, and heavier are relatives that have their existence in qualification. So when we describe [an area of] white as large (*polus*), given that large and small (*oligos*) are relatives occurring 10
in the area of (*peri*) quantity and not in that of qualification, we clearly do not so describe them properly or in their own right, but [only] because the surface, which we saw belongs to quantity, is large. So what he was saying earlier was not that many (*polus*) is in itself a quantity but that it is a relative in [the category of] quantity. And it is certainly not obligatory to refer this to quantity, unless incidentally so for someone who accepts that the many and few is in quantity.[105] 15

6a11 But it is above all with regard to place that there seems to be contrariety of quantity. For people consider up contrary to down.

Since he has proved that the large and the small are neither quantities nor contraries, he says that if anybody is absolutely bent on detecting contrariety in 20
quantity he should take the case of up and down, since these are furthest apart from one another and on that account admit of the definition of contraries. (For contraries are defined as 'the things in the same genus furthest apart from one another'.) However, he doesn't approve of this. For in reality up and down do not occur in nature,[106] but [only] the periphery (*to perix*) and the centre, which are not 25
contraries but relatives, since a periphery is around (*perix*) a centre.[107] Up and down, on the other hand, ought to be separated from one another by the distance at the diameter. But earth, on to which all heavy things fall, has the status (*logos*) of centre in relation to the universe. So how can we describe the place of earth, i.e. the centre of the universe, as contrary to the place of fire, i.e. the concave (*koilos*) [inner surface of the] sphere (*periphereia*)[108] of the moon? These are not separated 30
from one another by the diameter of the universe, and so are not furthest apart, for the things that are furthest apart are separated by the *whole* diameter.[109] 100,1
Therefore they are neither contraries nor up and down, but, as I said,[110] relatives

(for the periphery is around a centre) – unless someone were to premiss that all of the earth at once is down in that for those dwelling on any part of it the earth is beneath their feet and down and the heavens up. But if someone wants to speak of down in relation to its surface and call the sphere up, the same thing will be found to be both up and down, for the upper surface of the earth is down in relation to the heavens but up in relation to its own underneath surface. And, moreover, each of the hemispheres will be both up and down, changing their relationship according to their different motions. But there is nothing that has opposites in it at the same time and with respect to the same thing. And so it is not possible for up and down in the strict sense to occur in nature,[111] unless of course someone should wish to call all of the earth at once down in the manner described above. Up and down are positional (*thesei*), like the roof over our heads; for in relation to us that is up, in relation to those above it, down.

6a13 Considering the region towards the centre down because the greatest distance from the centre is to (*pros*) the limits of the cosmos.

Those, he says, who want up and down to exist in nature because earth is at the distance of a diameter with regard to each limit of the cosmos on that account want earth to be down.

6a15 They seem to derive the definition of the other contraries from these as well, for they define the things in the same genus that are furthest apart from one another as contraries.

Because, he says, they considered earth to be down and [because] this is separated by the greatest [possible] distance in regard to each limit of the cosmos, I mean that of a diameter, and [because] down is contrary to up, and these are included under one genus, quantity, they apply their definition to all the [other] contraries as well, saying that contraries are the things under the same genus furthest apart from one another.

6a19 Quantity does not seem to admit of more and less.

Having stated that it is a distinctive feature of a quantity to have no contrary and having shown that this belongs to all of them, he did not add 'but this is not peculiar (*idios*) to quantity because it is also a property of (*huparkhein*) a substance', as he did under substance,[112] because this was clear from what had been said about substance.[113] After all, if he said there 'but to have no contrary is not peculiar to substance because it is also a property of a quantity', it is clear that here too it will not be peculiar to quantity because it is also a property of a substance. And so nothing is contrary to a quantity; rather, if anything, one ought to say that a quantity is *receptive* of contraries, just as we said[114] that there is no contrary to a substance either but it is receptive of contraries. 'What', they ask, 'aren't thick and thin, and wide and narrow, which are contraries, [instances] of quantity? To this we reply that these are not quantities but [things that] have their being in quantities, like the large (*megas*) and the small (*mikros*). For a thing we call thick is one that has a large (*polus*) extension in depth and a thing we call wide one with a large (*polus*) extension in width, and a thing we call narrow or thin one with a small (*oligos*) extension in depth or width. And everything we said[115] about those other things, I mean large and small and many (*polus*) and few (*oligos*), we shall also say about these; for these too are cases of relatives.

6a19 Quantity does not seem to admit of more and less.

He has moved on to another distinctive feature of quantity, [namely,] not to admit of more and less. And this is plausible, for it was stated[116] that where there is contrariety more and less also arise from the mixture of the contraries. However, it should be noted that he once more rejects this [as a distinctive feature] as also belonging to substance and moves on to another distinctive feature and says:[117]

6a26 But most distinctive of quantity is to be called both equal and unequal.

This is distinctive of quantity in the strict sense[118] since it belongs both to it alone and to all of it. For a line is said to be both equal and unequal to a line and a place to a place and a surface to a surface and a body to a body and a time to a time and an utterance (*logos*) to an utterance and a number to a number. If ever we use (*legein*) equal and unequal in the case of anything else, it is not in its own right but derivatively. We say, for instance, that this white body is equal to this other white body, and the same goes for unequal, but not qua white things but qua bodies, which are cases of quantity. Rather, it is like and unlike that are properly used of things of this kind, for a white thing is said to be like or unlike [another] white thing, and the same goes in the case of other such things.

On Relatives

6a36 Called relatives are things such that they are said to be just what they are 'of' other things.

Before the teaching on relatives, we must consider these five things: first, their position in relation to the [other] categories; second, the reason for the title [of the section]; third, their mode of existence; fourth, their division into species; fifth, the mode of instruction.[119]

First, then, their position. For what reason has he placed the section (*logos*) on relatives and not that on qualification after the section on quantity even though qualification has a kind of (*tis*) form and existence in its own right whereas they don't have existence of their own but have their being in the other categories, and things that exist independently are ranked higher than those that have their being only in a relationship? For it [*sc.* a quality] must first be something in its own right and only then enter into a relationship with another thing.[120]

Well, we say that he does here as well[121] just what he did in the case of quantity, [when] he placed his exposition of it second [after substance] because he had mentioned it in the section on substance, so as not to leave the reader (*akroatês*) too long in ignorance as to just what quantity is; for, since he has mentioned the relatives in the section on quantity, where he said[122] that the large and the small and the many and the few are instances of relatives, so as not to leave us too long in ignorance as to the nature of the relatives, he provides his account of them straight away.[123]

Why has [the section] been given the title *On Relatives* and not *On the Relative* so that the title is in the singular? We answer that it is because relatives are a kind of relationship (*skhesis*) and a relationship is seen in a minimum of two things that he has used the plural in the title. Right, for example, is right of left, and something couldn't be on the right on its own, and a father is the father of a son, and someone couldn't be a father on his own without being so called in relation to a son. In the case of substance it is possible, in fact necessary, for a single thing on its own to be a substance, as, for instance, a man [is]. And the same goes in the case of quantity, for two cubits by itself can be referred to as a quantity.[124]

It is also possible for the things themselves to be referred to in the plural as 'relatives' and the category itself in the singular as 'the relative',[125] in the way that with quantity and the other categories we also refer to the category in the singular, indicating by the title not the things in it but the nature that is predicated of [all of] them in common. [This is possible] because the relationship, even if it is [embodied] in more than one thing, is nevertheless a single thing at base (*en hupokeimenôi*), like the seed and the fruit and the way up and the way down. After all, the relationship of the master to the slave, which is called slavery when we start from the slave and ownership (*despoteia*) when we start from the master, is [a] single [thing]. And the same applies in the case of student and teacher, etc. But, so as to show, as we said,[126] that the category of the relatives is never present in a single thing, he has on that account made the title *On Relatives* in the plural.

About their [mode of] existence we have the following to say.[127]

Some[128] say that none of the relatives exist by nature (*phusei*) but that they are a creation of our thought, claiming that on that basis (*houtôs*) the relatives do not exist by nature but [only] by imposition (*thesei*), because it is possible for someone on the right to come to be on the left and a father is also a son and a slave is a slave [only] by imposition; for no one is a slave by nature, since the same person may also become the master of another person at the same time [as being a slave]. However, these people are wrong. For these [relations] are observed in nature in the same way that the parts of the body are seen to be in a relationship, that to one another. For one [of these], namely, the liver, is placed (*tattein*) by nature on the right, another, namely, the spleen, on the left, and the liver could never be on the left or the spleen on the right, but if their position were switched, the organism (*zôion*) would be destroyed. And god only rules and all of us are ruled by him; and soul, and nature, only move the body, and the body is only moved by them and does not move them in return.[129]

Some, in diametrical opposition to these, claimed that all things are relative, one of these being Protagoras the sophist. This man used to say that nothing at all has a definite nature. Hence he would say that it is not possible for anyone to make false statements. For each person makes statements about things – which have no definite nature but have their being in relation to us – on the basis of what appears and seems to be the case to him. For this reason people suffering from jaundice say that honey is bitter and are actually telling the truth, for they are saying what seems and appears so to them, while healthy people, equally truthfully, say that it is sweet. And the throat of a dark pigeon standing in the sun appears purple to some, like gold to others,[130] and of some other [colour] to others, according to the different position of [the pigeon] and the observers. And the same applies for everything else: what seems true to one person another thinks false, and what seems noble to this person is considered mean to another, and the opposite is true [as well]. So it is by convention that we call a thing bitter, by convention that we call a thing sweet, and nothing is either. And so nothing at all has any defined existence, but [all things] are relatives.

Aristotle refutes this man in the third[131] book of his work the *Metaphysics*.[132] He says that if everything a person believes to be the case is actually true, then when mad people think that fire nourishes and doesn't burn, when fire is brought into contact with them, it ought to nourish them and not burn them, and when they think that bread burns, bread ought to burn them and not nourish them. And Plato too refutes him in his dialogue *Theaetetus*, where he sets out to refute this very position. There, after many other proofs, he elegantly advances this argument. 'Given, Protagoras, that we claim that what you are saying is not true' he says, 'are we making a true statement when we say of you that you are making a false statement or are we making a false statement? Well, if we are making a true statement, Protagoras is making a false one when he says that what anyone says is [always] true (for we are making a true statement when we say that you are saying this wrongly (*pseudês*)), and if we are making a false statement, then it is possible to say things that are false and not everyone who says something is making a true statement'.[133]

Others besides these[134] have correctly stated that some things are relative, others per se. Things such as right and left are relative, things such as body and man per se. (A man qua man isn't a relative.)[135] These relatives do not have existence of their own but have their being in the other categories. When, for example, I mention a father, I have mentioned a relative in [the category of] substance, when many or few, a relative in quantity, when whiter or blacker, one in qualification, and the same goes for the rest.[136] Some[137] aptly liken them to suckers, which do not have [separate] existence of their own but have their being on [the parent] plants. They also liken them to logs that support one another, for when one of these is removed the other will not stay (*einai*).[138]

Their division is this. Of relatives, some are said on the basis of (*kata*) homonymy, as, for instance, like is like like; others on the basis of heteronymy. Of those based on (*kata*) heteronymy, some are from superiority or inferiority [of things] to one another, like many and few and large and small and greater and lesser; some are based on ruler and ruled, as a master is master of a slave; some are based on judger and judged, as the perceptible is perceptible[139] by the senses and the knowable is known by knowledge; or on partaker and partaken, as a knowledgeable person is called knowledgeable through partaking in knowledge; or on cause and caused, as a father is the father of a son; or on agent and patient, as the striker strikes the person who is struck; or on a difference of place, as the person on the right is to the right of the one on his left.[140]

The mode of instruction he uses is this. He does not immediately give us the sound definition of the relatives but first presents the definition of the relatives the ancients subscribed to, then shows that a great number of absurdities follow from this definition, and only after that (*houtôs*) himself gives another definition of his own[141] of them,[142] one that belongs to the relatives alone and to all of them. For, so as not to appear to be running the ancients down, he presents their definition first, and having shown in an inoffensive manner that its consequences are absurd, [only] then (*loipon*) validates his own definition.[143]

One should be aware that relatives[144] begin in every case with the nominative case and are given (*apodidonai*)[145] relative to (*pros*) one of the oblique [cases]. And sometimes they reciprocate relative to the case relative to which they are given, as for example, a father is the father *of* a son and the son the son *of* a father, and at other times they do not reciprocate relative to the case relative to which they are given but relative to another, as for example in the case of perception and the perceptible. For perception is perception *of* the perceptible (here the giving (*apodosis*) is relative to a genitive), but they do not reciprocate relative to a genitive, but to a dative, since the perceptible is perceptible *by* perception. And the giving is often relative to an accusative too, as when we say 'the striker strikes the person who is struck', and this makes reciprocation relative to a genitive, for the person who is struck is struck by *the striker*.[146]

6a36 Called relatives are things such ...

He has used 'called' because he isn't satisfied with the statement (*logos*), for he will show that many absurdities result from the definition (*horismos*) and will propose another definition himself.[147]

6a36 ... that they are said to be just what they are *of* other things ...

As a man on the right, for instance, is said to be on the right of another man not qua man but qua [being] on the right.[148]

6a37 ... or [to stand] *in relation to* something else in some other way.

Because, in saying 'are said *of* other things', he made the giving relative to a genitive, so that that you won't imagine that relatives are only given relative to a genitive, he says 'or in some other way', that is, the giving may [also] be relative to a dative or an accusative.[149]

6b2 Things of the following types are also instances of relatives: a state, a condition, perception, knowledge, position.

Because the preceding [examples][150] are instances of quantity and these instances of qualification, he has with reason decided to separate them, saying 'things of the following types are *also* [instances of relatives]'. Or else, because he gave the earlier [examples] relative to [the] genitive case and they had their reciprocation again relative to a genitive, whereas these reciprocate relative to a dative, he fittingly lists these as though making a fresh start. In listing the examples, he teaches us procedures (*tekhnê*) for the conversion of relatives. For these, as I have already said, being given relative to a genitive, make reciprocation relative to a dative. A state, for instance, is a state *of* the possessed. Here the giving is relative to a genitive, but the reciprocation relative to a dative, for the possessed is possessed *by* the state.[151] And in the same way a condition is a condition *of* the conditioned (*diathetos*)[152] and the conditioned is conditioned *by* the condition, and knowledge is knowledge *of* the known and the knowable is known *by* knowledge.[153]

6b11 Also, lying and standing and sitting are particular positions.

Wishing to claim that lying and standing and sitting are relatives, he argues this from their genus, namely, position, which is the genus of the cited [postures], and which is a relative; for a position is the position of someone in [the] position (*keimenos*), and if the genus is a relative, it is clear that its species, i.e. the things listed above, are as well. For either the whole body is upright and it is called standing, or the whole of it is in a horizontal position and it is called lying, or some part of it is upright (*histasthai*) and some part reclining (*keisthai*) and it is called sitting.[154]

If these [postures] are included under the relatives, one should ask what we are going to include under being-positioned (*keisthai*).[155] We reply that standing is one thing, to be standing another, lying one thing, to be lying another, sitting one thing, to be sitting another, because standing and lying and sitting indicate the relationship itself, but to be standing, to be lying, and to be sitting do not indicate just the relationship but also the substance itself, the one that is lying or the one in which the lying is [taking place], and similarly in the case of the other [postures].[156] So the former [terms], in that they indicate a relationship, are included under relatives, and the latter, which, along with the relationship, also indicate the things to which the relationship applies, are included under being-positioned; for, just as what is in time is one thing and time another, and what is in place one thing and place another (for time and place are continuous quantities while what is in place is included under 'where' and what is in time under 'when'), so too is it with these, as has been stated – which is also what [Aristotle] himself

has added [here when he says] by way of clarification: 'to be lying or to be 20
standing or to be sitting are not themselves positions but are derived[157]
paronymously from the aforementioned positions'. And if a thing is named
paronymously, it is not the same [kind of thing] as the one from which it is
named. After all, to be standing is named from standing, to be lying from lying
and to be sitting from sitting, and just as they were derived from the species of
position, so too was being-positioned derived from their genus, i.e. position, 25
[and being-positioned] is one of the categories, being the genus corresponding
to[158] to be standing, to be lying, and to be sitting. And so one species of relatives,
i.e. position, has given birth to one category, [namely,] being-positioned. And
there is nothing surprising about this seeing that time too gives birth to [the
category] when (*pote*) and place to [the category] where (*pou*), and they [*sc.* time 30
and place] are species of quantity – not in that time itself is 'at a time'(*pote*) or
place 'somewhere'(*pou*), but that the things that occur in time and place are.

> **6b15** There is also contrariety in relatives. For example, virtue is contrary to vice,
> both being relatives, and knowledge to ignorance.

Having discussed the relative[159] from the perspective of the views of the ancients 108,1
with regard to it, he now wants to give its distinctive feature, and he first sets out
what appear to be distinctive features of the relatives but in truth are not (as he
also did in the cases of substance and quantity), lest someone, considering
(*prosballein*) them superficially, should think that they really are distinctive
features.

First he says that it is a distinctive feature of theirs to be receptive of contraries. 5
For vice, he says, is the contrary of virtue, knowledge of ignorance, and injustice
of justice. (Each of these is said in relation to (*pros*) something else. Virtue, for
example, is said to be the virtue of a good man, and knowledge knowledge of the
knowable or that of a knowledgeable person, and vice the vice of a bad man; and
they obviously reciprocate.)[160]

However, not all the relatives are receptive of contrariety. And this is 10
reasonable. Since the relatives are, as we said,[161] like suckers and do not have
separate (*aphorizein*) things (*pragmata*) so as to have (*pros*) an existence of
their own[162] but are found in the other categories, they mimic those [categories]
that they are attached to and whenever the categories are receptive of contraries,
the relatives that subsist in them also possess contrariety, and whenever they
contain nothing contrary, nor are the relatives in them receptive of contrariety.[163] 15
For instance, since nothing is contrary to a substance or a quantity, nor will
there be any contrary to the relatives that subsist in association with (*peri*)

them, to the triple for example. For triple is a relative (it is the triple *of* something) and yet does not exhibit (*ekhein*) any contrariety, since it is, as I said,[164] combined with (*sumplekein*) a category[165] containing no contrary, namely, quantity. And the same goes in the case of substance, for instance for master [and] son [and] right [and] left: there is nothing contrary to these because the things they are combined with (I mean men) are included under a category that contains no contrary. However, since there is a contrary for quality, there is also a contrary for the relatives associated with it. Virtue and vice, for instance, are contraries, and knowledge and ignorance. For these are qualifications. But one should note that these are contraries to one set of things but [related] as relatives to another. For instance, virtue is the virtue *of* a good man and a good man is good *through* virtue, and similarly vice is the vice *of* a bad man and a bad man is bad *through* vice. So [virtue and vice] are relative to these things, but contraries [to others], vice to virtue and a bad man to a good. With reason, then, contrariety is (1) observed in relatives and (2) it is not a concomitant of all of them.

One should enquire how it is that he says virtue and vice and knowledge and ignorance are instances of relatives. We reply that he is not stating doctrine when he says this but speaking casually (*lelêthotôs*)[166] in his desire to discredit (*kakizein*) the definition given [earlier].[167] For if relatives are characterized by being said of other things, these too will be relatives, since they too are said with reference to other things; for virtue is the virtue of a good man and vice the vice of a bad man, and knowledge the knowledge of a knowledgeable person and ignorance the ignorance of an ignorant person. However, it follows from this argument that all of the categories [derived] from accidents, I mean the nine [other than substance], are also instances of relatives, for all of them are said to be *of* substance. [This is] because they supervene upon it. Whiteness, for example, is said to be the whiteness of a white thing and two cubits two cubits of, say, log; and when and where and acting and being-affected and the rest are said *of* something; for 'when' is not anything in its own right, but 'when' is some [aspect] (*ti*) of substance, and the same goes for the rest. And substance itself, when considered as a part, is said in relation to something else; for a part is said to be a part *of* a whole, and a whole is said to be a whole *for* its parts. But this is absurd – I mean that all of the categories should be said in relation to something – since that the other categories are distinct from the relatives is clear from the following [consideration]. If [the other categories] were relatives, the things in relation to which they are said would have to be included in their definition, since when defining relatives we necessarily also mention the things in relation to which they are said. For instance, if you are going to define a father, it is necessary to mention a son as well, for you will say that [a father] is father of a son. But in defining the other categories[168] there is no need to mention what they are said in relation to. In defining two cubits long, for instance, you will have no need to mention any of the other things of which two cubits long is said, for example a log, and the same goes in the case of quality and the other [categories]. If, then, on the one hand the categories are said in relation to something else (for accidents are said to be [accidents] of substance and the parts [parts] of the whole) but on the other hand they are not relatives, it is clear that the definition of the relatives has been badly formulated, since it takes in the other categories. In fact, that which is said of another thing does not derive its being from being said of another thing, but relatives do derive their being from being relative to something [else]; for if something *is* 'of' another thing, it is also said of another thing, but if something is *said* of another thing, it does not also automatically (*êdê*) derive its being from[169] being said of another thing.

One should be aware that those who say that Plato defines the relatives in this way and that he believes that the existence of relatives lies in their being said of other things misrepresent the philosopher. Apart from other considerations (*kai gar*), one can see from what is said in the *Gorgias*[170] that he characterizes them by their *being of* and not by their *being said of* other things;[171] for he says, 'if there is something that acts, there must also be something that is acted on' ([observe that] he has said 'be' and not 'is said [to be]').[172]

> **6b19** Relatives seem to admit of more and less. For 'similar' and 'dissimilar' are called more or less [so], and 'equal' and 'unequal' [too] are called more or less [so].

Having rejected the previous one, he moves to another distinctive concomitant of relatives, that relatives admit of more and less. For we say that this thing is more or less like that, as when we say that the white on a wall is more like that of a garment than that of snow. And this concomitant is like the one before it, for this one too is not concomitant to *all* relatives. For one father is not said to be more a father that another father, and similarly nor is a son. And this is reasonable, since it was stated[173] that where contrariety is seen there is also more and less, and where contrariety does not exist, nor does more and less. So since contrariety is present in relatives, more and less is also present in them, but since contrariety is not present in all of them, on that account more and less is not present in all of them either.[174] Perhaps someone will ask whether, if in things in which contraries are present more and less also occur through the mingling of [those] contraries, it is for that reason also the case that in quantity, because there are no contraries, there is therefore also no more and less; and again, how is it that, if being equal and unequal is characteristic of quantity, he says here that unequal is called more or less [unequal]. For we said[175] that if the relative occurs in a category with contrariety (*enantion*),[176] it too admits of contraries, but if in a category that does not admit of contraries, it does not admit of[177] contraries either. So if the equal and unequal[178] is a relative existing in quantity and nothing is contrary to a quantity, [then] the equal and unequal are not contraries either. And where there is no contrariety, there is no more and less either. Therefore the unequal is not called more or less [unequal]. For if the more and less comes about through the mixture of contraries, and the equal is not mixed with the unequal, then nor could anything be more or less unequal. For the less unequal is called less unequal because it partakes to a greater degree (*mallon*) of the equal. And, besides, if a thing is more or less unequal, it is also less or more equal. For the less unequal is more equal than the more unequal, as, for example, the less light is more dark than the more light. So if it is not possible to be more or less equal than the equal (for that which departs from the equal in the direction of either more or less is no longer equal), then nor is there a more or less unequal. For the unequal is more [in the nature of] privation and indeterminateness, not the contrary of the equal. So perhaps he was mistaken in asserting here that the unequal is more or less so without considering his words carefully, or perhaps this has been added [to the text] by certain people as an interpolation.

6b28 All relatives are spoken of in relation to reciprocating (*antistrephein*) [correlatives]. For example, a slave is called the slave of a master and a master is called the master of a slave.

He has moved to another concomitant of relatives, one that is strictly peculiar to them, [namely,] that they are spoken of in relation to reciprocating [correlatives]. To learn what it is to be spoken of in relation to reciprocating [correlatives],[179] let us first learn what reciprocation (*antistrophê*) is, and before that what revolution (*strophê*) is. Revolution, then, is starting from and returning to the same point.[180] Because of this we also say that the universe revolves (*strephesthai*), since, moving in a circle, it starts from and returns back to the same point. And we also say that we go around in a circle (*strephesthai*) when we end up in the same place that we started from. Reciprocation is, as it were, 'equiversion'[181] (*isostrophê*); for amongst the ancients *anti* means 'equal' (*ison*); for example, 'godlike' (*antitheos*) is equivalent to 'equal to the gods' (*isotheos*) and 'a match for men' (*antianeira*) [means] 'equalling (*isousthai*) men', and we call our largest digit the thumb (*antikheiron*)[182] because it has strength equal (*isos*) to the rest [together]. 'Equiversion' is when one thing is not predicated any more of another than that is of it. For example, the father is no more spoken of in relation to a son than the son is in relation to the father. Relatives, then, are spoken of in relation to reciprocating [correlatives]. For example, a slave is the slave of a master and a master the master of a slave.[183]

> **6b33** However sometimes they will differ verbally (*kata tên lexin*) in the ending [of the words].

Since he has given [examples where the relative is] relative to a genitive, he has added that relatives are not only given relative to a genitive but relative to some other case, on account of which they do not always reciprocate in the same case either. But these matters have already been discussed[184] by us above.[185]

> **6b36** At times, indeed, they will not seem to reciprocate – if that in relation to which a thing is spoken of is not given appropriately but the person who gives it makes a mistake.

Relatives should preserve equality with regard to one another so as to be able to reciprocate in the way that 'human' and 'capable of laughter' reciprocate. But if they are unequal, the greater follows from the lesser, as 'animal' does from 'human', but the lesser doesn't from the greater; for human doesn't follow from animal. This, then, is the rule for relatives. Equality[186] [is seen in cases] such as 'father of a son' and 'double of a half', which, of course, reciprocate.[187] But if they are unequal, they no longer reciprocate, as he says himself, [when he says] 'if "wing" is given as "of a bird", "bird of a wing" does not reciprocate'. [This is] because not every wing is the wing of a bird. There are some winged creatures that are not birds. For of winged creatures, some are split-winged,[188] like ours,[189] and these alone are called birds (as he himself said in the *History of Animals*[190] [where he states] that split-winged creatures are called 'bird'), some, like bats, are membrane-winged, some, like beetles, sheath-winged, and these [last two groups] are not birds. Since, then, 'wing' and 'bird' are not coextensive but 'wing' is broader than 'bird', one must make them coextensive for them to reciprocate. [Now] unequal things are made coextensive when the lesser is increased or the greater decreased. So if in this case we broaden the narrower [term], i.e. 'bird', by calling 'bird' a 'winged creature',[191] and thereby produce [the statement] 'a wing is the wing of a winged creature', then they reciprocate, since 'a winged creature is a winged creature by [virtue of] a wing'.¹⁹² Again, if 'rudder' is described as (*apodidonai*) the 'rudder of a boat', then there is no reciprocation, for one cannot say that 'a boat is a boat by [virtue of] a rudder', since many boats, skiffs for instance, do not have rudders. So, since these too are unequal (for 'boat' is broader than 'rudder'), if we narrow the broader of them, I mean 'boat', by saying 'ruddered' instead of 'boat', then, becoming equal, they do reciprocate; for 'a rudder is the rudder of a ruddered [craft]'¹⁹³ and 'a ruddered [craft] is a ruddered [craft] by [virtue of] a rudder'.¹⁹⁴ Also, a head too is called the head of something – of an animal. But if it is given [as] *relative to* an animal, there is no reciprocation, because once more the statement (*apodosis*) is not appropriate, for a head is said to be the head of an animal but an animal is not said to be an animal by [virtue of] a head, because there are some animals with no head, for instance, crabs, grubs, earth-worms. So again one must narrow the broader [term], I mean 'animal', and make it 'headed', and in that way reciprocation will be preserved. For a head is the head of a headed [creature], and a headed [creature] is headed by a head. So in the case of the bird we have broadened the narrower [term], I mean 'bird', and in the other cases, I mean 'boat' and 'animal', we have narrowed the broader one.¹⁹⁵

> **7a5** At times it may perhaps even be necessary to create a name if there is no existing name (*onoma*)¹⁹⁶ in relation to which [a thing] would be appropriately given.

Lest someone should say 'What! If people invent names and alter each of them as they please, won't the result be that the normal usage of names is done away with in its entirety, everyone inventing names as they see fit, and consequently everyone will seem to be talking nonsense, saying, for instance, 'headed' instead of 'human being' or 'ruddered' instead of 'boat', or anything else anyone may invent?', he says to this¹⁹⁷ that it causes no difficulty if we think up names for things to which common usage hasn't thought to allocate them.¹⁹⁸ For common usage allocates names to the things it is familiar with, while the arts, inasmuch as they are the discoverers of new things, must allocate names to the things discovered by them to facilitate (*pros*) reference to them. For instance, the geometer, having discovered that some triangles have two equal sides, some three equal sides, and some three unequal sides, has called the first kind isosceles, the second equilateral, the third scalene,¹⁹⁹ and, similarly, the musician has given names to the various scales²⁰⁰ and called one chromatic, another diatonic, and so on. Here too, then, since common usage has neglected to allocate names to these things, we must allocate them. [Usage] has, for example, named the boat but has not distinguished those that are ruddered from those that are not ruddered, and it has named the animal but has not separated by their appellation those that have heads from those that do not. Therefore, as was stated,[201] there is nothing absurd about our creating names in such cases. How one should allocate names and from what sources, he has revealed in the continuation, saying:[202]

> **7a18** Perhaps one would most easily grasp things for which there are no [existing] names in this way – if names [derived] from the original [names] were also assigned to the [things] with which they reciprocate.

He now gives us a rule by which we shall be able to create a name appropriately should a name not be found in common usage.[203] One should, he says, assign a paronymous name [derived] from the first, and appropriately predicated, [names] to the [things] of which they are predicated, and in this way we shall find that they reciprocate. For instance, from 'rudder' [one might] call the boat of which the rudder is predicated 'ruddered', and from 'head' call the animal that has a head 'headed', and likewise in other cases. And this he also says casually (*lelêthotôs*) in his desire to discredit the definition.[204] For if relatives are those things that are said to be *of* other things, head and rudder and wing will be relatives, which is absurd. For qua parts of substances these are indeed said to be relatives (for the part is a part of a whole and the whole a whole for its parts), but qua wing or rudder or head they are not relatives but substances, for each of them is seen [to exist] in its own right. For instance, if the head or hand has been cut from the whole, it is none the less called a head or a hand, but they are no longer called parts, for a part is seen [to exist] in the whole. In the case of relatives, if they are taken away from the things in relation to which they are said, their own name is immediately taken away as well. For instance, a father is said to be the father of a son, but if the son is taken away, the father's being a father is also taken away. Things that are said [to be][205] *of* other things, on the other hand, even should they be taken away from the things of which they are said to be, none the less preserve their name. For instance, a head is said to be the head of an animal, and if it is taken from the animal, it is none the less called a head, and a rudder [is said to be the rudder] of a boat, and a wing [the wing] of a bird, and when taken from the things of which they are said to be [part], they too none the less retain (*tunkhanein*) their own name.

> **7a25** I mean that even among those [relatives] that are admittedly spoken of in relation to reciprocating [correlatives] and for which there are [current] names,

none reciprocates if it is given in relation to some accident and not in relation to just what [the correlatives] are²⁰⁶ called.

Here the argument is from the a fortiori. What is surprising, he asks, if reciprocation is not preserved in the cases mentioned on account of their not having been properly given, when not even things that are admittedly relatives and said in relation to reciprocating [correlatives] and for which there *are* [current] names do not reciprocate if the giving does not take place properly? For instance, if someone were to give a master not in relation to a slave but in relation to a man by saying 'a master is the master of a man' he would not be able to turn this round and say 'a man is the man of a master'. That would be ridiculous. There is no difficulty in saying that a master is the master of a man, but to say a man is the man of a master is quite absurd. And so in the case of these [things] too, because there has not been an appropriate giving, reciprocation is not preserved either; for we have not given [the relative] in relation to [something] equal since man is wider.²⁰⁷ So, as has been stated,²⁰⁸ the reciprocating [entities] must be equal to one another if they are to reciprocate. This indeed is why distinctive features²⁰⁹ reciprocate with the things of which they are distinctive features, since they too are equal to one another.

He says all of this in support of the definition that states that relatives exist by being said of other things and tries to show that under this definition relatives reciprocate, wanting to [first] strengthen [the case for] it as much as possible so as not to seem to be condemning by default, and thus refute it fairly later, showing that even after such stout advocacy many absurdities nevertheless result from it.²¹⁰

7a31 Also, if that in relation to which something is spoken of has been appropriately given, all the other things that are accidental being stripped away and only that in relation to which it was appropriately given left, [then] it will²¹¹ be spoken of in relation to that [thing].

He is giving us a rule for [recognizing] appropriately given [correlatives] of a thing. He says that if something is referred to by a number of names [and] then something else is predicated of one of those names and you want to know whether the predicate has been properly predicated for that name, [then], after stripping away all of the other names that are accidental to the subject and leaving only the one in relation to which the predicate was given, if you find that it reciprocates with what was predicated of it, you can know²¹² that the earlier (*to proteron*)²¹³ [predicate] was appropriately given, since it [*sc.* the term of which the predication was made] would not reciprocate if it [*sc.* the predication] had not been properly given. For example, if a slave has been given as the slave of a master, since being human and bipedal and receptive of knowledge [only] incidentally apply to a master, if you strip all of these away from him and imagine (*hupotithenai*) that they don't belong [to him] at all and leave only his being a master, you will none the less find that reciprocation occurs in the proper manner; for a master is called the master of a slave. However, if a slave is not given in relation to a master but in relation to a human being, when everything else is stripped away from the human being, I mean [being a] master and bipedal and the rest, the reciprocation will not be preserved, since it is not possible to turn [them] around (*antistrephein*) and say 'the human being is a human being of a slave', and so the slave was not appropriately given in relation to the human being.

He says, 'when all the other things that are accidental to a master are stripped away, for instance, being bipedal or receptive of knowledge or a human being',[214] and there is nothing surprising about his calling these things 'accidental', for he does not mean accidental *tout court* but things that would be accidental with regard to the relationship of the slave[215] and be predicated of [a master] secondarily, whereas 'master' is predicated [of him] primarily and per se. For the relationship of relativity (*tôn pros ti*), having no independent existence, may, as I said earlier,[216] sometimes be present in substance, sometimes in quantity or qualification or some other category. And so, without absurdity, one says in the case of 'double', which is a relative, that when it is in, say, a log, the log is accidental to it, when in a stone, the stone is, and when in surface or time, surface or time is, the relation per se being attended to (*theôrein*) in thought.[217]

> **7b15** Relatives seem to be simultaneous by nature, and for most this is true, but for some not true.[218] A double and a half are simultaneous, and when there is a half there is a double.

He has given another distinctive concomitant of relatives in addition to (*meta*) their being said relative to reciprocating [correlatives], [namely,] their being simultaneous by nature. Simultaneous by nature are things such that when one of them has been assumed the other is of necessity implied (*suneisagein*) along with it and when one has been eliminated the other is also eliminated, and of which it is never the case that the one exists and the other does not. For when saying 'slave' one of necessity simultaneously thinks of the master as well, and when there is a double there must also be a half.

'And for most', he says, 'this is true'. He says 'for most' because he is about to raise a puzzle with regard to certain other cases that appear not to be simultaneous by nature.[219]

> **7b22** But it does not seem to be true for all relatives that they are simultaneous by nature. The knowable for example would seem to be prior to knowledge.

Against what was said above he brings the objection that being simultaneous by nature does not seem to apply to all relatives. Knowledge and the knowable for example, while being relatives, are not simultaneous. If knowable things are eliminated, knowledge is also eliminated, for if the knowable did not exist, of what would there be knowledge? But nothing prevents there being knowable things in the absence of knowledge. And so these instances of relatives are not simultaneous by nature.

The 'prior' is of two kinds (*dittos*), the [prior] in time and the [prior] in nature. Prior in time is that whose separation from the present is greater, as is the case with the past; for we say that the Persian[220] wars were prior to the Peloponnesian because their separation from the present is greater. In the case of the future, on the contrary, it is that whose separation from the present is less that is prior. Tomorrow, for example, is prior to the day after tomorrow. Such then is the prior in time. Prior in nature, on the other hand, is that which [when eliminated] also eliminates [the other] but which is not also eliminated [when the other is] and that which is entailed[221] [by the other] but which does not entail [it], as is the case with animal and human being.[222] The knowable, then, would seem to be prior to knowledge in nature, for if the knowable does not exist, knowledge does not exist, but if knowledge does not exist, the knowable can exist. For instance, they say that Thales of Miletus was the first to understand[223] the cause of lunar eclipses having recognized that the moon gets its light from the sun because its illuminated part always faces (*neuein*) the sun, for which reason when it is waxing during its departure (*apostasis*) from the sun, it has its illuminated part towards the west, the sun being more to the west at that time, while its horn-shaped and unilluminated part faces the east. When [on the other hand] it comes to be completely face to face with the sun, being diametrically opposed to it, then all of it is illuminated, the whole of it facing (*prosballein*) the whole of the sun (I'm using 'whole' of the part facing us); and when it begins to wane with its approach (*sunodos*)[224] to the sun, then, in contrast, its illuminated part faces the east, the sun being more to the east at that time, and its unilluminated and horn-shaped part towards the west. From this then he came to understand lunar eclipses, because whenever it fell into the so-called shadow of the earth, the sun being vertically opposite it in the hemisphere below the earth, the result was that it suffered total eclipse, the rays of the sun not striking it at all. Of course, unless it is a full moon, this does not occur.[225] If, then, Thales was the first to understand a lunar eclipse, it is clear that before him the knowable existed – I mean of course the lunar eclipse – but there was no knowledge of it. So it is clear that the knowable pre-exists knowledge both in time and in nature and that, while being relatives, they are not simultaneous. In the same way, if there is no perceptible there is no perception either (for of what will there be perception?), but if there is no perception, nothing prevents perceptibles (e.g. fire, earth, and the like) from existing.[226]

7b24 For mostly it is of things that already exist that we acquire knowledge.

[Aristotle] himself has explained 'mostly', saying 'in few cases if any could one find knowledge coming into existence at the same time as the knowable'. He says this on account of things introduced through an art,[227] since these do not exist in advance but acquire existence at the time they are introduced by the art, for natural things pre-exist knowledge, but artificial things acquire existence at the same time as [there is] knowledge of them. For instance, someone or other invented a mattress for sleeping on. Here knowledge comes to exist simultaneously with the knowable. You may see this most especially in the case of discoveries in mechanics. For example, of how one can move heavy objects, or move water to a higher level, and so on. For it is clear that these and other similar discoveries are made simultaneously with [there being] knowledge of them and do not exist prior to knowledge of them. But it may even be the case that artificial things are of an opposite nature (*antipeponthotôs*) to natural ones. For in the case of natural things, the knowables themselves, as was stated,[228] pre-exist knowledge of them, but in the case of things that exist through art, knowledge of them must exist first, and [only] then does the knowable come into existence; for clearly the idea of a door and how it might be constructed came first and [only] after that came the outcome of the idea. Unless one were to say that even if the knowledge of the ship pre-existed in the mind of the person who first thought of it before the ship came into existence, even so the knowledge did not properly speaking yet have existence, since it was as yet unclear whether the reality was going to follow upon the idea.[229] For perhaps something of that kind has only got as far as visualization and cannot come to fruition (*eis ergon*), as the story about Daedalus tells of his having the idea of giving himself and his son Icarus wings. And so when [and only when], simultaneously with the knowledge of some knowable, the knowable itself also comes to fruition, is it then really the case that the knowledge is also, without ambiguity, knowledge in the strict sense. And so, in the case of artificial things, it does happen that knowable and knowledge simultaneously coexist with one another.

120,1 **7b27 Further, when the knowable is eliminated, it eliminates knowledge as well.**

Having shown (*ektithesthai*) the temporal priority that belongs to (*epi*) the knowable (he says: 'for mostly it is of things that already exist that we acquire knowledge'), he now further shows the priority in nature that belongs to (*epi*) the knowable by virtue of its also eliminating knowledge [when eliminated itself] but not also being eliminated by it [when it (*sc.* knowledge) is eliminated].[230]

7b31 Take, for example, the squaring of the circle, if it is in fact a knowable; there is as yet no knowledge of it, but the knowable exists.

Geometers say that a square is a figure that does not just have four sides and four angles but one that has four sides that are equal and four angles that are right angles. This is how they say the right angle comes about. When a straight line set upon a straight line makes the angles that are internal and facing in the same direction equal to one another, each of the angles is a right angle, and the standing straight line is said to be perpendicular to the one it stands on. That, then, is a right angle. An acute angle is one that is less than a right angle, an obtuse angle one that is greater than a right angle;[231] for with the inclination of the standing straight line, one of the angles becomes greater, the other less. The lesser angle, then, as was stated, they call acute,[232] since sharp shapes (*onkos*), which are suitable for piercing, like a dagger,[233] come with it, and the greater angle, obtuse, because blunt shapes, like a pestle, which is suitable for grinding, (*ôthein*) come with it. They say that some figures are rectilinear and others curvilinear, and that rectilinear figures are triangular, or tetragonal, or hexagonal, or with any other number of angles one can think of, and they call circles curvilinear.

Now geometers ask how a square equal to a given rectilinear figure, say a pentagon, can be constructed. Indeed they have even taught this using a [standard] method. And just as they have asked [this] in the case of rectilinear figures, so too do they ask in the case of the circle too how one can find a square that is equal to a given circle. But many god-like men have sought this and not found it. Archimedes alone found anything very close, but he didn't find the exact [solution].

Aristotle, then, says: if the squaring of the circle is a knowable, since up to the present there is as yet no knowledge of it, it is clear that the knowable is prior to knowledge.[234] But this example is no more such as to establish that knowables are prior to knowledge in nature than (*all' ê*)²³⁵ that they are so in time; for although the squaring of the circle is a knowable, knowledge of it has not yet been found. But the next one (*to epipheromenon*) is such as to prove that the knowable is prior to knowledge in nature too.²³⁶

7b33 *Further, if animal is eliminated there will be no knowledge, but there may [still] be many knowables.*

Having previously shown that the [present] concomitant is defective in the case of one example of relatives, I mean the knowable, he now shows this universally for all cases.²³⁷ If animal is eliminated, he says, all instances of knowledge (*epistêmai*) are also eliminated (for all instances of knowledge are in the soul), but the knowables exist no less in their own right. And so the knowable is prior to knowledge in nature.²³⁸

7b35 *The circumstances with perception are similar to these, for the perceptible seems to be prior to perception.*

Having deployed [the above] reasoning in the case of knowledge and the knowable he now deploys it in the case of perception and the perceptible and shows by means of the same arguments that the perceptible is prior to perception, for [when eliminated] the perceptible also eliminates perception, but perception does not [when eliminated] also eliminate the perceptible. For if perception is in an animal, and if an animal is an ensouled body, and if all body is perceptible, it is necessarily the case that when the perceptible is eliminated, body is also eliminated along with it, and when body has been eliminated, there is nothing ensouled [left] either, and if there is nothing ensouled, there is no animal either, and when the animal has been eliminated, there is no perception either, because perception has its being in animals.

As we have shown, then, when the perceptible has been eliminated, there will be no perception either, because all perception has its being in body and is observed in association with it alone; for incorporeal things have eluded all perception, neither themselves falling under perception nor being capable of perception. But this certainly does not reciprocate; for when perception has been eliminated, the perceptible is not also eliminated. Why is this? Because every animal is ensouled and everything ensouled is a body, but not every body is automatically also an ensouled animal or every body perceptible, and so even when animal has been eliminated, nothing prevents many other things from existing, for instance, fire, earth, water, air, sweet, bitter, and the like. From these considerations, then, it is established that perceptibles are prior in nature to perceptions, because they eliminate perceptions along with themselves but they are not eliminated along with [them], and they are implied along with perceptions but do not imply them along with [themselves].[239]

8a6 Further, perception comes into being simultaneously with that which is capable of perceiving (for an animal and perception come into being simultaneously), but the perceptible exists even before perception exists; for fire and water and the like, of which the animal is made up, exist even before an animal, or perception, exists at all.

Here the argument is again[240] from the a fortiori and from that which is more immediately given in relation to the perceptible, I mean that which is capable of perceiving; for that which is capable of perceiving is capable of perceiving the perceptible, and that which is capable of perceiving is what partakes of perception. So what – he says[241] – am I saying?[242] That perceptibles pre-exist perception, given that that which is capable of perceiving, I mean of course the animal, with which perception naturally comes into being, gets its existence from perceptible things, I mean fire and water and the other elements. And that which comes to be out of something [else], especially [out of something that functions] as its matter, is posterior to that from which it has come to be, both in nature and in time. And so, he says, the perceptible would appear to be prior to perception.

For [Aristotle] this is the extent of the difficulty. But he has not supplied the solution to the stated objections. In response to them one must state that relatives are conceived of in two ways: either as separate entities (*pragmata*) without ties, or as bound to one another in some relation, like father and son. In this pairing (*en toutois*), if we think of the father as Sophroniscus and the son as Socrates, Sophroniscus will be prior to Socrates, for Sophroniscus is prior when we think of them as [separate] entities. But if we think of them as 'father and son', they will be simultaneous, being bound [together] in the relation. Now knowledge and the knowable are also like this. If you think of them as [separate] entities, the knowable pre-exists knowledge, but if you think of them as a relation, they exist simultaneously. For there would not even be anything knowable, if there were not knowledge of it. For instance, the stars, which are knowable will, when conceived of as [separate] entities, be prior to knowledge of them, but if we conceive of them as relatives (I mean as knowables), they will be simultaneous with the knowledge of them. For they would not even be knowables if there were no knowledge of them – [knowledge] from which they are moreover paronymously named.[243] By what would they be knowable? The knowable is knowable by knowledge, so if knowledge does not exist, how will they get a paronymous name from what does not exist? The answer is that (*alla*) they exist as [separate] entities, but not as knowables. We shall also say the same of perception and the perceptible.

Besides, there being things that are potentially [something] and others that are actually [that thing] – [things that are] potentially [something] are those whose nature it is to be something but which as yet are not, [those that are] actually [a thing], those that have displayed that natural potential in actuality (*energês*); an example of [a thing that is] actually [something] is a fully literate person (*grammatikos*), in whom no aspect of literacy (*tekhnê grammatikê*) is wanting,[244] of [one that is] potentially [something] a child, who has the potential to become literate – in the case of all relatives, whatever the state of one, the other will be the same; if one of them is actually [something], the other will also be actually [that thing], and if one is potentially [something], the other will also be potentially [that thing]. So, whenever the knowable or the perceptible are actually [knowable or perceptible], knowledge and perception will also be actually [knowledge or perception], and if the former pair are [only] potentially [knowable or perceptible], the latter pair too will be [only] potentially [knowledge or perception]. So if someone were to have conceived of the lunar eclipse as a knowable before Thales, it will have been potentially and not actually knowable, and the knowledge of it too will certainly have been conceived of beforehand as a potentiality (*dunamei*). For if the knowledge of the lunar eclipse had not existed potentially before Thales, it would not have emerged into actuality in his time; for anything that did not earlier have the potential to come into being cannot come into being at a later time. In the same way that a horse, not having the potential to become literate, will never become actually literate, if knowledge of the lunar eclipse had not existed potentially before Thales, it could not have been brought to actuality by him. And since that knowledge became actual in his time, the knowable, [*sc.*] the lunar eclipse, also became actual [then]. And we shall once more[245] say the same in the case of perception and the perceptible.

And now, if [the solution to] the squaring of the circle [is something that] can [ever] be found, it is clear that it is at present [only] potentially knowable and that knowledge of it will exist [only] potentially. And if, on the other hand, it is not possible that it will ever be found by human beings, it will not even be potentially a knowable but exists as an entity but is not even potentially a knowable, just as the number of [grains of] sand is not even potentially knowable to human beings.

By means of this argument we also solve that well-known puzzle inflicted upon us by the lawyers. These people claim there is such a thing as a masterless slave. It goes like this. They say a dying man said in his will, 'let A, provided he does B, have my household slave C'. Think about it, they say. In this situation, as long as the legatee hasn't performed the prescribed act, the slave is masterless. Our response is that here too the potential and the actual hold the solution to the problem. The one man is not actually a master, the other actually a slave, but each of them is [only] potentially so. However, as soon as the legatee performs the prescribed act and becomes an actual master, the bequeathed servant will also become an actual slave. And so the statement to the effect that relatives are simultaneous in nature is sound in every case.[246]

8a13 There is a problem as to whether *no* substance is spoken of as a relative.

Having completed [his account of] the ancients' definition of relatives and said as much as was possible in its favour, and having then stated the concomitants of relatives and [now] being on the point of giving his own definition, he first, beginning here (*enteuthen*), exposes the absurdity attendant upon the definition that has been given. This absurdity is that, under the definition that has been given, the parts of secondary substances are found to be relative, that is, substance [is found to be] accident. For, as has often been stated,[247] of the ten categories, one is substance, while the [other] nine are those of accident, of which one is the category of relatives. So if the parts of substances are relative, it is clear they will also be accidents. And if the parts are accidents, so of necessity is the whole, for the whole is made up of the parts. [And] therefore substance too will be accident, and what could be more absurd than that? At this point (*entautha*) we are given a division (*diairesis*) of substance along the following lines.[248] Substance is either universal or particular, either whole or part. Therefore, there being four divisions (*tmêma*), six pairings once more[249] result, and two of them, those that bring contraries together, cannot, as has often been stated, [actually] occur (for the same thing cannot at the same time be both universal and particular or both whole and part), but the other four, I mean the subaltern[250] and the diagonal, do occur. For either[251] (1) the universal combined with the whole makes man *tout court*, which is both universal (it is predicated of individuals and embraces them) and a kind of whole (it is a kind of wholeness (*holotês*) of its own parts, for example of animal and rational). Again, (2) the universal combined with the part makes the universal part, for example head *tout court* or hand *tout court* – universal because it is predicated of every particular head or hand, part because it is one of the parts of animal. And (3) the particular combined with the whole makes the individual man, like Socrates, who is particular because he is not predicated of anything, a whole as embracing his own parts. Again, (4) the particular combined with the part makes the individual head or the individual hand, like those of Socrates; for these are particular because they are those of Socrates alone, a part because they are seen in his wholeness, for part differs from particular in that the part belongs to many things but the particular to just one.[252]

Of these [pairings], three, he says, would not be considered relatives, but one, that of universal part, that is to say, a head [or] a hand, would seem, as far as the definition of relatives that has been given goes, to be a relative.[253] That first substance[254] is not relative is, he says, clear, since Socrates is not said to be the Socrates *of* someone else. And nor would a part of him, I mean a particular part, as for example an individual hand – not even it[255] would seem to be relative; for nobody is going to say that the individual hand is an individual hand *of* someone. That would be laughable. And nor is secondary [substance], the one that combines universal and whole – I mean man *tout court*. For nobody is going to say that man is man *of* someone or ox ox *of* someone, but, rather, an ox or a man is said to be a possession of someone, and man is not said to be man *of* someone or ox ox *of* someone. So, he says, only the one [*sc.* the pairing] combining universal and part, only this will seem to be a relative according to the definition that has been given, I mean head *tout court* and hand *tout court*; for the head is said to be the head *of* someone and the hand the hand *of* someone.[256]

But to me it seems to be the case that the particular and part too is relative as far as the definition given earlier goes. For if those things were said[257] to be relatives that are said to be just what they are *of* other things, and not only the universal part, as for instance the hand *tout court* is said to be *of* the man *tout court*, but the individual hand too is said to be *of* the individual man (for we say that this hand is [the hand] *of* Socrates, and both common parlance and the usage of the ancients are full of this [way of speaking], for we say, for example, 'I wrote this with my own hand',[258] 'I struck the hand *of* this fellow, or his head'; 'for such were the feet *of* the man, such the hands';[259] 'all the feet *of* Ida of the many streams were shaken';[260] 'the head *of* Zeus does not nod assent')[261] – and so, if the particular part too is the part *of* someone, then it too will be a relative.[262] The absurdity that appears to follow according to the text[263] is [in fact] easy to resolve; for it is not even necessary to say that an individual hand is the individual hand of someone, since we don't say that the universal hand is the universal hand of someone either but that it is the hand of [universal] man. So in just the same way we also call the individual hand the hand of someone, of Socrates for instance, without further qualification.[264]

So two parts of the above-mentioned (*proekkeisthai*) diagram,[265] the universal part and the particular part, will be relatives and, as I said,[266] it will turn out that substance is accident.[267] This absurdity, then, (I mean that the parts of substances should be relatives) is, he says, impossible, or [at least] difficult, to resolve working with (*kata*) the previously given definition of relatives.

In this fashion, then, he discredits the definition that has been given by means of *reductio ad absurdum*. *reductio ad absurdum* is as when, wishing to prove something, we take its opposite and show that some absurdity follows from it, and then conclude from this that the reason this absurdity followed for us was that the granted premiss was false; for an absurdity does not follow from any true premiss, and if that premiss was false, then the one opposed to it is true. This is the sort of thing I mean. Wishing to show that the soul is immortal, we assume the premiss contrary to that, i.e. that it is mortal, and then we show that some absurdity follows from that so as to thereby validate the contrary. For example [as follows]. If the soul is mortal, there will not be subterranean places of correction, but our life is [only] as long as it appears (*mekhri tou phainomenou*) and the soul perishes along with the body. So there will be neither any reward for good deeds nor any retribution for bad. For if we see that many of the just pass the whole of their lives in dire straits while most wrongdoers live out their lives in great repute and affluence, and if there is no scrutiny after this life of our conduct during our lifetime, the life of men being limited just to this [lifetime], then nobody is going to receive his just deserts, and if nobody is going to receive his just deserts, there will be no providence. For if, when a good ruler governs a city, one can see that everything in the city proceeds in an orderly fashion and that good men are honoured with gifts and marks of appreciation and wrongdoers publicly scorned and subject to constant punishment, how much more will it be the case, given that god is good essentially and knows and foresees everything at a glance (*mia epibolê*), that nothing disorderly will arise in the life of the universe (*ta hola*)? Therefore there will not be providence unless there is scrutiny of our conduct during our lifetime. But what is more impious than this absurdity? If there is to be no providence, nothing there is will be [well]-ordered. For what is not overseen by providence is disorderly inasmuch as it is swept along without [visible] cause (*ek tautomatou*) and just anyhow (*hôs etukhe*). But that life is not [actually] without [any] cause and [a matter of] chance (*tukhaios*) is clear from the following. Uncaused (*ek tautomatou*) and chance (*ek tukhês*) [events] are very rare and the by-products (*parakolouthêma*) of other [factors], in the case of the uncaused, of natural forces (*hormê*), in the case of chance, of purposive [behaviours]. For instance, a rock tumbles down, being brought down from a high place by natural impulse (*hormê*),[268] and, because it has been abraded (*prosrêgnunai*) by the earth and its protuberances smoothed away, has become suitable for a seat. So its becoming suitable for a seat is said to have come about without [any] cause because it was a by-product of (*epakolouthein*) the natural downwards impulse of the stone. And a stone that tumbles down from a high place rarely becomes suitable for a seat. Again, a horse, becoming thirsty during a war, bucks away from its master and runs off to drink, and when an engagement occurs and his master perishes along with everyone else, the horse survives. So the horse is said to have survived by accident (*ek tautomatou*). And but rarely does a horse throw its master during a war and survive because of it. Chance [occurrence] too is rare and the by-product of purposive impulses. For instance, someone comes [to town] to bathe or pray[269] and chances upon a book for sale that he has long been looking for and buys it. This is a chance [occurrence]; for it is not through any forethought or because he has gone where books are normally sold that he has bought the book. And this too would be very unusual.

Accidental and chance [occurrences], then, are very rare; those that are the products of a craft (*tekhnêtos*) or of nature (*phusikos*), and those that come about as a result of forethought in general, on the other hand, are among those that occur for the most part or even invariably. The carpenter, or the builder, for instance, for the most part achieves his particular goal rather than[270] failing to. And the doctor [usually] heals rather than not healing; for if he with equal frequency (*ex isês*) healed and failed to heal, nobody would even call him in, and [that would be] even more [the case] if he healed less often [than he failed to]. And nature for the most part produces someone with five fingers and only very rarely someone with six, and that through a surplus of matter; the moon always wanes as it comes into conjunction with the sun and waxes with its departure from it; the sun always creates winter solstices when it enters Capricorn and summer solstices when it moves into Cancer, and doesn't ever behave differently; and fire is always borne upwards and water always flows downwards; and, in the same way, in the case of all things that are the products of a craft or of nature, and of things that are the result of forethought in general, one can observe [that it is a case of] 'always' or 'for the most part' and never the opposite.

It is clear, then, that the cosmos is not uncaused, and nor are its parts. And if it is not uncaused, it clearly has a cause that presides over it and which arranges its affairs (*ta kath' hauta*) in an orderly fashion (*euruthmôs*), [a cause] that we call providence. So, there being providence, everyone will of necessity get their just deserts. And if this is true, and we see, as I have already said,[271] many people to all appearances meeting with experiences in this life that are the reverse of their own actions,²⁷² then human existence (*zôê*) is not limited to this life. So there will certainly be scrutiny of our conduct during our lifetime after life here [on earth], during which providence will allot to each his just deserts. And if this is so, then the soul is immortal and does not perish along with the body; for it must remain after the body has been let go (*luein*) and not perish, so as to receive its just deserts after life here [on earth].

Observe how here, wishing to show that the soul is immortal, we have assumed the premiss contrary to that one, namely, that it is mortal, and shown that an absurdity follows from it, namely, that it follows (*eisagesthai*) from it that there is no providence, and in this way established that it is immortal. For if an absurdity follows from saying that the soul is mortal, and no absurdity can follow from a true premiss, then that [premiss] is false. So the [premiss] contrary to it, namely, that it is immortal, is true; for what is contrary to what is false is of necessity true.

This, then, is the *reductio ad absurdum*, which the philosopher too uses here. For he wants relatives to be characterized by *being* 'of' other things and he hypothesizes what is the contrary of this and the view held by others, I mean that they are characterized by *being said* of other things, and he shows the absurdity that follows, i.e. that the parts of secondary substances are also relatives because they too are said of other things. And having thus ruled out this view as false, he validates his own. And, in a manner drawing the above conclusions, he says:²⁷³

> **8a28** Now if the definition of relatives has been given adequately, it is either extremely difficult or impossible to show that no substance is spoken of as a relative.

He said this – I mean 'extremely difficult' – because it somehow gives the impression that it admits of a defence. The definition ran²⁷⁴ 'those things that are said to be just what they are of other things'; so [one might argue] the head is a relative not qua head or body, but as being a part, for the part is a part *of* the whole. But this isn't true. The head is not said to be *of* something else as being a part, but precisely because it is a head. And so, according to the previously given definition that states that relatives are characterized by being said of other things, the parts of substances will also be found to be relatives. For a head is indeed said to be the head *of* something. And so it is not possible for the definition of relatives that was given [above] to escape this absurdity. For this reason, because he had said 'extremely difficult', he added 'impossible', showing the indefensibility of the absurdity.²⁷⁵

> **8a31** But if [it has] not [been given] adequately, but relatives are rather things for which 'being is the same thing as being in some way related to something', perhaps something may be said in reply to the above.

Now he sets out his own definition of relatives and says: 'but if not adequately', 25
(i.e. if the definition of relatives has not been passed down to us by the ancients
in an adequate (*autarkôs*) and complete form) 'but relatives are rather things for
which being is the same thing as being in some way related to something' (i.e.
things whose existence lies in their entering into (*anadekhesthai*) a relation of
some kind with something else) 'perhaps something', he says, may be said in
reply to the above'. In reply to what? In reply to the above puzzles to the effect 30
that the parts of substances will appear to be relatives. For if, he says, the definition 130,1
is given as we have just given it, we can easily respond to the above absurdities.
What the response is, he has added himself: 'The earlier definition does hold
good for all relatives, yet their being called what they are of other things is not 5
the same thing as their being relatives'. For it is not the case, he is saying, that if
something is said of something else its being also lies in its being said in relation
to something else. For if a thing is 'of' something else, it is also said of something
else, but if a thing is *said of* something else, it is not automatically (*êdê*) also *of*
something else. A father, for example, being the father of a son, has his being in
being the father of a son, and is of course also called the father of a son. But a 10
head, while being called the head of an animal, does not also have its being in
being said to be [the head] of an animal. Even severed (*apotemnein*) from the
animal it is still both said to be a head and is a head. But a father sundered from
(*apotemnein*) a son neither is a father nor any longer spoke of in relation to a son.
And so with reason it was said that the earlier definition holds good for relatives
but not that the second does for the first,[276] Homer also teaches this: 15

> let the head of Odysseus then no longer sit on his shoulders
> and let me no longer be called the father of Telemachus.[277]

For, no longer being a father, as a result of no longer being one, neither can he be
called one. And so 'being called' is a concomitant of 'being', but not vice versa.
And if this is so, then it is not the case that if the parts of substances are said to 20
be 'of' other things, they will on that account be relatives.[278]

One should enquire just why he has included the relatives [themselves] in the
definition of the relatives by writing 'being in some way related to something', for
one should not include the thing to be defined in the definition. Our reply to this
is that relatives are of two kinds. Both the things themselves in which the
relationship occurs and the relationship itself are called relative, as for example, 25
the category where and the category when on the one hand indicate the things
[between which the relationship holds], I mean the substance and the time or
place, and on the other hand also indicate the bare relationship itself which the

substance has with the time or the place. So because the things are clearer [to us] than the relationship in that they are perceptible, on that account he includes them in the definition so as to base his instruction on the clearer [of the two].

8a35 From this it is clear that if someone knows some relative definitely he will also know that in relation to which it is spoken of definitely.

Having given his own definition of relatives, he derives a corollary from it in the manner of the geometers. By a corollary they [sc. the geometers] mean something that becomes apparent with the proving of something else, as for example, when we were earlier[279] seeking to prove the immortality of the soul, it also became apparent that providence exists. So, here too, as we seek the true definition of relatives, it has become apparent along with this that if someone knows one relative definitely he will also know the other definitely, and if he knows one indeterminately he will also know the other indeterminately. For example, if someone knows that Sophroniscus is a father he will also know that Socrates is a son, for if he does not know that Socrates is a son, he will not know whether Sophroniscus is a father either.[280] Some say to this that if someone's body is completely covered up but he has his head or his hand uncovered (*gumnos*), in the case of this person it is possible to know the part, the hand, say, or the head, definitely (for we know that it is certainly a part), but of whom it is a part, that we do not know. Therefore, they say, it is not the case that someone who knows one [of a pair] of relatives definitely will know the other definitely. But we reply that qua head or qua hand we perceive (*ginôskein*) it definitely but qua part we do not perceive it definitely but only indeterminately, for we do not know of whom it is a part, but just as we know this [sc. that it is a part] indeterminately, so too do we perceive whose part it is indeterminately.[281]

It is possible that he also adds this in the belief that he is solving the aforementioned puzzles. For since he said [earlier] that there are some relatives that are not simultaneous by nature, the knowable, for instance, pre-existing knowledge and perceptibles being by nature prior to perception, because for the most part, he said, we acquire knowledge of things that already exist, he therefore says here, in resolution of the present [difficulty], that if relatives are identical with things for which 'being is the same thing as being in some way related (*pôs ekhein*) to something',[282] then it is necessarily the case that whatever the state (*hôs an ekhei*) of one relative the other will be the same. And so if knowledge is potential, the knowable will also be potential, and if one of them is actual, the other will be too. But we have already spoken about this in detail.[283]

> **8b7** In the same way, if he knows of something or other (*tode ti*) that it is more beautiful ...

132,1

For one who knows of something that it is more beautiful must also know definitely what it is more beautiful than and in what respect it is more beautiful. If he does not know in what respect it is more beautiful, he does not know whether it is more beautiful either. How could he, not knowing the difference on the basis of which it is said to be more beautiful than the other thing?

5

> **8b9** ... he will not know in an indefinite way that it is more beautiful than an inferior thing. That sort of thing is conjecture (*hupolêpsis*), not knowledge.

By 'conjecture' he here means a vague and insecure comprehension (*gnôsis*) tantamount to opinion, while knowledge is a well-grounded comprehension. And so, since [some person] knows in an indefinite way and not with [real] knowledge that something or other is more beautiful than an inferior [thing], inasmuch as his comprehension is error-prone (*planasthai*), he may one day suppose even in the case of the lowest of all things, I mean matter, that it is more beautiful than something, being ignorant of the difference on the basis of which it is more beautiful and than what it is more beautiful, which is absurd. Through these [considerations], then, [Aristotle] proves in the case of the head and the hand and all of the parts of substances (which are themselves also substances) that they are not relatives – if, that is to say, it is possible to know them definitely but it is unnecessary to know the things of which they are 'said to be' definitely, and[284] it was said[285] with regard to relatives that if one knows one of them, one then necessarily knows the other. And so the parts of substances are not relatives.[286]

10

15

> **8b21** It is perhaps difficult to make strong statements on such matters without repeated examination of them. However, to have reviewed the difficulties associated with each of them is not without value.

20

He says this in a very philosophical vein. For since he said the head and the hand qua substances are known definitely but qua parts [only] indeterminately unless it is known whose head or hand they are, on that account he says that anyone who has not thoroughly examined such [issues] should not make strong statements about them. And not only about this, but about anything. Nevertheless, raising puzzles in connexion with such matters is a necessity, for puzzlement (*aporia*) is the beginning of finding the way (*euporia*) and a road to learning. He says these things because he does not want us to rest content with his words, but to examine such questions for ourselves as well and not [just] be moved to action by others.[287]

25

133,1

On Qualified (*poion*) and Quality (*poiotês*)[288]

8b25 By a quality I mean that by which people (*tines*)[289] are said to be qualified in a certain way.

Here we enquire in its turn[290] into the position of quality [among the categories], the reason for the title [of the section], the division of quality, and the order of the division of [its] species.[291]

First, then, [its] position. This is clear from what has already been said.[292] As we said [then], the section on quality should [arguably] have been placed before the [one on] relatives, because it is seen [to exist] on its own, while the relatives have their being in relationship to something else, and things that exist in their own right are ranked higher (*timiôteros*) than those that do not have being in their own right, and [also] because when the qualified thing is eliminated, the relative which subsists in it is eliminated along with it, as [is the case with] the whiter, the hotter, teacher and pupil, and the like, but when the relatives do not exist, nothing prevents every quality from existing; for we stated[293] that the relatives do not have any existence at all of their own but supervene upon (*episumbainein*) the other categories. But, as we [also] said[294] [then], because the philosopher had mentioned the relatives in the section on quantity, it was necessary that he deliver his teaching about them straight away, so that we would not be long left in ignorance of their nature. So much on their position.[295]

But why exactly does he make the title twofold – [i.e.] *On Qualified and Quality* – rather than single as he does in the case of the other categories? Our reply is that a qualified thing (*poion*) is one thing, a quality (*poiotês*) another. A quality is the universal quality itself, that from which participating qualified things are paronymously named, for instance, universal whiteness or blackness, whereas a qualified thing is the body that partakes of the quality and is named paronymously from it, for instance, a white body or a hot [one]. So a quality is grasped by the mind alone, but a qualified thing is subject to sense-perception. Since, then, the name of quality is twofold,[296] either as it is just by itself and perceived (*noein*) by mind alone, like the genus of quality itself, or as grasped by sense-perception, on this account he has also made the title twofold. And he has put '[the] qualified' first because it is better known as being perceptible [to the senses], and one should always begin instruction with the better known. And one can say besides (*allôs*)[297] that quality itself is a *poion*; for *poion* is predicated of a qualified thing (*poion*) and of a quality, being [the] more general (*koinoteros*) [term], and so quality too is said to be a *poion*,[298] just as 'name' (*onoma*), for instance, is predicated in common (*koinôs*) of both name and verb.²⁹⁹ If he talks of qualified things, he is not speaking primarily of these, but [doing so] for the sake of quality proper, so that the account of it will be clear as starting from what is better known.³⁰⁰

He divides quality into four species. The first of these he calls state and condition, the second capacity and incapacity, the third affective qualities and affections, the fourth figure and shape.³⁰¹ In order to see the reason why there are only four species of quality and neither more nor fewer and why he has imposed this order upon them, let us carry out a division of quality.³⁰²

Well then, a quality either has to do with (*kata esti*) capacity and incapacity³⁰³ or with actuality – with capacity in the way that the child is potentially literate, with incapacity in the way that the horse has an incapacity to absorb (*dekhesthai*) grammar. And should a quality have to do with actuality, it is either perfective of or harmful to the subject or neither perfective nor harmful. And if it is either perfective or harmful, it either does not produce an affection in the area of (*peri*) our perception or does produce one. And if it does not produce an affection, it [sc. the quality itself] is either lost with difficulty or easily lost. And if it is lost with difficulty, it is called a state, if easily lost, a condition. For instance, [qualities that] have to do with actuality, are perfective and do not produce an affection are health and, in the case of the soul, virtue;³⁰⁴ and harmful [ones] are illness and vice. For health and virtue are both perfective of their subjects, since they are in accordance with nature, and do not produce an affection, because they do not fall under (*hupopiptein*) any of the senses³⁰⁵ – except for the concomitants of health such as a good complexion, or of disease – which is harmful – such as pallor; but health itself or illness itself and the like do not fall under any of the senses.³⁰⁶

If, then, these are long-lasting and lost with difficulty they are called states, for we are said to possess virtue or vice as a state (*en hexei*) – and health and illness too,³⁰⁷ which is why³⁰⁸ we are said to be in a good state (*euektein*)³⁰⁹ when our health is at a high pitch (*epiteinein*).³¹⁰ Moreover there is an illness called hectic fever (*hektikê*), and [when ill] we are, conversely,³¹¹ said to be in a bad way (*kakhektein*). But if they are short-lived and easily lost they are called conditions.

He says that this – I mean state and condition – is the first species of quality. And they call the kind of quality that is lasting and lost with difficulty a state and the kind that is easily lost a condition. Thus, we say that the person who possesses the skill (*hexis*)³¹² of rhetoric is the one who knows not only the methods of rhetoric³¹³ but can also counter the difficulties he is confronted with, but [as for] the person who has not altogether successfully mastered the methods of rhetoric but has come to be qualified in it in some other way,³¹⁴ we do not say that that person possesses the skill of rhetoric but that he is in a certain condition (*diakeisthai pôs*) with regard to it.³¹⁵

10   Well, but isn't a state also a condition? The person exhibiting (*ekhein*) a state is certainly in a certain condition with regard to it. We reply that the word 'condition' has two senses (*ditton esti*), one more generic, which is predicated of 'state', the other more specific, which is distinguished from 'state'. Here, then, he has not used the generic 'condition' but the specific one, the one that is distinguished from 'state'.[316]

15   One should note that the word 'state' (*hexis*) is used of things of which the word 'good state' (*euexia*) is also used, since a good state is the intensification of a state. So if we normally only use the word 'good state' in the case of animate beings (for nobody would say that fire was 'in a good state' (*euektein*) with regard to heat or snow with regard to cold[317]), then the word 'state' will also only be used in the case of animate beings.[318]

20   And if a quality that has to do with actuality is perfective or harmful and produces an affection of our senses[319] it is called an affective quality, as producing an affection of our senses – a perfective [quality being one] like the heat in fire or the sweetness in honey, a harmful [quality one] like sourness in wine or putrescence in fruit and in other bodies. It is with reason that the former are called perfective, since honey and fire are endowed with form by them, and the latter harmful, because they are destructive of the subject, yet all of them produce an affection of our senses. But these [qualities] are not said to arise as the result of an affection, since they have not arisen as the result of some change in the subject – I'm talking about the perfective [ones] – but are their substantial qualities, by way of which they are characterized.[320]

There is no need to subdivide this section (*tmêma*) [of the division], like the other, into the hard to lose and the easily lost.[321] That [section] was seen only in animate beings, in which both harmful and perfective qualities of their nature come and go while the subject remains the same, which is why they were divided into the long-lasting and the short-lived. This section, on the other hand, is seen in inanimate things, in which both qualities that are perfective of a subject and those that are harmful to it are coextensive with their subjects and when they fade away (*marainesthai*) cause their subjects to fade away along with themselves (or at any rate they fade away along with their subjects),[322] as is the case with the rose and the apple, for when their perfume and bloom perish, they cause the subject to perish along with themselves. And, moreover, harmful qualities also stand in the same relationship (*hôsautôs ekhein*) to the subjects in which they occur, being coextensive with them and perishing along with them, as is the case with sourness in wine or putrescence in fruit and other bodies.

If a short-lived harmful quality may also be found in some things, such as tarnish in silver or the like, in the first place perhaps one would more properly call such things affections that are classified under quality. But since harmful quality as a whole was earlier classified along with perfective, because in the other part of the subdivision (I mean the one that includes[323] perfective or harmful qualities that do not produce an affection) it shares all the features of perfective quality (for each was either a state or a condition and was only seen in animate beings), for that reason, having of necessity been classified with it in the other part of the division, in this present one [too] they have been carried along with it in all respects, not having been divided into long-lasting and short-lived and being characterized by their producing an affection rather than by their arising out of an affection. And they, I mean the perfective quality and the harmful quality, have been classified together so that the division will not, through having become [over]-complex[324], be difficult to take in and need to be divided into the same sections.[325]

If the quality is neither perfective nor harmful, it has either gone deep or is superficial. And if it has gone deep, it is either lost with difficulty or easily lost. If, on the one hand, it is lost with difficulty, it is called an affective quality, as arising from an affection, like the sweetness in a sauce or congenital pallor. It is not [so-]named because it produces an affection of our senses, although it too produces one, but because it arises out of an affection, since we have named it from what is more strictly speaking (*kuriôtaton*)[326] more characteristic (*mallon huparkhein*) of it; for its coming to be through a change in the subject, i.e. through an affection, characterizes it more than does its producing an affection of our senses. If, on the other hand, it is easily lost, i.e. short-lived, if it does not readily give way and is not readily got rid of (*ekptuein*), it is said to be the kind of affection that is classified under quality, like the pallor resulting from long illness or the darkening that comes from much exposure to the sun; for these too are included under quality because the distinctive concomitant of a quality is maintained in their case too, [namely,] that things that participate in it are named paronymously from it. But if it does readily give way it is said to be the kind of affection that is classified under [the category] 'being-affected', as [is the case] if someone has gone pale through fear or turned red from shame. He doesn't even consider calling these [conditions] qualities because those who share in them are not named paronymously from them, for nobody, he says, would call someone who turned red from shame red-complexioned or someone who turned pale from fear pale-complexioned.[327]

From these is constituted the third species of quality, namely, affective qualities and affections – I mean the kind of affective quality that produces an affection and the kind that arises out of an affection and the kind of affection that is classified under quality and the kind of affection that is classified under 'being-affected'; for the first three are affective qualities,[328] the fourth an affection.

But how is it that we say that these, I mean pallor and redness, have gone deep although they are only seen on the surface? We reply that such a quality has not appeared on the surface without a change in the interior. For just as those who have been ruddy-complexioned from birth have come to be like that as a result of [having] a particular (*toiosde*) constitution, the heat in them having become excessive and moved to the surface, so too have those who have turned red or white from fear or shame not done so without an internal change.[329]

And if a quality that has to do with actuality is neither perfective nor harmful and is superficial, if it occurs in inanimate things and mental representations (*phantasta*), it is called a figure, if in animate beings, a shape. 'Mental representations' are as in mathematical objects (*mathêmatika*) of all kinds (I mean triangles and the circle and the other figures), for these have being only in mental representation (*phantasia*). 'Inanimate things' are logs and stones and the like, for mental representations (in other words, figures), by occurring in inanimate bodies, cause them too to be disposed in this way or that in accordance with the different kinds of figures. 'In animate beings' [means] as in all living things; for shape is only seen at the surface.[330]

What? Don't we also say that a statue (*andrias*)[331] has shape? Not in the first instance. In the first place it is said to have figure, in the second shape too; for, because it is the copy of an animate being, in which there *is* shape, 'shape' is, rather loosely (*katakhrêstikôteron*) applied to it.

You [now] have the fourth species of quality, I mean figure and shape. The [following] diagram of the division will make its organization (*methodos*) easier for us to grasp.

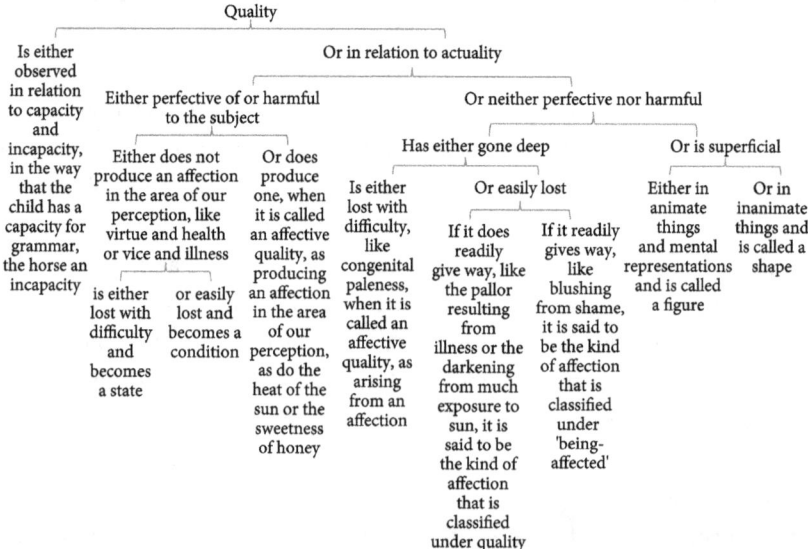

The [above] division has made it clear to us why there are only four species of quality and neither more nor fewer. Concerning their order we have the following to say.

He has placed the species [consisting] of state and condition first with good reason. For since these occur in the ambit of animate beings and animate beings are ranked higher than all inanimate things, the quality that is seen in (*kata*) them has with good reason also been assigned the first place. And with good reason the second species is the one to do with capacity and incapacity. For since capacity and incapacity are a kind of natural propensity (*epitêdeiotês*) (the child has a certain natural capacity to take in grammar and rhetoric and the horse a natural incapacity to take in such things, and fire has by nature the capacity to heat, and the same goes for other such things) and [since] the works of nature (*ta phusika*) occupy second place after animate beings, the species of quality that involves capacity and incapacity, being seen in natural objects (*pragma*), with good reason also occupies second place. And since one must first have a certain natural propensity and then either do something or have something done to one in accordance with it (for if the propensity did not pre-exist, a person (*tis*) would neither have anything done to him nor do anything; for instance, since asbestos does not have a propensity to burn, it will not burn even if one applies fire to it ten thousand times, but wood, having the capacity to burn, will burn when fire is applied to it),[332] on that account the affective qualities and the affections occupy third place among the species of qualities – because, as was stated, a person would not be able to do anything or have anything done to him that involved (*kata*) them[333] unless there pre-existed in him a certain capacity that was ready (*epitêdeios*) to receive such [things]. Figure and shape, being seen only at the surface (the affective qualities and the affections penetrate all the way to the interior), have been assigned the last place. So much for the order of the species [of quality].[334]

One should be aware that the same quality can be designated in more than one way. For instance, heat when in fire is an affective quality as producing an affection in the area of (*peri*) our perception; when in us, as in the case of a fever, an affective quality as arising from an affection; when in iron being hardened by fire and, as it were, resident in it, an affection of the kind that is classified under quality; and heat that has arisen in us, perhaps because we have got close to a fire in passing, an affection of the kind that is classified under [the category] 'being-affected'.[335]

8b25 By a quality I mean that by which people (*tines*) are said to be qualified in a certain way.

Why is it that he presents his teaching about quality (*poiotês*) by means of the qualified (*to poion*)? We reply that the qualified is, as has been stated,[336] more

140,1 evident inasmuch as it is apprehended by the senses; and in general we come to a notion of quality by way of the qualified, for it is after observing the white in milk and that in snow and that in white lead that we come to the notion of whiteness, and similarly, after tasting honey and a date and a fig that we come to the notion of sweetness. In presenting his teaching, then, he starts with the
5 qualified because it is more evident. And that which actually (*autos*) partakes is a qualified thing, that which is partaken of, a quality.³³⁷

8b25 But quality is among the things that are spoken of in many ways.

By saying this he is not indicating that it is spoken of homonymously but that it is spoken of in different ways (*diaphorôs*), for to be spoken of 'in many
10 ways' [can] mean either 'homonymously' or 'in different ways', as here. If 'homonymously' had been understood,³³⁸ the division would have been into different senses, but since 'in different ways' is understood, on that account the division is as of a genus into its species. In that case isn't quality a genus? So why is one of its species referred to as first, another as second?³³⁹ We reply that it is not qua quality that one is first, the other second, but that they differ solely
15 in point of worth, as human being likewise does from horse.³⁴⁰

8b26 Let one species of quality be called state and condition.

The first species of quality is state and condition. A state, he says, differs from a
20 condition in that a condition is easily lost and a state lost with difficulty, and because a state is in every instance also a condition but a condition is not necessarily also a state.³⁴¹

8b29 Such are the branches of knowledge and the virtues.

He is not referring to the absolutely stable (*aptaistos*)³⁴² branches of knowledge here but simply to any established (*monimos*) skill (*tekhnê*), and so in this sense
141,1 grammar and carpentry and the other manual skills are branches of knowledge, since each of them is an established state. We talk of knowledge in three senses. We describe as knowledge the kind that has a stable (*aptaistos*) subject matter (*hupokeimenon*) and is always concerned with things that are the same and
5 unchanging. In this sense geometry and astronomy and arithmetic are knowledge. But medicine is not knowledge in this [sense] because it concerns itself with fluctuating subject matter. We also call knowledge the kind that starts out from self-warranting principles. This is knowledge in the true sense (*ontôs*) [and] what people call 'unhypothetical' (*anupothetos*) philosophy because it starts out from common conceptions. On this basis you will not call geometry or astronomy

or any similar [discipline] knowledge since they do not start out from self-warranting principles but from principles needing proof. For the principles of geometry are the point, the line, the surface, and the like, and the geometer defines each of these, describing the point as 'that which has no part' and the line as 'a length without breadth',[343] and the rest in keeping with their nature (*hôs ekhei*), but qua geometer he does not know the proof of these things, I mean the reason why the point is without parts or the line a length without breadth, but refers the construction of proofs of them to the first philosopher,[344] for no branch of knowledge proves its principles itself. Branches of knowledge, then, that do not start out from self-warranting principles would not be instances of knowledge in the strict sense; as Plato says,[345] 'for a person who has principles he does not know, and whose intermediate steps (*mesa*) and conclusions are based on things he does not know – how could this be knowledge?'. According to a third account there is also practical knowledge that knows what one should assume in advance and what should come after that; in this sense both medicine and all the manual skills are knowledge. And this is the sense of knowledge that the philosopher has used here.

By virtues he here means the perfect virtues, those that know both the what and the why.[346] For of virtues some are natural, the kind that those who have a sort of natural temperance or those who are gentle by nature, or even some irrational creatures, are said to have, as the turtle-dove and the crow [are said to show] temperance and storks justice;[347] others ethical, knowing that justice and virtue *tout court* are fine things but not knowing why they are fine things, their possessors having learned this from their parents or teachers as matters of right opinion; others civic – along with the what these also know the why; and others purificatory. The purificatory virtues differ from the civic in that the civic are oriented towards inferior things and seek after the more respectable pleasures, paying heed to time and place and quantity, whereas those who practice the purificatory virtues (*kathartikôs energein*) are indifferent to inferior things and utterly despise pleasures. [Finally,] there are other virtues that are contemplative.[348] Here, then, as was stated,[349] he means the perfect virtues, [namely,] the civic and the purificatory and the contemplative.[350]

8b31 Unless a great change is brought about by illness or something else of that kind.

For someone who has come down with a lengthy illness or who has become involved in other matters is likely to lose knowledge through inattention.

8b35 [Those qualities³⁵¹] that are easily changed and alter quickly are called conditions, for example heat and coolness, illness and health, and anything of that kind.

For a person is said to be in conditions of some kind where these are concerned, not to be in states.

9a1 Unless even one of these should, through length of time, eventually become naturalized and either inveterate or very hard to shift – one would perhaps call that a state.

For that sort of thing is no longer called a condition but a state. He says 'naturalized', i.e. converted to [part of a person's] nature and having itself become [that] nature because of long-time habituation.

9a5 For those who do not have much mastery of a branch of knowledge are not said to be in a [knowledgeable] state.

For the man who, in the field of rhetoric or grammar, is ready to answer any questions that may be put to him about any rhetorical or grammatical topics (*theôrêma*) and who gives a [good] account of them and readily resolves the difficulties associated with them – this man is said to possess the skill (*hexis*)³⁵² of rhetoric or grammar. And if someone else is [only] moderately qualified in these [disciplines], he is not said to possess skill in them but to be in this or that condition in regard to them.³⁵³

9a10 States are also conditions but conditions not necessarily states.

Just as 'word' (*onoma*) is predicated of both noun (*onoma*) and verb, and in the one case *onoma* is the genus of noun and verb and in the other opposed to verb, so too is condition predicated of both state and condition, and the one kind of condition is predicated of state and condition as [their] genus, the other opposed to state as a species. And so a state is in every case also a condition, because condition is its genus, but a condition is not also a state, because state is used in opposition to it.³⁵⁴

9a14 A second genus of quality is that in accordance with which we describe people as having a talent for boxing or running³⁵⁵ or as healthy or sickly.

This is the second species of quality, I mean the one having to do with capacity and incapacity. But why has he called it 'genus of quality'? After all, it [*sc.* quality] is a highest genus. They [*sc.* the commentators] reply that he said genus instead of species so that nobody would take it to be an *infima species*. At any rate, he did not say 'highest genus' but 'genus' in order to indicate that it is a subaltern genus – in the way that we might say that animal is a genus *of substance* instead of [saying that it is] one *under substance*.

He is then, as I said, giving the second species of quality, the one having to do with capacity and incapacity, 'in accordance with which we describe people as suited to boxing or running or as healthy or sickly'. And by those suited to boxing or running he means people with a constitution (*phusis*) suited to something of that kind, that is, those who are potentially such [*sc.* potentially boxers or runners].

The first species of quality – state and condition – is observed as an actuality (*energeiâi*), the second as a potential (*dunamei*). For it is one thing to speak of a boxer, another of a person suited to boxing, or of a runner and a person suited to running. The one, the boxer or the runner, is in actuality, the other, the person suited to boxing or the one suited to running – [i.e.] the person who is not yet actually such [*sc.* a boxer or a runner], but has a natural potential, that is, the capacity to become such – in potentiality. And the person who is actually a boxer or a runner is no longer so described because of a natural capacity, but is displaying (*ekhein*) a state or a condition.

But how is it that he also calls incapacity a quality? It is because we are also in this or that condition on account of it. It is because the horse is in such a condition that we say that it has an incapacity to absorb (*dekhesthai*) knowledge. And, in general, in cases where capacity is observed so is incapacity, for someone who has a capacity to be affected has an incapacity not to be affected and someone who has a capacity not to be affected has an incapacity to be affected. And besides, since opposites have the same genus, if (a) one wishes them to be opposed as contraries, under whichever genus one of the contraries is included the other will also be included under that [genus], since white and black, which are contraries, are both included under the same genus, quality (so if capacity is included under qualification, incapacity too will be placed under the same [genus]); or (b) if one should wish them to be opposed as things [that are opposed] as privation and state, one will include them under the same genus in that case too. For whatever the state is said to belong to, the privation will also be said to belong to. A case in point is an eye, for both sight and blindness belong to it. So whichever genus the state is included under, the privation will be included under the same one.[356]

9a16 For it is not because they are in some condition that such people are said to be [so] qualified.

[This is] equivalent to: 'We do not speak [of them in this way] because they are actually such [sc. a boxer, etc.] but because they have such a capacity'.

Capacity has three senses. A person may be said to have a capacity either (1) to act, or (2) to be affected, or (3) to not be affected. We say, for example, that (2) a sickly person has the capacity to be affected by a lot of walking or by exposure to the sun, (3) that a healthy person has the capacity not to be affected by such things, and (1) that a carpenter has the capacity to make a door.[357] Incapacity will have the same number of senses as capacity: someone who can be affected has an incapacity to be not affected, and someone who cannot be affected has an incapacity to be affected – but someone who can act does not in every case have an incapacity to not act.

So why didn't we link (*paralambanein*) the capacity to not act with the capacity to act in the way that we linked the capacity not to be affected with the capacity to be affected? We reply that it is because there are some things that only have the capacity to act and in no wise also have the capacity to not act. Thus Aristotle himself says in *On Interpretation*[358] that one kind of capacity can go either way, but the other only has one of [two] contrary [possibilities], and [that] any rational capacity goes either way, while a non-rational one only has one of [two] contrary [possibilities]. For example, a doctor can heal but just as easily not heal, and while a carpenter has the capacity to make a door, he equally has the capacity to not make one. On the other hand, while fire has the capacity to heat, it does not also have the capacity to not heat, and, similarly, while snow has the capacity to chill it does not also have the capacity to not chill, and while god has the capacity to do good things, he does not also have the capacity not to.

And it is reasonable that rational entities should have a capacity that can go either way, because in their case capacity does not keep pace with wish (*boulêsis*), since they cannot in every case achieve what they wish for (*boulesthai*), and they do not in every case wish for what they are capable of achieving. The divinity (*to theion*), however, does have capacity that matches his will (*boulêsis*).[359] For if we say that he[360] wills (*boulesthai*) but cannot achieve what he wills, the willing is senseless, just as the man who wishes for things he cannot achieve, like [being able] to fly or being immortal, is senseless. On the other hand, if we say that he has the capacity [to do something] but does not will it, he will have that capacity to no good purpose, since if he has the capacity to do something but does not will to do it, he certainly will not do it and will not bring that capacity to actualisation, so the capacity, remaining inactive, will exist to no good purpose. On account of this, in the case of god, we only speak of ability (*to dunasthai*) and never of inability (*to mê dunasthai*) because what he is able to do is also what he wills and, willing it, he certainly also does it and does not do it at one time and not do it at another but does it in every case. For he can do whatever he wills, and everything he can do he wills.

Here by *boulêsis* we mean 'will', not 'deliberating' or 'deliberation', for properly speaking 'deliberation' does not even apply in the case of god, not at any rate if deliberation is, as Aristotle says,[361] nothing other than[362] deficiency of wisdom.[363] For we deliberate when we do not know what we should do and whether this thing or that is what should be done. For it is in matters where there is a choice that deliberation takes place, if, that is to say, choice is nothing other than choosing one thing before another, and deliberation takes place with a view to choosing things, and we deliberate when we are at a loss, and we are at a loss when we are lacking in wisdom – because for a person with wisdom all the things that ought to be done are a matter of knowledge, for [wisdom] is the most perfect virtue [of all]. So if the divinity is absolute wisdom (*autophronêsis*), he will have no need of deliberation if that takes place through lack of wisdom.

It was for these reasons, then, that Aristotle said that only a rational capacity can go either way. And if we must put it more precisely, all appetitive capacity can swing (*tên rhopên ekhein*) in either direction, but all capacity other than the appetitive, whether the kind that is superior to it or the kind that is inferior to it, has [available to it] only one of the two opposed alternatives (*antiphasis*), as we have already shown[364] in the cases of fire and snow. If, then, it has been shown that in the case of some things there is only room for the capacity to do [something] and not for the opposing alternative (*antiphasis*) as well, with good reason he has not opposed 'to not do' to 'to do' as he did 'to be unaffected' to 'to be affected', since we want to talk about every capacity, but not every capacity is in every case accompanied by an incapacity.

They [*sc.* the capacities], and their negations (*apophasis*),[365] should be diagrammed as follows:

can do	cannot do
can be affected	cannot be affected
can be unaffected	cannot be unaffected
(affirmation)	(negation)

For the above reasons, then, [Aristotle] himself presents this species of capacity[366] in three parts,[367] [referring to] the [capacity] to do [something] in the words 'for example, people are said to be suited to boxing or running not because they are in a certain condition but because they have a natural capacity to do something easily' – here is the capacity to do [something] – 'and they are said to be healthy because they have a natural capacity not to be easily affected in any way by chance events' – here is the second [part] – 'and they are said to be sickly because they have a natural *incapacity* to be not easily affected in any way by chance events' – here is the third [part]. (Sickly people have a capacity to be easily affected by anything and an incapacity to be unaffected, healthy people the reverse.) He was speaking precisely when he said that healthy things are not affected by chance events – by [the sun's] heat or wind, for instance – for they would be affected by a sword or by fire or by something else of that sort. Sickly things, on the other hand, have a capacity to be affected by chance events and an incapacity to be unaffected.

9a24 Similar to these [are] the hard and the soft.

For the former has a capacity not to be divided easily and an incapacity for the same thing, and the soft has a capacity to be divided easily and an incapacity not to be divided.

9a28 A third genus of quality is affective qualities and affections.

Again[368] he has said genus instead of species. This [species of quality] is seen in four guises.[369] An affective quality is either present to the whole species, as white is to all snow, or not to the whole of it, yet naturally and from birth, as black is to Ethiopians. And if [it is present] to the whole [species], it is either constitutive of the subject or not. A constitutive [quality is one] such as the whiteness and coldness of snow and the heat and dryness of fire, and [one that is] not constitutive [one] such as the blackness of ravens and the whiteness of swans, for blackness is not, as has often been stated,[370] constitutive of the raven, because, robbed of its feathers, it is no longer black but is none the less a raven, and, from another perspective (*allôs*), because we do not include such qualitative differences in their definition either – unless perhaps for want of substantial differentiae (*diaphora*);[371] after all, it is not at all surprising that, being human, we do not discover the substantial differentiae in all cases and on that account are compelled to characterize things by means of such [differences].[372]

Further (*toinun*), if a quality is present to the whole species and is constitutive, it is called an affective quality as producing an affection on (*peri*) our senses, but if it is present to the whole species but is not constitutive, it is called an affective quality as arising from an affection. If, on the other hand, it is not present to the whole species, it is either long-lasting or short-lived. If it is not present to the whole [species] and is long-lasting, it is again called an affective quality as arising from an affection, like the sweetness in a sauce or pallor [present] from birth or ruddiness, and if, while not being present to the whole species, it is short-lived, if it does not readily give way and is not easily lost, it is referred to as the kind of affection that is classified under quality, as are pallor after long illness or the chill resulting from a long period of wintry weather, and if it is easily lost and readily and immediately gives way, it is referred to as the kind of affection that is classified under [the category] 'being-affected', as is the pallor caused by unseemly fear or the redness caused by shame. Aristotle does not think it correct to call [phenomena] of this [last] kind qualities since the things that partake of them are not named paronymously from them. Again, a diagram will make the division easy to grasp.[373]

30
148,1

5

		an affective quality			
is either present to the whole species			or not to the whole of it		
is either constitutive of the subject: an affective quality as producing an affection on our senses; e.g. the heat in fire	or not constitutive: an affective quality as arising from an affection; e.g. the blackness of crows	is either long-lasting: again an affective quality as arising from an affection; e.g. pallor from birth	or short-lived		
				either not readily giving way: an affection classified under quality; e.g. pallor after long illness	or readily giving way: an affection classified under being-affected; e.g. redness caused by shame

These four species of affective qualities are seen not only in the sphere of (*peri*) the body but in that of the soul as well.[374] For if a person has the best disposition (*hexis*) for scientific thought (*theôria*), or rational thought *tout court*, such a disposition will be referred to as an affective quality – as producing an affection on our senses and not as arising from an affection – because a disposition of this kind is constitutive and perfective of the substance of the soul. And it produces an affection not, it is clear, on the bodily senses but on those referred to as the divine and rational senses. At any rate, we are said to perceive words and insults (*hubris*) through (*kata*) the soul, evidently, and not the bodily senses. One would say that those who are mad or irascible or similarly afflicted thanks to their physical constitution have an affective quality of the kind that arises from an affection, and those that have become that way through illness, an affection of the kind that is classified under quality. On the other hand, we would say that those who have been angered or experienced some such [emotion] because they have lost control (*ek sunarpagês*)[375] in a crisis have the kind of affection that is classified under [the category] 'being-affected'. However, it is

10

149,1

5

clear that we are misusing these terms when we speak in this way, since strictly speaking all of the above are really included under state and condition.

Affective qualities are to be understood in two ways. A subject is said to have an affective quality either (1) because it has been affected and some quality has come to be in it as a result of the affection, or (2) because our senses are affected in the perception of these qualities, although they have not come to be in the things in which they are present as the result of an affection but naturally, as in the case of fire; for heat has not come to be in fire as the result of an affection, because it is present in it essentially and is formative of it. The same goes for the sweetness in honey or the whiteness in snow and the like. However, white flesh has its whiteness from an affection, because the white is accidental to it and is not present to it essentially and is not formative for it. And we shall say the same of blackness too, and in the case of a sweet sauce and the like.

Now the senses are affected in these cases too, but since it is more proper in their case to say that they have come to be as a result of an affection than that they produce an affection, because the former belongs to them primarily and they [only] also produce an affection secondarily, we have named them from what is more significant (*kurios*); for in the case of things where both apply, it is perhaps better for the name 'affective quality' to derive from what is more significant. And so in the case of honey, since sweetness does not come to be in it as a result of an affection (for it is characteristic of it), on that account, from its producing an affection on our senses, it is called an affective quality.[376]

9b11 That many changes of colours take place as a result of an affection is clear.

Having stated that the colours are affective qualities on the ground that they (*autas*)[377] come to be in [things] through an affection, he establishes [this] and shows that it is so.

9b19 Such symptoms as.[378]

He has said that colours are symptoms because they supervene on other affections in the way that pallor follows a long illness. There is also substantial colour, as white is to white lead or snow, or red to blood, or the black in the ink of a squid.[379]

9b27 For in the same way we are said to be qualified in virtue of them.

A quality is that in respect of which people are said to be qualified. So if they are not said to be qualified through affections that are easily lost, it is clear that these are not called qualities.[380]

9b33 Similarly affective qualities and affections are also spoken of with regard to the soul.

For affective qualities and affections are observed not only in connexion with the body but in connexion with the soul as well.[381]

9b35 For those that appear straight away at birth as a result of certain affections that are hard to shift are called qualities.

For just as blackness in the Ethiopian, being congenital, is called an affective quality, so too is congenital insanity (*ekstasis*)[382] or irascibility called an affective quality.[383]

10a2 And similarly other mental disorders (*ekstasis*) that are not inborn (*phusikos*) but have come about through any other circumstances (*sumptôma*).

Again, just as loss of colour resulting from a long illness is called an affective quality, so too is madness, or anything else of that kind, resulting from some occurrence (*sumptôma*) called an affective quality.[384]

10a11 A fourth genus of quality is figure and the external shape associated with (*peri*) each thing.

This is a fourth species of quality. (He is once more[385] using 'genus' in place of 'species'.) It consists of figure and shape. 'Figure' is wider than 'shape', for every shape has both figure and shape, but not everything that has figure also has shape. This is why he has put figure before shape since it is [therefore] more important and more universal.

Moreover it was stated[386] above that figure is seen in the case of inanimate things or mental representations, shape in the case of animate beings[387] or natural things, and that even if we on occasion use the word 'shape' in the case of inanimate things, we do so, somewhat incorrectly, on account of their being copies of animate beings.

These [sc. figures and shapes] too are with reason [called] qualities because things that partake of them are disposed in a particular way in accordance with them and are named from them.[388]

10a12 And also, in addition to these, straightness and curvedness and anything like them.

For a straight line is named (*legein*) paronymously from straightness and a curved one [paronymously] from curvedness and straightness and curvedness are affections of the line.[389] For it should be noted that of these four – [I mean] the point, the line, the surface, and the solid (*sôma*)[390] – which are in sequence with one another, the point, inasmuch as it is without parts, has received neither affection nor figure, much less shape, the line, having a single dimension, has received only affection (it is either curved or straight or whatever else it may be called), the surface, having two dimensions, I mean that of length and that of breadth, has received both affection and figure. (The affections of surface are narrowness and wideness, its figures, triangle, square, and things of that kind, for because every surface is bounded by lines – the limits of a surface are lines, says Euclid[391] – it has on that account with reason also received figures; after all, figures are composed of lines.) And body, for its part, having the three dimensions, [i.e.] those of length, and depth and breadth, has received affections and figures and shapes. [Among its] affections are thickness and thinness and [it has received] figures since it is cubic or cylindrical or the like. And in addition the animate body (*sôma*) also receives a shape.

10a16 'Porous' and 'dense' and 'rough' and 'smooth' might seem to signify a qualification, but such [designations] appear to be foreign to the classification (*diairesis*) of qualifications. Each seems rather to reveal a certain position of the parts.

Because the things that partake of these are disposed in a certain manner with regard to porosity (*manôsis*) or density (*puknôsis*)[392] or roughness or smoothness and are named from them, they have something of the appearance (*doxa*) of [being] qualities, but this is not true and they will be included rather under being-positioned, since they indicate a certain position.[393] For example, a dense [object] is one whose parts are positioned so close to one another that it cannot admit a body of another kind, a porous [object] one that has parts so spread out that it can admit a body of another kind. Again, we call 'smooth' something that has parts which are equal to one another and that project equally, 'rough' something that has parts that are unequal to one another in their projections. For instance, an apple is smooth, since its surface is uniform, while the face is rough[394] because it is made up of non-uniform and unequal parts – the mouth, the nose, the eyes, and the rest – some of them occupying a prominent position, others a sunken one. So it seems to be more the case that their parts indicate a certain position.[395]

The rough and the smooth are by common consent (*homologoumenôs*) included under being-positioned for the above reasons, but here he has only included the porous and dense that are artificially produced, for it is these that are included under being-positioned. For instance, if someone should make a strap porous by stretching it for [in that case the strap] is not made porous everywhere, but the position of some of its parts is altered by their being further away from one another. Again, if someone should fill his hand with nuts, the body [produced] from all of them is said to be porous (*manos*) because it is not single (*hen*), for what is not single is said to be porous. And similarly with the dense. If we think of the nuts as crushed together, the body [produced] from all of them will be dense. And again, if someone should make a tightly packed and compressed (*puknousthai*) fleece of wool loose (*araios*) by carding it, we describe it as open-textured (*manos*).

Given that he is addressing beginners, he with good reason here includes this artificially produced porosity and density under being-positioned because these things[396] are said to be dense or open-textured (*araios*) according to the position of their parts. They are not qualities, neither possessing natural porosity nor density nor being dense nor porous throughout but only with respect to the position of their parts; and nor, moreover, do their parts take on the same porosity as the whole. In the physics course,[397] on the other hand, he wants the natural density and porosity present in one and the same subject to be a quality. For instance, if water, which has a natural density and is dense throughout the whole of itself, throws off this [condition] and becomes rarefied, it turns into air, with the result that a pint of water would make, say, ten pints of air. And this does not happen because the water is divided into small portions (as though someone were to fill his hand with dust and throw it into the air and the dust take up more space because its particles (*morion*) had been dispersed) since, if that were the case, we too would necessarily make air when we dispersed water into small [droplets]. And if someone says 'but we can't split the water up into [droplets] that small', well, even if we can't actually do it, even if we [can only] mentally hypothesize it, even then it isn't possible.[398] For the parts of water are in every case [themselves] small volumes of water (*hudation*), because the parts are the same in substance as the whole, and what a thing is composed of is also what it is dissolved into. So if water is composed of identical parts that are [themselves] water (for the parts, as we said, are the same as the whole), it will certainly, when decomposed, also be separated into these. And the air [that was produced] would not have been continuous either but would have been interspersed with empty spaces. For the parts of water must be either continuous or separated. (They cannot be in contact, for when in contact they immediately become continuous because of their fluidity.) If, then, they are separated, air is not continuous, which is false and contrary to evident fact. And if they are joined together, the whole [that results] will again be water and not air. And so water does not produce air by being divided up but by altering completely and changing its qualities (*alloiousthai*).

That these [sc. porosity and density] *are* qualities Aristotle shows[399] clearly in the *Physics*. He says that, just as body, being receptive of qualities, changes in its entirety in line with them, becoming black after being white and white after being black, so too, since both density and porosity are qualities, does body, as one would expect, change in line with these, and, taking on density, become water, and, becoming yet more dense, become earth, and, switching from density to porosity, become air, and becoming yet more porous, become fire.

Natural porosity and density, then, the kind present in a single subject, is a quality, but if it is not present in a single body but more than one, it is not, even if it is natural, referred to as a quality but as a position, as [are], for example, the density or porosity of teeth.[400] For even though this is from nature, nevertheless, because it does not occur in a single subject but in more than one, [sc.] the teeth, this is not referred to as a quality but rather as a position. But enough on these [matters].

Given that Aristotle says[401] that straightness and curvedness are qualities but says, as we said earlier, that roughness and smoothness are not qualities but the rough and the smooth are just a [certain] position of the parts [of a thing], certain people raise the question as to whether, if 'a straight line is a line which lies evenly (*ex isou*) with the points on itself'[402] or, again, 'one whose mid-parts are in line with its ends', the straight and the curved may not also indicate only an arrangement of the parts [of a thing]. After all it is clear that here too a certain position of the parts of the line creates the straight line, [a position] such that (*hôste*) no part of it bends out or in but, due to their evenness (*isotês*)[403], the mid-parts are in line with the ends. And the curved differs from straightness solely by the position of the parts, for it is when its[404] parts are bent and some turn out and others in that curvature comes about. So either the rough and the smooth are qualities or, if they indicate only a position of the parts, the straight and the curved will indicate the same.

Such, then, is the nature of the difficulty [they raise]. We resolve it in the following manner. It is not the same thing to talk of a curved (*kampulos*) line and of a bent (*keklasmenos*) one. A bent line does not, in so far as it is a straight line, depart from the form of a straight line,[405] but one line simply becomes two and creates an angle. A curved line, on the other hand, is of a different form from a straight line, because 'curved' means 'circular' (*peripherês*),[406] and that a circular line (*periphereia*)[407] differs in form from a straight one is clear on many counts. First, every part of a circular line fits onto every other, just as all the parts of a straight line for their part fit onto one another, but no part of a straight line fits onto any part of a circular one. Second, if figures constructed from straight lines differ in form from those constructed from circular lines, then the straight line will also differ from the circular in form. Also, not one straight line, not two, but at least three [are needed to] produce a figure (hence the triangle, which is contained by (*ek*) three straight lines, is the first and simplest of the rectilinear figures), but the circumference (*peripherês*), being [a] single [line], produces the figure of the circle; for 'a circle is a plane figure contained by one line', etc.[408] If, then, the straight line and the circular have taken (*tunkhanein*) a different form, then they do not differ solely by the position of their parts. But the rough and the smooth do differ solely by the position of their parts. Hence, nor is the subject altered in form through them, but while the form of the surface remains the same, [that] same [surface] becomes rough or smooth. It's as though there were a rectangular field, then someone, digging it over, excavated some parts of it and raising others [so that] it becomes rough while remaining rectangular. And if he levels off (*perixein*) the raised parts again and fills in the cavities, it becomes smooth without having departed from the form of a rectangle or taken on any additional quality but just having changed the position of its parts.

And so Aristotle properly called straightness and curvedness (i.e. circularity) qualities but said that the rough and the smooth differ only in the position of their parts.

10a25 Perhaps some other type of quality may come to light, but those most spoken of are pretty much these.

Having given us the four species of quality, he comes to a conclusion and states that these are the types of quality. But wanting us not to rest content with what he has said and to remain idle and [only] be moved to action by others, but to have some self-motivation and ask questions for ourselves as well,[409] he says that perhaps another type of quality may come to light.[410] But in truth there is no other type of quality over and above those given (*paradidonai*), as both the division[411] and the investigations of more ancient and perspicacious men have shown.

10a27 The above-mentioned, then, are 'qualities', and the things called paronymously after them are 'qualified'.

Having talked about quality he now talks about the qualified; and in fact he has made the title about both.[412]

Qualities are things like whiteness and blackness, the qualified that which partakes of the qualities, for instance the white body and so forth. The qualities are partaken of, the qualified things partake of [them]. The qualified things are named (*legein*) paronymously from the qualities, as has often been stated.⁴¹³ But not all of them are named from them paronymously, but some are named from them homonymously or not named (*onomazein*) from them at all. This is why he has also said 'or [named] in some other way'.⁴¹⁴

10a29 In most cases, indeed in almost all, they are called paronymously.

Because at the beginning of the section on quality he said that a quality is that from which the things that participate [in it] are named paronymously, talking about it [there] in rather general terms and not with precision (for this is not a concomitant of every quality), he now takes up the story (*logos*) again and states more precisely that in most cases the statement that its participants are named paronymously from a quality is true (white is [so] called from whiteness and the grammarian from grammar, for example), but in the case of some qualities,⁴¹⁵ because there are no names for the qualities, the things that participate [in them] are not called from them paronymously. This happens in the case of the second species of quality, that according to capacity and incapacity, for neither the person suited to running nor the person suited to boxing, [sc.] the people with a natural capacity (*epitêdeiotês*) for these [activities], are called paronymously from these capacities. There are not even names for these capacities because common usage is concerned with giving names to things that are completed and in operation; for instance, the person suited to boxing or the person suited to running are [so] called from the actual sciences,⁴¹⁶ I mean that of boxing (*puktikê*) and that of running (*dromikê*). And why do I say in the case of capacities for which there are no names when even in the case of some qualities that do have names the things that participate [in them] are not named paronymously from them? For example, the person who participates [in virtue] is not called 'virtued' from [the name] virtue but 'good'. At times moreover the things that participate are called from the qualities homonymously, as a woman grammarian (*grammatikê*) is from grammar (*grammatikê*) and a musical one (*mousikê*) from music (*mousikê*). Hence, as I said,⁴¹⁷ because he is here giving us the account of the qualities more accurately, he has added the [words] 'or in some other way from them'.⁴¹⁸

10b12 There is also contrariety with respect to qualification. For instance, justice is contrary to injustice and whiteness to blackness.

He moves on to the distinctive feature of quality, employing the same model (*kanôn*) of presentation (*didaskalia*) as [he does] in the case of the other categories. He says that it is a distinctive feature of quality to be receptive of contrariety. [And] reasonably, for contrariety is properly seen in association with quality, since even in the case of the other categories contrariety was observed with regard to quality. Indeed even substance is receptive of contraries because of it[419] and those of the relatives that are receptive of contrariety were drawn from the category of qualification. As I said, then, contrariety is properly seen in association with quality. But contrariety is not present in every quality. To the qualities [falling] between opposed qualities there is no opposite, for instance to red or yellow or the like. And nor is there any opposite to [geometrical] figures, I mean to the triangle and the circle and the like. And equally[420] there is contrariety in the case of qualified things, since the white is said to be contrary to the black and the hot to the cold.[421]

> **10b17** Further, if one of [a pair] of contraries is a qualification, the other will also be a qualification. This is clear from particular cases if one examines[422] the other categories.

For that whichever category one of [a pair] of opposites is included under the other will also be included under that [same category] is clear from our not being able to refer it to another category. [This is so] because contraries have the same genus.[423]

> **10b26** Qualified things (*poion*) admit of a more and a less; for one thing is said to be more or less white than another.

Another concomitant of the qualified is to admit of a more and a less; one white [thing] is said to be more white than another – and whiter than itself. But this too is not a concomitant of all [qualified things]. [And] with reason, for it was stated[424] that where contrariety and the mingling of contraries is seen there is also a more and a less, but where there is neither contrariety nor the mingling of contraries nor is there a more and a less.[425]

> **10b30** For if justice is said to be more or less than justice one could raise difficulties.[426]

That to say that it admits of a more and a less will not apply to (*harmozein*) the whole category is clear from the difficulties that some people, not wanting justice to be more or less than justice or health than health and so on, raise in this connexion. Aristotle has not provided us with a detailed account of these matters, but we have the following to say about them.

We say that by general consent qualified things admit of a more and a less in the stated fashion, but the quality itself as definable by definition,[427] i.e. justice and health and the like, does not admit of a more and a less, for justice itself in itself could not be more or less [justice] than justice. For if something does not admit of the definition of justice, it is not justice at all. For just as [beings] that the definition of man applies to are men no matter what (*ouden hêtton*) but those to which even the least thing in the definition doesn't apply (like rationality or receptivity of knowledge in the case of irrational beings or mortality in the case of the angels)[428] are not men at all, in the same way if something does not admit (*ekhein*) the definition of justice, or that of health or of some such thing, in every detail (*aparallaktôs*), such a thing is not justice or health or any other such thing.[429] However, the corresponding qualified entities[430] do admit of a more and a less to the degree that each partakes of the quality to a greater or lesser extent, for we describe someone who partakes more of paleness (*leukotês*) than darkness (*melania*) as paler than someone who partakes more of darkness than paleness. And similarly we describe as more just a person who has enjoyed (*span*) a closer association with the just (*to dikaion*) and [more] healthy a person who has partaken of health more than another person. And likewise in all such cases. For just as, for example, those standing around it do not all get an equal share of the heat in a fire, but those who are closer get more to the degree that they intercept more of the radiant heat (*aura*) and those who are further away less, and yet the heat of the fire is one and the same, so too in the case of all qualities one must believe that they do not in themselves admit of intensification or abatement, but once present in corporeal subjects, in which it is indeed their nature to be mingled (*mignunai*),[431] either intensify or abate according to the greater or lesser admixture of their contraries.[432]

11a5 Triangle and square do not appear to admit of a more or less, and nor does any other figure.

Through this too he establishes that a more and less does not exist for every quality, for it does not for any figure either. No triangle is more or less [a triangle] than [another] triangle, since each of them admits the definition of triangle in equal measure; and nor is [one] circle [more or less a circle] than [another] circle even if it is ten thousand times as large, for each of these too admits the definition of circle in equal measure. And the same applies in the case of other things that the same definition exactly fits.[433]

11a9 Of the things that do not admit [the definition of triangle or circle] none will be called more the one than the other.

What he means by the above[434] is this. In things in which one observes a more and a less, he says, the same definition (*horismos*) must apply, but not exactly; for if it applies exactly, they will not admit of a more and a less. For instance, a healthy thing is one consonant with (*summetrôs ekhein*) health. This definition will apply to a gymnasium, to foodstuffs, to urine, and to a number of other things.⁴³⁵ Now, since all of these admit the same definition, but not without some variation (the gymnasium does so as being protective of health, food as being productive of it, urine as being indicative of it), they also fittingly (*eikotôs*) admit of a more and less. You will, for example, say that the gymnasium is more healthy than food, since the former preserves existing health, while the latter restores lost health, and that food is more healthy than urine, since urine only has to do with (*metekhein*) healthiness to the extent that it indicates a healthy condition. If, on the other hand, either exactly the same definition or an entirely different one belongs to any things, they do not admit of the more and the less, for the latter are absolutely different, the former absolutely the same. Take a man and a horse. Nobody would say that the man is more a man than the horse or the horse more a horse than a dog,⁴³⁶ since these are completely different things. But nor [would anyone say that] one man is more a man than another man as far as concerns their essence, or one horse more a horse than another horse, since these are in every respect the same as one another and admit of exactly the same definition.⁴³⁷ On the other hand, since the white in snow and that in a garment admit of the same definition (*logos*), though not exactly, the one is properly (*eikotôs*) said to be more [white] than the other. After all, it is not in the same way that each admits of the same definition (*horismos*). Snow possesses whiteness as part of its nature and as constitutive of its own being and in such a way that it does not admit of its opposite; a garment possesses it possibly through an artificial process and not as constitutive of its being or in such a way that it does not admit of its opposite. And the same goes for black and the rest. [It is] on this account,⁴³⁸ then, [that] the polygon is not said to be more a circle than the triangle, since neither of the stated [figures] admits of the definition of circle. And nor of course is a circle said to be less a polygon⁴³⁹ than other circles, again for the same reason.⁴⁴⁰

> **11a15** None of the things mentioned is peculiar to quality, but things are called similar and dissimilar only in virtue of qualities.

Just as in the case of substance and the other [categories] he first rejected the [merely] apparent distinctive features and later gave the actual distinctive features, so too here, after rejecting two concomitants of the qualified (*poion*)⁴⁴¹ ([namely,] that contrariety belongs to it and that it admits of a more and a less) as not being concomitants of every qualified thing, he singles out being called similar and dissimilar, since this is not said in the case of any of the other categories.⁴⁴² But it is not quality (*poiotês*) itself that admits of similarity and dissimilarity but qualified things. Each quality, considered on its own and not in a subject, [remains] one and the same. So how could it be similar or dissimilar to itself? However, once it has entered a subject, it does admit of similarity and dissimilarity, either being constantly present to (*phoitan*) the same things in an unmixed state (*eilikrinês*), or receiving the admixture of its contrary in a uniform manner and thus rendering its subjects similar to one another with respect to it,⁴⁴³ or [rendering them] dissimilar by not being present uniformly but admitting of a greater or lesser admixture of its contrary in its subjects. On account of this, then, in order that we may apply the distinctive feature to the whole category, let us do what we did in the case of substance.⁴⁴⁴ [There], adding something to its assigned distinctive feature and stating that the distinctive feature of the category of substance is that the individuals in it are, while remaining numerically one and the same, receptive of contraries by turns, we thereby made the concomitant a distinctive feature of the whole category. Let us then do the same here too, stating that the distinctive feature of the category of quality is that the individuals in it are said to be similar or dissimilar.⁴⁴⁵ For in this way the concomitant will apply to the whole category and to it alone.

11a20 We should not worry that someone may say that although our proposed subject was quality we are counting in many relatives.

Since his topic was quality and he had included states and conditions under quality, [and these] were in fact relatives (for he himself had earlier⁴⁴⁶ included them under the relatives, saying that a state is the state *of* the possessed and a condition the condition *of* the conditioned), perceiving the resulting puzzle, he solved it in two ways, first somewhat superficially, the second time more rigorously. The first solution is as follows:⁴⁴⁷

11a23 For in virtually all such cases the genera are said in relation to something but none of the particulars is.

Here is the first solution of the puzzle. He says that the genera of qualities are classified under the relatives but their species under the qualified. For instance, knowledge is a relative, since knowledge is a genus and is called knowledge *of* the knowable, while geometry is not a relative, being a species of knowledge, but is classified under the qualified.⁴⁴⁸ And the same applies in the case of state and condition and all such things: a state is the state *of* the possessed and the possessed is possessed *by* the state, and a condition is the condition *of* the conditioned and the conditioned is conditioned *by* the condition.⁴⁴⁹ However, health or illness, being species of state or condition,⁴⁵⁰ are qualities; for it is in relation to these [*sc.* qualities] that we are qualified in this or that manner and it is paronymously from them that we are said to be literate or skilled speakers or healthy or anything else of that kind. And we are said to be knowledgeable not simply because we partake of knowledge but because we partake of one of the particular kinds of knowledge, of grammar or music or some other. This, then, is the more superficial solution. It is superficial because the genera in all the categories are included under the same category as [their] species are. The more rigorous solution is as follows:

> **11a37** Further, if the same thing turns out to be both qualified and relative, there is nothing absurd about its being numbered in both of the genera.⁴⁵¹

For just as the father and the son are included under substance, and included under relatives as well, though from different perspectives, so too is there nothing absurd about states and conditions too being included [in their own right] under quality as entities but under relatives as having taken on (*anadekhesthai*) some relationship.⁴⁵²

Of Acting and Being-Affected⁴⁵³

> **11b1** Acting and being-affected admit of contrariety.

Some⁴⁵⁴ of the categories are simple while some owe their existence to the coupling or combination of the simple ones. The simple ones are the four [already] mentioned, substance, quantity, relatives, qualification, and the remaining six come into being as a result of the combination of substance with one of [the other three⁴⁵⁵] or with itself. So that we can see that this is so – I mean that the categories in the strict sense are the four mentioned and that the other six arise from the combination of these with one another – let us obtain the stated [propositions] by division.

Of the things there are, some exist in their own right, as does substance, while other have their being in other things. Of the things that have their being in other things, some are seen in a relation, i.e. the relatives, while others are not in a relation (*askhetos*). Of the things that have no relation, some are divisible, as are quantities (indeed we said⁴⁵⁶ that this, [I mean] divisibility, was a distinctive feature of quantity), while others are indivisible, as are qualities.

These, then, are the categories in the strict sense, those primarily so named, while the other six arise when substance is combined with the other three – I mean with quantity, the relative, and qualification – or with itself. Substance combined with quantity produces two categories, [namely,] when and where. For combined with time it produces when, since when indicates neither simply a substance nor simply a time but a substance that is in time. And combined with place it produces where, for where indicates neither just a place, because a place is not in a place, nor yet a substance, but a substance that is in a place. Again, substance combined with qualification produces two other categories, that of acting and that of being-affected, since acting and being-affected occur in relation to a quality. For someone who acts on something does so by heating it or cooling it [or by producing a change] with regard to some other quality, and someone who is affected is affected by being heated or darkened (*melainein*) [or affected] with regard to some other quality. Again, substance combined with relatives produces being-positioned (*keisthai*), and we said[457] that position (*thesis*) was a relative. And combined with itself [substance] produces 'having',[458] for 'having' indicates the arrangement of a substance around a substance.[459]

Although Aristotle has given the definitions and the concomitants of the [first] four categories, he has given neither the definitions nor the division into species of the remaining six on the ground that we can gather[460] these from what he has said. Therefore it is for us to give the definition and division into species of each.

(1) Acting (*poiein*) is operating (*energein*) on something. There are two species of this. Either the agent (*poioun*) acts (*poiein*) on itself, as the soul knowing itself, or it acts on something else, as fire acts on us when heating us. (2) Being-affected is being qualitatively changed by something. There are two species of this. A thing is either affected as being brought to destruction, like a log that is burned by fire, or as being brought to perfection, as when we say that vision is affected by the visible, because vision is brought to perfection by visible things in that it takes its own peculiar operation (*energeia*) from [them].[461] And the pupil is affected by the teacher, he too being perfected and not destroyed. (3) Being-positioned is to have a certain position. There are three species of this: lying,[462] sitting, standing. For either, as has often been stated,[463] the whole body is reclining and is said to be lying, or part of it is reclining and part upright and it is said to be sitting, or the whole of it is upright and it is said to be standing. (4) When is that which is indicative of time or that which is in time. There are three species of this: present, past, future. (5) Where is that which is indicative of place or that which is in place. There are six species of this: up, down, right, left, in front, behind.[464] It is only reasonable that the different kinds of place are six in number. For if, as has been stated by us,[465] place is the limit of the container by which it contains the contained, and if that which is contained is body, and if every body

has three dimensions, and if each dimension is regarded as bounded[466] by a straight line and not by any other [kind of line] (for if someone wants to know the measurement of the vertical (*kata mêkos*) dimension of, say, a wall, he will measure it along a perpendicular, and a perpendicular is a straight line;[467] and, likewise, if he wants to know the measurement of its horizontal (*kata platos*) dimension or of its depth [i.e. thickness], he will measure it by stretching a measuring cord [along it], and that is also a straight line), and every straight line has two extremities – if then [as I was saying] every body has three dimensions, and if each dimension is marked off (*kharaktêrizein*) by a straight line, and if every straight line has two ends (*peras*), it is only reasonable that a body has six boundaries (*peras*). So if a body has six boundaries, the place that surrounds it will of necessity also have six boundaries, since the place surrounds the body in every dimension. So, to speak of animate beings, the boundaries of the vertical dimension are the upper (*anô*) and the lower (*katô*), those of the horizontal, the right and the left, those of depth, the front and back. (6) Having is an arrangement of a substance around a substance.[468] This is either a case of a whole surrounding a whole, as a cloak surrounds the whole body, or a whole surrounding a part, like a ring on a finger.

11b1 Acting and being-affected admit of contrariety.

One must ask here why the philosopher does not include acting and being-affected under the relatives but says that they are separate (*heteros*) categories. After all, the agent (*poiôn*) acts on someone who is affected and the person who is affected is affected by an agent, so these[469] too are relatives.

To this we say that infinitive verbs are indicative solely of the nature of actions (*energeia*) or affections (*pathos*) because they only indicate an action or an affection, but other verbs, or participles, indicate the relation of substances to an action or an affection. 'Acting' and 'being-affected', then, being infinitive verbs,[470] are indicative of the action (*poiêsis*)[471] or affection (*pathêsis*) themselves and are not relatives. After all, nobody would say that 'acting' does something to 'being-affected' or that 'being-affected' is affected by 'acting'. However, the person who is affected and the agent *are* classified as relatives because the agent acts on someone who is affected and the person who is affected is affected by an agent.

Aristotle does well to ask in the physics course whether, if motion [arises] from acting and being-affected, it is regarded (*theôrein*) [as being] in the agent or in what is affected, and says that it is [regarded as being] in what is affected.[472] For motion is a path (*hodos*) from the potential to the actual (*energeiâi*),[473] and action (*energeia*) is the projection itself of a state (*hexis*).[474] So the things that move are those that are deficient and are changing from an imperfect state to a perfect one. At any rate things with a greater number of deficiencies exhibit a greater number of motions, while things with scant deficiency show scant movement. For instance, divinity, being in need of nothing, is also entirely motionless. If, then, the agent is in a perfected state with respect to the very thing it is doing (*poiein*), it will not move with respect to what it is doing, while the person who is affected, in that he has need of the agent to advance the potential present in him to actuality, is with reason said to be moved, being advanced from [only] potentially being to actually being what it is its nature to be. And so the motion is single, being regarded (*theôrein*) as only in the person affected, but the account of the motion can be twofold, for it can be regarded as in both the agent and the person affected, because when we think of the motion as starting from the agent and ending at the person affected, we call it 'acting', but when we think of it as starting from the person affected and ending at the agent (*to poioun*), we call it 'affection', as we likewise do in the case of teaching and learning. And so the motion is single with respect to its subject but differs in account. Relatives, on the other hand, not only differ in account but are also different in their subject. And so acting and being-affected, since they occur in connexion with (*peri*) a single subject, motion, will not be relatives, if, that is, relatives need (*thelein*) to have not only a different relation but different subjects too.[475]

So why didn't he use the title *Of Action*[476] (*poiêsis*) *and Affection* (*pathêsis*)?[477] We reply that action is twofold. Both the path itself, e.g. the activity (*energeia*) of the builder, is called 'action' and the end-product (*telos*) of the activity itself, e.g. the house.[478] So, lest error should arise as a result of this ambiguity (*homônumia*) and we should think that he is talking about the end-product, he gave it the present title *On Acting and Being-affected*, that is, on the activity itself, or the path.

Acting and being-affected too admit of contrariety and of more and less. This is only reasonable. Contrariety is only observed in qualities and acting and being-affected consist of a combination of substance and quality. And we have often stated[479] that it is the things that also admit of contrariety that admit of more and less. But since not every quality admits of contrariety or of more and less (shapes, for instance, [do not]), admitting of contrariety and of more and less quite reasonably does not hold good for (*parakolouthein*) every predication (*katêgoria*) of acting and being-affected, but in the case of one derived from a quality that does admit of more and less exactly the same applies for it, and in the case of one deriving from a quality that does not admit of contrariety there will not be anything contrary to it either.[480]

11b15 On the one hand (*men*),⁴⁸¹ about the proposed genera what has been said is sufficient.   10

On the basis of this brief remark some commentators have supposed that the subject (*skopos*) of the *Categories* is just concepts. Aristotle, they say, only knows of the genera that are later in origin and conceptual. The universal ones, he says   15
in *On the Soul*,⁴⁸² are either non-existent (*ouden*) or posterior, and the kind that are prior to the many he does not want to exist at all but calls them twitterings⁴⁸³ and superfluous nonsenses.⁴⁸⁴

On Opposites

11b16 On the other hand (*de*), concerning opposites we must say in how many ways they are usually opposed.   20

The account of the categories is complete and he [now] begins the section [that comes] after the categories, for we said⁴⁸⁵ at the beginning of the book that this book is divided into three parts, into the one [that comes] before the categories, the one on the categories themselves, and the one after the categories,⁴⁸⁶ and that in the one [that comes] before the categories he talks about words that he will   25
use in the teaching of the categories which are not known to us from everyday usage, in the second section, about the categories themselves, in the third, i.e. the   168,1
present one, about certain words that he has used in the teaching of the categories of which we have some notion but not a detailed one.⁴⁸⁷ And that this present section is not foreign to (*apartan*) the aim (*skopos*)⁴⁸⁸ of the *Categories*, as some have thought,⁴⁸⁹ is clear from what has [just] been said and clear too from the   5
very continuity of the writing (*phrasis*); for having used the conjunction (*sundesmos*)⁴⁹⁰ 'on the one hand' at the end of the previous section, he has added the [antithetical] conjunction 'on the other hand' in this one. For after saying 'On the one hand, about the proposed genera' in that [section], at the beginning of this one he says 'On the other hand, concerning opposites'. And so from this too the coherence (*sunekheia*) of the aim is evident.

He teaches about opposites first, for he also made mention of them in the   10
discourse on quantity⁴⁹¹ when he said that the large is opposed to the small not as contraries are but as relatives are. Accordingly he wants to teach [us] here in how many ways oppositions are stated. Opposites, then, he says, are opposed it four ways: as relatives, or as contraries, or as privation and state, or as affirmation and negation.⁴⁹²   15

We must ask just why the kinds of opposites are only four in number and neither more nor fewer and what the reason is for their being in the above order.

So that we may learn why they are only four in number, let us say this. Opposites are opposed either as statements (*logos*) or as things. Those that are opposed as things are either seen in some relation [to one another] or are not in a relation. And if they are not in a relation, they either change or do not change into one another. So then, (1) opposed as statements are affirmation and negation, e.g. 'Socrates is walking' [and] 'Socrates is not walking'; (2) opposed as things and having a relation are the relatives, e.g. father and son, right and left, knowledge and the knowable; (3) [opposed] as things and not in a relation and changing into one another [are] the contraries, e.g. black and white, hot and cold; (4)[opposed] as things and[493] not in a relation and not changing into one another [are] state and privation, e.g. sight and blindness.[494] [This last is the case] because, while state changes to privation, e.g. sight to blindness, privation certainly does not change to state, e.g. blindness to sight, since here by privation he means the complete eradication of the form and of the very potential – whereas in the physics course[495] by privation he does not mean the complete eradication of the potential (for in that[496] [work] he also wants privation to change into state), but only the absence of the actuality.[497]

Division, then, has shown us the reason why the kinds of opposites are only four in number. We shall now say why he placed the opposition between relatives first, that between contraries second, that between state and privation third, that between affirmation and negation fourth.

We say, then, that he began with those that display the milder opposition. I mean the relatives. These not only do not destroy one another by their opposition but even entail one another. For given one, a father, say, the other, i.e. a son, is also implied, and when one is eliminated, the other is eliminated along with it, because they are responsible for one another's existence.

The opposition between contraries, e.g. white and black, takes second place. Their opposition is somewhat stronger because they not only do not entail one another but even destroy one another, since when one is present the other does not hold its ground. They do, however, change into one another, examples being hot and cold [and] white and black.

Things [opposed] as state and privation take third place. Their opposition is stronger than the opposition between contraries, since contraries change into one another, but the privation never changes to the state. For nobody will ever see again once blind – not at any rate according to the laws of nature or art – unless perhaps by some divine power.[498]

Things opposed as affirmation and negation are in last place. For their opposition is [yet] stronger, because in the case of all things, existent or non-existent, they divide the true and the false. For example, it is said that Socrates is either on the right or not on the right, and this division is clearly true whether Socrates be on his own or with others or totally non-existent. For should he be on his own, the division that says that he is not on the right is true. And if he is with others, the same applies; for among others he is either on the right or not on the right but either in the middle or on the left, and both of these mean not on the right. And if he is totally non-existent, it is true to say that he is not on the right. For how could a totally non-existent person be? And a sound is said to be either clear (*leukos*) or not clear, a stone to have or not have sight. You will find this opposition holds true in every case, not only in the case of particular oppositions but in the case of universal ones too; for [all] things that exist are either on the right or not on the right, are either clear or not clear, either have sight or do not have sight. And this opposition does not only hold in the case of corporeal things (*sômata*) but in the case of incorporeal things too: they too do not have right-hand position, since they are not even bodies, and nor are they clear, and nor do they have our [kind of] sight. And not-being too is neither to the right nor clear nor in possession of sight.

Affirmation and negation then, as was stated earlier, divide all things that exist and all things that do not exist, but the other oppositions in no wise do. (1) The opposition between relatives is not said [to hold] in the case of all things, for should someone be alone, he is not said to be [either] on the right or on the left. And nor is any of the incorporeal things, such as soul, for [soul] is neither on the right nor on the left. And nor is (2) the [opposition] of contraries; for sound is not said to be [in every case] either clear (*leukos*) or indiscernible (*melas*), for there is also the kind called muted. And nor is it the case with colours that they are [in every case] either light (*leukos*) or dark (*melas*); there are also the in-between ones, the greys and off-whites and the like.[499] And nor is it so in the case of (3) privation and state. A stone is not said to be [either] blind or to have sight.

So it is with good reason that he has mentioned the [opposition] of relatives first, that of contraries second, that of privation and state third, and that of affirmation and negation fourth, beginning with the [relations] that display a milder opposition and advancing to those that are more strongly opposed.

11b19 Each of these is opposed, in outline, [as follows]: in the case of the relatives, as the double to the half ...

By this he gives us some idea of these [oppositions], conducting (*gumnazein*) the argument using examples, then, after that, he distinguishes each separately from

the rest so that nobody will imagine that they embody the same opposition. For in fact some people have supposed that the contraries embody the same opposition as the relatives; for a contrary, they say, is contrary *to* a contrary.[500] To this we say that on the one hand the things that admit of contrariety are qualities,
25   things like white and black [and] hot and cold, [and] nobody would say that white is white *to* black or that black is black *to* white. But contrariety itself, on the other hand, *is* a relative. And there is no absurdity if contrariety, being a relative, is seen in other things. After all, we said [earlier][501] that relatives have no existence of their own but subsist in the other categories.[502]

30   **11b21** ... in the case of the contraries, as bad to good.

By good he does not mean here the [kind that is] above being (*huperousios*)
171,1   (for bad is not opposed to that), but the contrary of bad. Good is in fact twofold. One kind exists per se, the kind that belongs substantially (*ousiôdôs*) to god, [and this] has no contrary (for there is no contrary to substance (*ousia*)). The other kind is accidental, the kind that is said in contradistinction to bad,
5   I mean the [kind that is] in us.[503] It is just like light, which we also said[504] is twofold. One kind is in the sun. This has no darkness opposed to it since it contributes to the substance of the sun and is [part] of its substance (*ousiôdês*). The other kind is in the air, having come to be in it accidentally. Darkness is opposed to this [kind], it too[505] supervening *per accidens* upon the departure of the light from the air. And comprehension (*gnôsis*) too is twofold, as Plato also
10   says.[506] One kind, which knows only truth, is intellective, and it does not admit of (*ekhein*) the opposed[507] falsehood; the other kind is discursive, and also opinion, which do admit of the opposed falsehood;[508] for it is possible to reason to (*dianoeisthai*) falsehoods or to opine [them] but impossible to intelligize (*noein*) falsehoods. For [in that case] the intellect would be devoid of intellect (*anoêtos*); for the intellect has either grasped the object of its intellection or not grasped it, says Aristotle,[509] and so is not subject to error. So it is to this
15   good here (I mean to the kind in [the sphere of] generation) that he says bad is opposed.

11b32 Thus things that are opposed as relatives are called just what they are *of* other things.[510]

He wants to show that the opposition of relatives is not the same as the opposition
20   of contraries and he shows this using the following second-figure syllogism: things that are opposed as relatives are called just what they are *of* other things

(e.g. right is said to be to the right *of* left); things that are opposed as contraries are not called just what they are *of* other things (white is not said to be white *of* black); therefore things that are opposed as relatives are other than those that are opposed as contraries.⁵¹¹

> **11b38** But contraries that are such that it is necessary that one or the other of them belong to the things in which they naturally occur or of which they are predicated – between these there is nothing [that is intermediate].

Having distinguished the opposition of relatives from that of contraries, he now wants to distinguish it from the remaining [types of opposition].⁵¹² And first (*proteron*) he distinguishes it from the opposition of state and privation.⁵¹³ And since an enumeration of the differentiae⁵¹⁴ of things opposed as state and privation helps him in this, he first gives us their differentiae.⁵¹⁵ And even before these he gives us the different kinds of contraries,⁵¹⁶ because he intends to distinguish these too from things opposed as state and privation immediately [afterwards].⁵¹⁷ And after the enumeration of the differentiae of things that are opposed as state and privation he further sets out the differentiae of things opposed as affirmation and negation,⁵¹⁸ since he lastly distinguishes these too from the other [kinds of opposition].⁵¹⁹ For if we understand (*eidenai*) the differentiae and the concomitants of each opposition, we shall readily understand the difference (*diaphora*) from one another of the oppositions as well.

First then, as was stated, he gives the division of contraries. It goes, in effect,⁵²⁰ like this. Some contraries are without intermediates, like even and odd, and some with intermediates, like white and black, since grey and the other colours fall between [them]. And of those with intermediates, some are such that both can be absent from a subject (it is not necessary for every body to be white or black; they can also be grey), others are such that one of them in particular, and not just whichever chances to be, is necessarily present to the subject, in the way that heat is to fire and cold never is and coldness is to snow and heat never is because that is the nature of each.⁵²¹

So much for the division and subdivision [of the contraries]. But the contraries with intermediates are further divided in another fashion:⁵²² of contraries with intermediates some have intermediates that are indicated by names, others [intermediates that are indicated] by definition (*logos*)⁵²³ and by the negation of the extremes. The intermediates between white and black, for instance, are called by names such as grey, off-white, yellow and the like, while the intermediate between bad (*phaulos*) and good (*spoudaios*) is not indicated by a name but what is neither bad nor good is indicated by the negation of the extremes.[524]

11b38 But contraries that are such that [it is necessary that one or the other of them belong] to the things in which they naturally occur or of which they are predicated – [between them there is nothing that is intermediate].

Some contraries belong to the subject accidentally, others per se. By 'naturally occur' he has indicated those that belong to the subject accidentally, by 'predicated' those that belong to it per se. As [Aristotle] himself says in his works on demonstration,[525] per se has two senses. One is that which becomes part of the definition of the subject entity, like 'animal' [and] 'rational' (for these belong per se to 'man' and are included in its definition); the other is that whose subject is included in the definition, like even and odd, snubness and hookedness. For when we define even and odd we mention the subject, namely number, since we call an even number one that is divided in two and an odd number one that cannot be divided in two. On the other hand, you will not necessarily mention 'odd' when defining number, for number is a plurality or collection of units, and at most [one would add that] every number is either even or odd. And when defining snubness and hookedness, we necessarily mention their subject, the nose, and say that snubness is concavity in a nose and hookedness convexity in a nose.[526]

12a1 [But contraries that are such that] it is necessary that one or the other of them belong [to the things in which they naturally occur or of which they are predicated] – between these there is nothing [that is intermediate].

What he wants to say here is this. Those contraries that are such that one of them must necessarily be present, whether per se or accidentally, have nothing between them, but those that are such that both contraries can be absent from the subject in which they are present, whether per se or accidentally, are not without intermediates but have something between them. Of the former [kind], an example of contraries that are present per se is the even and the odd, for there is nothing between them, and of those [that are present] accidentally, illness and health, for there is nothing between them either, but one or the other of them must of necessity be present in the body of an animal, if we count every departure of any kind (*hopôsoun*) from the natural state as sickness.[527] Of the latter [kind], an example of the per se [type] is something like heat in fire or coldness in water, since there is something between them, [namely,] the lukewarm, and of the accidental [type] something like black and white in us, since grey is in between.[528]

12a6 And odd and even are predicated of number.

For every number is either odd or even, and a number could not be found[529] that is not such.

12a13 And bad and good are predicated both of men and of many other things.

For it is not only in the case of man that we speak of bad and good but in the case of other things as well, for instance, a horse.[530]

12a20 In some cases names exist for the things between [them].

By this, as I have already stated,[531] he produces a subdivision of the contraries with intermediates in another way, having earlier already subdivided the very same [contraries] into those that can both be absent from the subject and those whose nature is such that they are necessarily present to the subject in the guise of one of the opposed [terms] (*antikeimena*).

12a26 Privation and state are spoken of in connexion with the same thing.

Having told [us] about the various senses of the contraries, he now turns to teaching about privation and state, for it was stated[532] by us that the teaching of these helps him in distinguishing them from the relatives, and not only [in this] but in distinguishing [them] from the other opposites too.[533]

12a27 To speak generally, each of them is spoken of in connexion with that in which the state naturally occurs.

There are three things one must look at in the case of state and privation: what is of a nature to receive [them]; when it is natural for it to receive [them] (that is, the period (*khronos*) during which[534] it is natural [for it to do so]); in which part it is natural for it [to receive them]. A privation is seen [only] in a thing in connexion with which we speak of a state. We don't say that a stone is deprived of sight, because it is simply not in its nature to have sight.[535] Nor do we say that a man is deprived of sight in his feet, because it is not in his nature to have sight in that part [of his anatomy]. And nor do we say that a [newborn] pup is deprived of sight, because it isn't natural for it to have it at that point (*kairos*). We do, however, speak of a man being deprived of sight where his face[536] is concerned, because it is a man's nature to have sight, and in that part, at that stage (*khronos*) [of his development]. Similarly, it is not simply someone without teeth that we call toothless (certainly not the newborn, since it's not in their nature to have them at that time), just as we don't call the pup blind either. It is a person deprived of his teeth by, say, age or some accident that we describe as toothless.[537]

12a35 *Being deprived and having a state are not privation and state.*

By this, the philosopher wants to show that being deprived is not the same thing as privation or having a state as the state.[538] In themselves state and privation are qualities, while the things that have the state and the privation are qualified things that are named from them paronymously, as in the case of whiteness and the white, since the former is a quality, the latter a qualified thing called after it paronymously. The philosopher shows this (I mean that a state is a different thing from possessing a state) not through the genera (I mean those of the state and of the possessor of the state and of the privation and the possessor of the privation)[539], but through the species (I mean those of sight and blindness and of the possessor of sight or of blindness), because the species are clearer than the genera. [This is] because in their case it is clear that blindness is one thing, the possessor of blindness another, and sight one thing, the possessor of sight another, since the first mentioned [items] are particular (*tis*) qualities, the second substances that partake of them. If, then, these are different, their genera are also different. For as sight or blindness stand to the possessor of sight or blindness, so do a state or a privation to the possessor of the state or privation, since it is also the case that as sight or blindness stand to state or privation, so too do the possessor of sight or the possessor of blindness to the possessor of a state or privation, for they are their species. If, then, these are different (I mean sight and the possessor of sight and blindness and the possessor of blindness), their genera are also different (I mean state and the possessor of a state and privation and the possessor of a privation).

12a39 *Also, if blindness were the same thing as being blind, both would be predicated of the same thing.*

And, besides, he says, if sight and the possessor of sight were the same thing, both would be predicated of the same thing. For just as mortal, man, and human (*merops*),[540] being the same thing, are predicated of a single subject, so too would these, if they were the same things, be predicated of one and the same subject. But as it is a man is said to *have* blindness or sight but is not simply said to *be* blindness or sight. And so it is clear from this too that these are different.[541] But even though they are different, they still, he says, show the same kind of opposition; for just as sight is opposed to blindness as privation and state,[542] so too is having sight opposed to having blindness on the basis of (*kata*) state and privation.

12b6 *And nor is the subject of*[543] *an affirmation or a negation [itself] an affirmation or a negation.*

And that nor is an affirmation or a negation the same as the things indicated by them he shows from the fact that the negation or affirmation are statements while the [items] indicated by them are things. 'Socrates is sitting', for example, is a statement while the actual seated Socrates is a thing, for it is a substance along with a certain activity, namely, sitting. But these too are opposed to one another with the same kind of opposition [as the statements]. For just as the statement 'Socrates is sitting' is opposed to the statement 'Socrates is not sitting', so too is the seated Socrates opposed to the not seated, for both these oppositions are opposed as affirmation and negation.[544]

12b16 *That privation and state are not opposed as relatives is clear.*

Having taught us about each opposition separately he now makes a distinction [between] them and [first] distinguishes things opposed as relatives from those opposed as state and privation, for he has already distinguished them from contraries. He again deploys the argument using species, namely, sight and blindness, because they are clearer.[545] First he gives the following proof,[546] once more[547] employing a second-figure syllogism: relatives are said to be just what they are *of* the opposed [person or thing] (a father, for example, is said to be the father *of* a son, and what is on the right is said to be on the right *of* what is on the left); but things [opposed] as state and privation are not said to be just what they are of their opposites (sight, for example, is not said to be sight *of* blindness); therefore things opposed as relatives are other than those opposed as state and privation. In this way he has first provided a proof on the basis of what is clearer and a matter of general agreement (namely, on the basis that sight is not said to be the sight *of* blindness), then subsequently also provides[548] a proof on the basis of the doubtful [proposition] that blindness is not even said to be the blindness *of* sight. For this does seem to be said.[549]

12b18 *Nor is sight*[550] *spoken of in relation to it in any other way.*

Equivalent to: 'however you may formulate the term (*onomatopoiein*) it is in no way said *in relation to* the opposed term,[551] whether you give it in relation to a dative or another case'; for sight is not sight *for*[552] blindness either.

12b19 *And likewise blindness would not be called blindness of sight.*

Having shown for the agreed case, namely, sight, that it is not said in relation to its opposite, he now shows this for the doubtful case; for blindness is said to be privation of sight, but certainly not blindness *of* sight.[553] But perhaps we do not do well to say that blindness is not said to be blindness of sight. For if, as he says himself, we talk of privation of sight and when something is predicated of the genus, there is every necessity that something should also be predicated of its species (for it is not possible for anything to be an animal that will not in every case be either a human being or a horse or one of the other animals), and in the same way there cannot be a privation either without there being in every case something of which it is said to be the privation, there is in that case (*oun*) every necessity that the privation that is opposed to that state at the level of (*kata*) the species should also be said to be a privation *of* it. After all,[554] the privation of sight is not privation *tout court* and absolutely universally but clearly a particular privation, i.e. blindness. So if privation of sight is a particular privation, and this particular privation is nothing other than blindness, then blindness is blindness *of* sight. For how could it be possible, when the genus is said to be *of* something, for the species not also to be said *of* something, if indeed it is not possible for the genera to be in existence without [at least] one of the species? So either the genus too, i.e. privation, is not said to be privation *of* sight or, if the genus is, [at least] one of the species certainly is.

But perhaps someone will say to this that if we talk of privation of knowledge, then by this argument there must be some species of this privation that will be predicated of knowledge or be said *of* it, but in fact, while the genus is predicated of knowledge, we do not find any species of it [*sc*. of the privation] [so] predicated. Well, to this one can say that we do not even have a named privation that is opposed to knowledge in the way that the privation opposed to sight is called blindness, one such that, if it had existed, it too would have been said in relation to (*pros*) knowledge, in the way that blindness is said to be the blindness *of* sight. For when we name privations with reference to (*kata*) the privations of states, as in the case of ignorance, illiteracy, imprudence,[555] and the like, clearly such [qualities] are no longer said to be [features] of the opposite but of the recipient. For ignorance (*agnôsia*) is not said to be the ignorance *of* knowledge (*gnôsis*), but the ignorance *of* the soul,[556] and [the same goes for] illiteracy and the rest; for they contain in themselves the opposite of which they are predicating the privation.[557] But even if the privation is said to be just what it is *of* its opposite ([and] not only the genus itself, but also any named species there may be under it [*sc*. under the privation]), even so the state is not said to be just what it is of the privation, whereas in the case of relatives each of the opposed [terms] is said to be just what it is of its opposite, as Aristotle says later. And so things opposed as state and privation may be distinguished from the relatives in this way.

And one would also say that it is not in the same way that relatives are said to be just what they are *of* their opposites that a privation is said to be the privation of a state. For [in the case of] relatives it is as being mutual causes (*sunaitios*) of one another that each of the opposed [items] is thus said to be *of* the other, whereas the privation is said to be *of* the state not as being the cause of its 15 existence, but on the contrary as being the cause of its non-existence. But perhaps it is possible to say something in support of (*sunêgorein*) Aristotle's statement to the effect that privation is said to be privation of sight but never blindness of sight. Note at any rate that we also talk of privation of light but never of darkness of light, yet darkness is nothing other than privation of light, just as blindness is 20 privation of sight, as has been shown at length by us elsewhere.[558] Rather, just as we talk of, say, maiming (*pêrôsis*) of the limbs but not of maiming of symmetry (*artiotês*) [of body] or uprightness or straightness, or whatever else one might call[559] the natural bearing (*thesis*) of the limbs, so too, quite clearly, do we talk of darkness of air but never of darkness of light. And nor therefore of blindness of sight, but if anything of blindness of the eyes, as we also [talk] of impairing 25 (*pêrôsis*) of the eyes. The eye means the part that has sight, but sight the faculty itself. But since, just as in the case of the other qualities too we often name the thing that is qualified by the same name as the quality, calling both the white-coloured body and the whiteness itself 'white', and similarly with hot and cold 30 and heavy and light and the rest, so too do we apply 'sight' not only to the faculty but to the organs [of sight] themselves, calling the eyes 'the sight', and we properly speaking say that blindness belongs to the eyes, but the eyes, as I said, are called 'sight'. For this reason, then, we also speak of blindness of sight, applying the word 'sight' not to the faculty but to the organs [of sight]. And Aristotle is saying 35 that 'blindness' is not said in connexion with (*pros*) the opposed faculty [*sc*. sight], which is true.

It remains then for us to explain how it is that, given that its genus (I mean 180,1 that of the privation) is said to be [the privation] of the state, each species of the privation is not also said [to be the privation] of some opposed state, if it is indeed true that in cases where a genus is said of something one of the species under the genus is in every case also predicated of it. My reply is that states are 5 certain entities (*pragma*) that are endowed with form and have [real] existence and therefore, as one would expect, being a genus, the state also has subordinate species with [real] existence and each having a particular physical form, whereas the privation is nothing but the absence of the state, and so is, by its own definition, non-being. So how do we search for species of what is non-existent as 10 though it existed?[560] And so, even though there is some more specific privation that is opposed to a particular state, it is not as something with existence that it is so opposed, but, once more, as not existing [and] through (*kata*) the negation of the state, as the unwise is opposed to the wise and the toothless (from 'tooth' and the privative 'less') to that which has teeth.

These particular privations, then, are, like the genus, said in negation of the state. And if on occasion there is found to be an established name for a privation, as the absence of sight is called blindness or the absence of light darkness, such a name is not predicated of the absence of the state, but of the affection (*pathos*) in the recipient or of something else that supervenes upon the absence of the state, in the way that 'darkness' (*skotos*) is derived from 'to shadow' (*skiazein*) and shadow (*skia*) is a blocking of the light that takes place in the air, or simply in the transparent [medium] – or, as Herodian states,[561] from 'to hold back' (*skhethein*), since it hinders (*epekhein*)[562] us from seeing, or holds us back (*epekhein*) from getting out (*proodoi*) and from most activities.[563] And 'blindness' (*tuphlôsis*), for its part, is perhaps from 'to smoke' (*tuphein*) – and 'blind man' (*tuphlos*) [too], as if a blind man[564] is someone who has smouldering eyes (indeed the poet[565] says, 'my empty eyes are smouldering'), as 'cripple' (*pêros*) is from: 'I suffer' (*pêthô*) – 'I shall suffer' (*pêsô*)[566] – 'cripple' (*pêros*); just as [we get] from 'I hesitate' (*oknô*) [the sequence]: [I hesitate] – I shall hesitate (*oknêsô*) – hesitating (*oknêros*). So such [privations] are plausibly said to be *of* the organs and not *of* the states, for they are conditions (*pathê*) of the bodies that underlie the states and not of the states themselves.

12b21 Also, all relatives are spoken of in relation to reciprocating [correlatives].

He shows by means of yet another syllogism that things opposed as relatives are other than those opposed as privation and state. What he says is in effect (*dunamei*) this: relatives are spoken of in relation to reciprocating [correlatives] (for just as the father is father of the son, so too is the son the son of the father); things [opposed] as state and privation are not spoken of in relation to reciprocating [correlatives] (for sight is not said to be sight of blindness); therefore relatives are other than things opposed as state and privation.[567]

12b26 And that nor are things that are predicated (*legein*) as privation and state opposed in the way that contraries are is clear from the following.

He has distinguished the opposition of relatives from the opposition of contraries and from that of things opposed as privation and state. He next now distinguishes things opposed as privation and state from things opposed as contraries.

According to natural sequence he should have distinguished the relatives from things opposed as affirmation and negation, but since he is about to distinguish things opposed as affirmation and negation from the other [oppositions] by means of a single argument, he on that account defers distinguishing relatives from affirmation and negation for the present[568] so as not to have to repeat himself. He repeats the enumeration of the kinds of contraries because he wants [to show[569] that] things [opposed] as state and privation [are] opposed to all [types of] contraries.

> **12b27** In the case of contraries with nothing between them it is necessary that one or the other of them be present in what they naturally occur in or are predicated of.

For it is entirely necessary that a number be either even or odd and an animal either sick or in good health.[570]

> **12b32** But in the case of those with something between them it is never necessary that one or the other of them be present in everything.

For not every body is necessarily either white or black, for there is also the grey; or, again, hot or cold, for there is also the lukewarm.[571]

> **12b35** Further, there was something between [just] those of which it was not necessary for one or the other to be present in the recipient – except [in the case of] those in which one [of them] is present by nature.

This was the third species of contraries, [the type] which [also] has something between [the contraries], but [in which] one or other of the contraries is of necessity present in the recipient because it is present in it by nature, as heat is in fire and white in snow. [In their case] it is not possible for one or other of the contraries ever to be absent from the recipient. It is, for instance, impossible for fire not to be hot or snow not to be cold, or for earth not to be heavy or fire not to be light.[572]

> **13a3** But in the case of privation and state neither of these accounts (*eirêmena*) is true.

Having reminded us of the different types of opposition between contraries, he now shows that in none of the types mentioned can the opposition of the contraries be the same as that according to privation and state. And first he distinguishes this last from the contraries without intermediates. This is what he says:[573]

13a4 For it is not necessary for one or the other of them always to be present in a recipient.

For in the case of opposites without intermediates one or the other was [as we saw]⁵⁷⁴ present to the subject, but in the case of things [opposed] as privation and state one or the other is not of necessity present to the subject, but [on the contrary] both may be absent. For example, a [newborn] pup is neither blind nor in possession of sight, and a recently born child is neither toothless nor in possession of teeth, whereas a number is in every case either even or odd and an animal is of necessity either sick or healthy. So the opposition of contraries without intermediates is not the same as that according to privation and state.⁵⁷⁵

13a8 But nor of those that do have something between [them], for it is necessary for one or the other of them to be present at some time (*pote*) to everything able to receive them.

He now distinguishes things [opposed] as privation and state from contraries with an intermediate, and first from those whose nature it is to be [able to be] absent from the subject with respect to both of the contraries. For in the case of things opposed as state and privation, whenever the subject is able to receive them, one or the other is of necessity present to the subject; for example, Socrates is of necessity either blind or has sight. But he is not of necessity either white or black. It is possible for neither of these to be present in him even though he is of a nature to receive either opposite.⁵⁷⁶

13a11 And not definitely one or the other of these but whichever has chanced to be the case; for it is not necessary for it to be blind or for it to have sight but whichever has chanced to be the case.

By this he again distinguishes things [opposed] as privation and state from contraries with intermediates, [this time from those] in whose case one or the other of the contraries is by nature definitely present to a thing that can receive them. For with privation and state, he says, it is not the case that one or the other [must] definitely be present to the subject when it is of a nature to receive them, but whichever has chanced to be the case (for Socrates is not definitely blind or definitely possessed of sight, but as chance has had it), whereas with contraries with intermediates in the case of which one or the other is by nature present to the subject, it is necessary that one [of them] definitely be present and its contrary never be present. Heat, for example, is definitely present to fire, and whiteness and cold to snow, their opposite[s] never. And this is so on account of the nature of the subject, since in their own right heat and cold have intermediates.⁵⁷⁷ And so the opposition of things [opposed] as privation and state is not the same as [that present]⁵⁷⁸ in either kind of contraries with intermediates.

> **13a17** Further, in the case of contraries, as long as the thing capable of receiving them is present, it is possible for change from one to the other to occur.

Having divided contraries and having shown separately that the opposition of things [opposed] as privation and state is not the same opposition [as that found] in any of the kinds of contraries, he now distinguishes them [*sc.* privation and state and contraries] from one another by means of a general argument as follows: contraries change into one another (for instance, hot changes into cold and cold into hot, and black into white and white into black); but things [opposed] as privation and state do not change into one another (even though sight changes to blindness, blindness does not also change to sight.); therefore contraries are not the same as things [opposed] as privation and state.⁵⁷⁹

He did well to say 'as long as the thing capable of receiving them is present', since it is on account of this that the change of contraries into one another takes place, for in their own right qualities are unchanging and they [only] undergo change when they enter a subject.

And he also did well to say 'it is possible', since contraries do not always change into one another, for those that by nature definitely belong to some subject never change into their contraries. For instance, the heat in fire would never change to coldness or the coldness or whiteness in snow change to heat or blackness.

> **13a22** And it is certainly possible to become bad after being good or good after being bad.

He does not show that it is possible to become a bad person after being a good one but does argue that it is possible to become a good one after being a bad one.

By a good man he doesn't mean here a perfect one and one who possesses the good as a matter of knowledge (*en epistêmêi*). The condition of such a person is not subject to change in that he not only knows that virtue is a good but also why it is a good. So it is not such a person that he is saying changes, but the one who is guided by right opinion (*orthodoxastikos*), for such a person will change for the worse when lead astray by false reasoning or deceived by wicked men, because he does not know the reason why virtue is a good.⁵⁸⁰

13a29 And if this keeps happening it will bring him over (*apokathistanai*)⁵⁸¹ entirely to the opposite state, unless that is precluded by time.

For it is likely that part way through the continuity [of the process] will be interrupted by illness or worries about his personal concerns (*pragmata*) or association with worse men; and also if a person begins to engage in philosophy in extreme old age and then is cut off in the middle of things by death before he can change to a state of perfect virtue.⁵⁸²

13a34 Nobody who has gone blind has [ever] recovered his sight.

Certainly by the law of medicine or nature no blind person has ever recovered his sight, although perhaps [it may have happened] as the result of some divine illumination.⁵⁸³

13a37 It is clear that things that are opposed as affirmation and negation are not opposed in any of the above ways.

He has distinguished the relatives from the things [that are opposed] as privation and state and from the contraries and these last from the things [that are opposed] as privation and state. Three pairings arise from this. Therefore there remain another three pairings, in accordance with the method that was given in the *Isagoge*.⁵⁸⁴ The method was as follows. One must multiply the given number (*plêthos*) by [that] number (*arithmos*) minus one and take the half of the number obtained, and state that that is the number of the pairings. For instance, the given [number of] things in our case is four. We multiply these by [that number] minus one, i.e. by three, and the result is four times three – [or] twelve. Half of this is six. So that is the number of pairings. So given that, as was stated, three [of the conjunctions] have been given us, the other three are left, [and] he now gives us these in a general statement, for he distinguishes the things [that are opposed] as affirmation and negation from the other three in a general statement, [namely,] 'for only in their case is it always necessary that one of them be true and the other false'.⁵⁸⁵ For example, if I say 'Socrates is sitting down' [and] 'Socrates is not sitting down', one of these is true, the other false.⁵⁸⁶ But none of the three others indicates either truth or falsity. For if I say 'father or son' or 'white or black' or 'sight or blindness' ten thousand times over, I have not indicated any truth or falsehood. The nouns by themselves, enunciated without verbs, do not indicate either a truth or a falsehood; when they are combined with verbs, *then* they are indicative of truth or falsehood. And verbs too, used on their own, indicate neither truth nor falsehood, but when used in conjunction with pronouns are expressive of truth or falsehood, as in 'I am walking' (*egô peripatô*). And in fact *peripatô*⁵⁸⁷ by itself potentially contains the pronoun [*egô*] within itself, since it too provides an indication of the [grammatical] person. Of course the infinitives – 'to walk', 'to run', for instance – because they don't indicate [grammatical] persons, don't indicate truth or falsehood: the [uninflected] verb on its own is empty [of extra content] and doesn't contain the pronoun even potentially, as [the inflected form] *peripatô* does. If, then, things [that are opposed] as affirmation and negation are expressive of truth or falsehood and not one of the other three indicates truth or falsehood, then the opposition of things [that are opposed] as affirmation and negation is not the same as any of these.

> **13b3** For neither with contraries is it necessary that one always be true and the other false.

He has added 'always' because sometimes when these are combined with subjects they become receptive of truth or falsehood, as, for instance, 'Socrates is well' [and] 'Socrates is not well'.[588]

> **13b10** In sum, none of the things that is said without any combination is either true or false.

Things that are said without any combination express nothing[589] [that is] either true or false; but relatives and contraries and things [that are opposed] as privation and state are said without combination; therefore they express nothing [that is] either true or false; and so they are not the same as the things that are said in affirmation or negation.

> **13b12** It might very well seem that something of the sort does occur in the case of contraries that are said *with* combination.

Anticipating the difficulty that one would have put to him, he both raises it and resolves it himself. He says that contraries that are said in combination with a subject divide the true and the false, because in the case of Socrates' being well or being ill the one is true, the other false. And further, having sight or being blind, or a father or a son – these too are receptive of truth and falsehood. Well, to this he replies that even though these [when] in combination appear to divide truth from falsehood, even then they differ greatly from affirmation and negation. Affirmation and negation always, both in the case of things that exist and of things that do not exist, divide the true and the false. For Socrates' being blind or not being blind, or being white or not being white, or being a father or not being a father, are, when he exists, of necessity always the one true and the other false, while, when he does not exist, the second [of each pair] is always true, since a

120 Translation

totally non-existent person is neither a father nor blind nor white. And somebody who says [either] that the soul is white or that it is not white, and [either that it] has sight or does not have sight, and [either that it] is to the right or not to the right, will be stating a truth in the one case and a falsehood in the other. However
25 contraries are not like this, but as long as Socrates exists one of them must be true and the other false (he must, for example, be either well or ill), while if he doesn't exist both must be false; for how could a totally non-existent person be either well or ill? In the case of privation and state, on the other hand, even when he exists it is not the case that one or other of the contraries is always true, but there are times when both are false, and when he doesn't exist both are always false. For
187,1 instance, [in the case of] Socrates' being toothless or having teeth, it is not the case that one or the other is always true [even] when he exists; in fact there is a time when both are false ([i.e.] when it isn't natural for him to have any). And when he doesn't exist, both are always false. For how under any circumstances at all could a totally non-existent person be either toothless or have teeth? And, similarly, in the case of the [newborn] pup both, i.e. the state and the privation,
5 are, whether [the pup] exists or doesn't exist, false – [I mean] having sight or being blind. And the same goes for relatives. Being on the right or on the left are not always either of them true even when there is [someone present]. At times both are false, [for instance] if someone is alone. And when there isn't [anyone present], they are again both false. And being a father or a son likewise. When there is no [person], both are false, and [even] when there is, there are times when
10 both are false. For if someone has neither a father nor a son, whose father or whose son would he be called? (Unless perhaps retrospectively (*kata mnêmên*), since he couldn't truly be called anyone's.) And so in this respect too the things [that are opposed] as negation and affirmation differ greatly from the rest. For if they always, both in the case of things that exist and of things that do not exist, divide the true and the false, and the rest, in the case of things that exist, don't always divide the true and the false, and in the case of things that don't exist,
15 never divide it, then affirmation and negation are not the same thing as the others. And besides, the very fact that these [other types of opposition] at times admit of truth or falsehood has supervened in their case for no other reason than that they have become affirmations, since in themselves they are not receptive of either of these. For 'Socrates is well', or 'is blind', or 'is a father', or anything of that kind, is
20 an affirmation. And so, on account of the affirmation, they have also acquired [the property] of at times entirely (*holôs*) dividing the true and the false.[590]

One should note that here (*epi toutôn*) again the things [that are opposed] as privation and state and the relatives occupy a middle position between the contraries and affirmation and negation. For, whereas affirmation and negation always divide the true and the false in the case of all existing things and non-existing things...[591]

[On Contraries][592]

13b36 The contrary of a good thing is necessarily a bad one; this is clear by induction from the individual cases (*kath' hekaston*).

Having completed his account of the opposites, he now gives us some theorems relating to the contraries. First is the theorem that the opposite of a good thing is in every case a bad thing while the opposite of a bad thing is not in every case a good thing but also sometimes [another] bad one. For instance, to justice, which is a good thing, is opposed injustice, a bad one, and to temperance, licentiousness, but what is opposed to taking more than one's due (*pleonexia*), which is a bad thing, is not in every case justice, but also taking less than one's due (*meionexia*), [the two being opposed] as defect to excess.[593] What? Is nature so unfair[594] as to oppose two things to one? After all we [normally] everywhere observe that one thing has been opposed to one, as, for example, fire to water, light to heavy, and moist to dry. We say, then, that the good thing is opposed to the bad as symmetry to asymmetry, but a bad thing [to a bad] not as symmetry to asymmetry (for both are disproportions) but as defect to excess. For while virtue is seen [to exist] in symmetry, a vice is observed on either side of it, one opposed to it through excess, the other through defect. For instance, whereas justice is seen [to exist] in symmetry, taking more than one's due is an excess and taking less than one's due a defect, each of them being a disproportion, for they are opposed [to justice] as disproportion to symmetry. And again, the defect of temperance is licentiousness, its excess[595] insentience (*êlithiotês*) and those of courage, cowardice and rashness [respectively], and of practical wisdom, low cunning[596] and folly (*anoia*).[597] Each of the deviations, then, is opposed to the virtue as a bad thing to a good and as disproportion to symmetry, but not thus to one another, but as defect to excess. And so one is opposed to one and not two to one.

14a6 Also, with contraries it is not necessary that if one exists the other does too.

This is the second theorem relating to the contraries. He says that if one of the contraries exists there is no necessity that the other should also exist. If, for example, we assume that all human beings are healthy, health will of necessity exist, illness not. And similarly in the case of illness, and whiteness and blackness, and the like. Aristotle says this looking at (*exetazein*) the things that take on the contrariety in their own right and not qua contraries. For white as an entity (*pragma*) can exist even apart from black, but as its contrary cannot be thought of (*theôrein*) on its own, because the contraries are relatives and have their being in relationship to other [things]; for a contrary is contrary to a contrary.[598]

14a10 Also, if Socrates' being well is contrary to Socrates' being ill, and it is not possible for both to hold (*huparkhein*) at the same time of the same person, it would not be possible when one of the contraries existed for the other to exist as well.

One should be aware that this is either said in confirmation[599] of the previous point or, seeing that we said[600] of the contraries that some are simple and others seen in combination with subjects, having shown by what precedes that in the case of the simple ones it is possible when one of the contraries is [present] for the other not to be, he now shows that this is also possible in the case of those that are seen in combination. For if the ill Socrates is contrary to the well Socrates, and it is impossible for contraries to be [present] in the same [subject], there is every necessity that when one of the contraries is [present] the other is not. For when Socrates is well, it is not possible for him to be ill at the same time.[601]

14a15 It is also clear that it is the nature of contraries to occur in [something] the same in either species or genus.

This is the third theorem relating to the contraries. He states that it is the nature of contraries to occur either in one and the same genus[602] or in one and the same species. For instance, whiteness and blackness occur in something one and the same in genus, I mean in stone, or horse, or man, in a word in animate and inanimate body, [all of] which are the same in genus, since their genus is body *tout court*. Health and illness, on the other hand, [occur] in something one and the same in species, for instance, in man, or horse, or, in a word, in any animal, [all of] which are the same in species, for body of animal is a species of body *tout court*. Similarly, it is the nature of justice and injustice to occur in the human soul, and this [sc. the human soul] is a species of soul *tout court*, or of the incorporeal.

Why, after saying 'in [something] the same in either species or genus', didn't he add 'or in number'? After all, 'the same', as we said earlier,[603] is the same in either genus or species or number – as 'difference' (*heterotês*) also is. ([Examples of things the same] in genus are man and horse, in species, Socrates and Plato, in number, a sword [and] a blade[604] and the like.) Our reply to this is that he omitted it either because it went without saying because we can supply it ourselves or because, even though the contraries occur in something numerically the same, they don't in the same part [of it]. Socrates, for example, is white in one part and black in another, and hot in one part and cold in another. For it is not possible for contraries to exist in the same part [of a thing] at the same time.[605]

> **14a19** All contraries must either be in the same genus or in contrary genera or be genera themselves.

This is the fourth theorem relating to the contraries. It is that contraries may either fall[606] under one and the same genus, like white and black (which fall under colour), or under contrary [genera], as do injustice and justice for example (the latter falls under virtue, the former under vice and vice is the contrary of virtue), or be genera themselves, like good and bad, for these do not fall under another genus but are genera on their own (*monôs*). What? Must we then add two further categories, that of the good and that of the bad, to the [existing] ten, so that the categories are no longer ten but twelve? To this we reply that he has not called them genera in the same sense as the other categories (I mean on the basis that they exist in their own right as the categories do), but just as Plato called those five well-known [kinds of his] (I mean being, sameness, otherness, motion, and rest) 'genera of existing things',[607] [namely,] because they are seen in all existing things and not because they exist in their own right, in just the same way has Aristotle said here that good and bad are genera not in their own right but because they are seen in all of the categories; for there is something good and something bad in substance and in quantity and in qualification and in the other categories. In substance good is perfection of its kind (*kath' hautên*), being in possession of the form proper to its nature (*logos tês phuseôs*) in full perfection and not being a monstrosity by exceeding or falling short relative to [that] form; in quantity (*poson*), the quantity (*posotês*)[608] appropriate to each thing; and in qualification, the colour appropriate to each thing;[609] and similarly for the other [categories].

But, if we look closely, good and bad will be seen not to be contraries at all but to be opposed as privation and possession. Each of [a pair] of contraries must be endowed with form and have a defined nature (*phusis*), as white and black do. But the bad does not have a defined nature (*hupostasis*). It is a kind of disproportion, and how could disproportion have a definite form? Hence vice is not even subject to definition, but just as privation is the side effect of (*paraginesthai*) the absence of possession [and] has no definite nature itself, so too is vice the side effect of the absence of virtue, whether due to excess or defect; for since it [*sc.* virtue] is seen [to consist] in symmetry, [it is a] deviation from due measure, whether due to excess or to defect, that has created vice.[610]

One should be aware that although he said that the opposites fall under contrary genera, he wasn't talking about their highest genus but about the proximate and subaltern genus, because all contraries must fall under the same genus. For even though injustice and justice fall [respectively] under vice and virtue, they too nevertheless come under a single common genus, I mean state or condition; and these last come under quality, which is the highest genus of all of the contraries. And it is reasonable that the opposites should fall under a single genus, for nature, aware of their mutual conflict, has been at pains to link them together both from above and from below,[611] from above by way of a common genus, from below by way of a common subject.[612]

On the Prior

14a26 *One thing is said to be prior to another in four ways.*

He mentioned the prior in the section on relatives, where he said that the knowable is prior to knowledge and the perceptible to perception.[613] On account of this, then, he enumerates its various meanings here, and he tells us that these are four in number, the first being the prior in time, the second the prior by nature,[614] the third the prior in order, the fourth the prior in worth. He says that [what is] 'first and most properly' called prior is that which is chronologically (*tôi khronôi*) older and more ancient. We say, for example, that Socrates is prior to Aristotle in time. He says that this is the first and most proper[615] meaning of prior because even everyday usage is accustomed to call the chronologically older above all 'prior'.

One should note that 'more ancient' is customarily also[616] used in the case of inanimate things but 'older' only in the case of animate beings.

14a29 *Second, that which does not reciprocate with respect to implication of existence.*

This, [namely,] 'that which does not reciprocate with respect to implication of existence' (i.e [a thing] in whose case the implication of existence is not reciprocated), is the second meaning of the prior. Those things are said to reciprocate with respect to implication of existence for which it is no more the case that the one follows the other than the other way round; for instance, father and son, right and left – for in their case whichever is assumed the other also follows. This, then, is [what is meant by] reciprocation. And here he says that 'that which does not reciprocate with respect to implication of existence' is prior. For instance, when two is assumed, one necessarily follows, but this implication is not reciprocated in the case of one, for if one is assumed there is no necessity for two to follow. Similarly in the case of animal and human being. When human being exists it follows that animal exists, but when animal is assumed, it does not necessarily follow that human being exists, for animal is prior to human being not in time but in nature.[617]

14a35 Third, prior is used (*legein*) with respect to some order, as with the sciences or with speeches.

The third meaning of the prior is the prior in order, as holds, he says, in the case of the sciences. In demonstrative science the premises come first and the conclusions follow and in the case of geometry the elements (*stoikheion*), he says, are prior to the diagrams. And geometers call the point, the line, the plane, and the like – all of the things habitually assumed in advance of the proof of the theorems – 'elements' and the theorems themselves 'diagrams'. And in the case of writing (*ta grammata*) the syllables are prior to the words (*lexis*) and the letters (*stoikheion*) to the syllables. And we shall say the same thing about speeches. First come the preliminaries (*prooimion*), the introduction to the pleading (*prokatastasis*) follows, then the pleading (*katastasis*), the statement of the case (*diêgêmata*) follows these, [and] then the main argument (*agônes*).[618] All of these only involve priority (*to proteron*) in order and not [priority] in nature or in time. For it is possible for the unskilled orator to deal with the main argument first, the preliminaries next, and the statement of the case after that, and for the[619] geometer to place the theorem first and the elements next; and so these things involve only priority in order.

Now, perhaps one could agree that the prior is spoken of only with respect to order in the other cases [mentioned above], but in the case of writing it is not only in order that letters seem to be prior to syllables or words (*onoma*) or sentences (*logos*). It is not even possible to reverse the order and learn the words first and then the syllables and then the letters, for if the letters aren't known, the others can't be known, and when the letters are eliminated, the others are also eliminated, but when they are eliminated, the letters can remain. And so it is not only in order but in nature too that the letters are prior to the things [formed] from them. Therefore he does not do well to say that the letters are prior only in order in the case of grammar (*grammatikê*).⁶²⁰ Unless perhaps he had an eye to the fact that even the illiterate can string together sentences and words but do not know the value (*dunamis*) of the letters. But clearly, even though through practice they may carry on conversations, they know the meanings of the sounds (*phônê*) [they make] but do not know the actual [phonetic] value of the sound (*phônê*) of the utterance (*logos*), being ignorant of its components.⁶²¹

> **14b3** Also, besides the things mentioned, the better and the more worthy [seem to be prior by nature].

This, the fourth type of the prior, I mean the more worthy, is what everyday usage calls the prior. This is quite remote (*allotrios*) from the [other] senses of the prior, for which reason [Aristotle] himself also rejects it⁶²² and goes on to mention a fifth type in its place so as to round out the four senses of the prior [that he had promised]. Hence too, when enumerating the various meanings of the simultaneous and setting one of the types of the simultaneous against each of the meanings of the prior, [it was] only to the present one [that] he did not oppose [one], completely banishing it from the meanings of the prior.

> **14b10** There would seem to be yet another type of priority besides those mentioned. For of things that reciprocate with regard to implication of existence, the one that is in some sense the cause of existence for the other may reasonably be said to be prior by nature.

He adds this as a fifth [type]. [He does so] because the fourth [type] was, as was stated,⁶²³ remote from the [other] senses of the prior, since it had arisen (*huparkhein*) from a decision on our part and not from the nature of things.

The second [sense] is contrary to the fifth, for whereas that does not reciprocate with regard to implication of existence and the one [thing] is not the cause of the other, this does reciprocate and the one [thing] is the cause of the other, as in the case of the father and the son.⁶²⁴ For these latter also mutually reciprocate with regard to implication of existence (whichever of them is posited, the other in every case follows), yet one of them is also the cause of the other, namely the father of the son. The same applies in the case of a fact (*pragma*) and a true statement about it, for they too reciprocate with regard to implication of existence, [but] the one is the cause of the other – for instance, [the fact that] Socrates is a philosopher and a statement about him asserting that he is a philosopher. Whichever, then, of these is posited, the other of necessity follows:

if the statement asserting he is a philosopher is true, Socrates must be a philosopher, and if Socrates is a philosopher, the statement asserting he is a philosopher is of necessity true. But even though these mutually reciprocate, it is nevertheless the case that the fact is the cause of the statement's being true. If the fact weren't so, the statement about it would not be true.

14b22 And so one thing may be said to be prior to another in five ways.

He has spoken about the prior but has not mentioned the posterior, because from his teaching about the prior that about the posterior was clear, since these are simultaneous and are relatives. Hence if one has been understood the other is also understood, for the prior is said to be prior to a posterior and the posterior said to be posterior to a prior. Thus posterior will be used in the same number of senses as prior. After all, whatever applies to one of [a pair] of relatives also applies to the other.[625]

On the Simultaneous

14b24 The things that are called simultaneous without qualification and most properly are those whose generation occurs at the same time.

He mentioned[626] the simultaneous too[627] in the section on relatives [in the passage] where he said 'relatives seem to be simultaneous by nature' and hence he appropriately gives an account of it now. And since the simultaneous is opposed to the prior, he gives a threefold differentiation (*diaphora*) of the simultaneous.[628] He opposes the first type to the first type of the prior, the second to the second and to the fifth, the third to the third, but opposes no type to the fourth; he[629] did, after all, state earlier that it [*sc*. the fourth type] is the most remote of the meanings of the prior.[630]

He says that the first type of the simultaneous, which he also says is the most proper one, is [the simultaneous] with respect to time, as when two or more people are born at the same time. He with reason says that this is the most proper[631] [sense]. After all, everyday usage applies 'simultaneous' to these things in particular – [i.e] to things that originate at the same time.

This [first sense] is, as we said, opposed to the first meaning of the prior, which was itself also said to be most especially and most properly called prior, I mean of course [the prior] with respect to time, as [seen in the case of] Socrates and Alcibiades, since Socrates is prior to Alcibiades in time. So if the prior in time would most especially and most properly be called prior, and [if] the simultaneous is opposed to the prior, the simultaneous in time would also be called most proper.⁶³²

14b27 And simultaneous by nature are things that reciprocate with respect to implication of existence while neither is in any way the cause of the existence of the other.

This is the second type of the simultaneous. It is opposed to the second and to the fifth senses of the prior. [It is opposed] to the second because there 'that which does not reciprocate with respect to implication of existence' was said⁶³³ to be prior – as [in the case of] one and two, for two doesn't follow from one in the way that one does from two – and here he calls simultaneous that which reciprocates 'with respect to implication of existence' – like double and half, for just as when there is a double it follows that there is a half, so too when there is a half it of necessity follows that there is a double. And it is opposed to the fifth because there that which reciprocates with respect to implication of existence but is the cause of its existence for the other⁶³⁴ was said⁶³⁵ to be prior, as was said to be the case with the father and the son – for even though these reciprocate with respect to implication of existence, since whichever of them is posited the other certainly also follows, it is nevertheless the case that the father is the cause of his existence for the son, and hence was said to be prior, while here things that reciprocate 'with respect to implication of existence while neither is in any way the cause [of the existence] of the other' are said to be simultaneous – I mean of course⁶³⁶ the double and the half, for these reciprocate, since when one is posited, the other is of necessity also introduced, and neither is cause of existence for the other.⁶³⁷

14b33 Co-ordinate (*antidiêirêmena allêlois*) [species] of the same genus are also said to be simultaneous by nature.

This is the third type of the simultaneous, which is opposed to the third meaning of prior, the prior in order, examples of which were letters in syllables, syllables in words and the preliminaries in speeches. Here it is things that have the same order [having derived it] from what is prior [to them] that are simultaneous, as do genera obtained from the same division, e.g. the corporeal and the incorporeals. These last have the same [degree of] separation from both substance and the *infimae species*, I mean [for instance] man and horse, angel and soul. In the same way the animate and the inanimate are called simultaneous, for they have the same [degree of] separation from body *tout court* and from animal. Also, the terrestrial, the aerial (*ptênos*), and the aquatic, and everything of that kind are called simultaneous, for none of them is prior to another, since they have one and the same [degree of] separation from the most generic genus, and likewise from the *infima species*. But if one were to divide the aerial, say, into birds and insects, then bird and aerial are no longer said to be simultaneous. Rather, aerial is prior, because it was obtained from the division of animal and bird from the division of aerial, and genera are always prior to species, since they do not reciprocate in respect of implication of existence; for, given the species, the genus of necessity follows, but given the genera, the species do not of necessity follow.

On Motion (*kinêsis*)[638]

15a13 There are six species of motion: generation, destruction, increase, diminution, qualitative change, change of place.

Discourse on motion is fitting for a natural scientist, for all natural things have their being in motion. In fact, nature as [Aristotle] himself defined it,[639] is the principle of motion and rest. Hence, in the physics course, he discourses on it at length and in great detail.[640] We should ask for what reason he has mentioned it here.

Some[641] have stated that since of the categories those of acting and being-affected were motions but he has not said anything about them, on that account he speaks about motion here. For perhaps, they say, motion is a genus, and acting and being-affected are, along with many others, species of motion.

Such has been the stated opinion of some on this subject. But one cannot accept such an argument. It was not the philosopher's intention to say any more about acting and being-affected than what was said at the start. And besides, as we said[642] at the beginning, moving is included under acting and being moved under being-affected, but motion itself is not, because motion is not acting (*poiein*); indeed, we said[643] that the motions are not categories but paths to the categories.

So what do we say? We shall say that just as he provided instruction on the preceding words because he had mentioned them in his teaching of the categories so too [does he now] in the case of motion. For he mentioned motion in the section on substance. After giving the distinctive feature of substance [as] that, [remaining] numerically one and the same, it is receptive of contraries by turns, and after raising against this the difficulty that this is perhaps not peculiar to substance (for it is not a property of [substance] alone but of statement and opinion as well, since they too, while remaining numerically one and the same, are receptive of contraries by turns, I mean of truth and falsehood), he added in resolution of the difficulty that these last are not receptive of contraries on the same basis as substance, since substance becomes receptive of contraries by itself moving, while they do not take on truth and falsehood by themselves moving but because other things move. It was, then, because he had mentioned motion there, that he considered it necessary to teach us about it.[644]

As I said previously,[645] motion is a suitable subject (*logos*) for a natural scientist, and indeed [Aristotle] himself devoted the last four of the eight books of his physics course to the subject of motion. Here he says as much about it as it befits a logician to ask about – how many species motion is divided into, what its species are, and which follow, or don't follow, from which.[646]

> **15a13**[647] There are six species of motion: generation, destruction, increase, diminution, qualitative change, change of place.

In the section on motion the following three things are investigated: how many species of motion there are and by what they are distinguished from one another, and third, in addition to these, which species of motion is opposed to which.

He himself has already enumerated the species of motion, stating that there are six. But so that we may also know scientifically why the species of motion are six and neither more nor fewer, let us derive (*paragein*) the statement (*logos*) from a division.

We say, then, that there are some three things that are observed in connexion with our nature: [its] substance itself, the things in the substance, the things around (*peri*) the substance. The things in it, to divide [them] into [their] major (*megas*) constituents (*meros*), are quantity and qualification (we said 'into their major constituents' because even though there are other categories in substance they certainly take their origin from these, as we said earlier[648]). Around substance is place. So there being these three things, motion of substance is generation and destruction, that of quality, qualitative change, that of quantity, increase and diminution, and that of place, change of place, which is referred to as locomotion (*phora*). One kind of locomotion, the up and down kind, is called rectilinear motion, another, the kind that goes round, like that of the heaven, is called rotation.[649]

Here, then, he says that these six are the species of motion – not dividing locomotion into rectilinear motion and rotation. In the physics course,[650] on the other hand, he wants change to be a genus and there to be three species of it, motion, generation and destruction; for there he opposes motion to generation and destruction because in that work (*en ekeinois*) he does not want the generation of certain entities that are lasting and endowed with form to be [seen as] a change in one of their associated accidents. Hence he says that things that move move in respect of quantity or qualification or place while retaining their original substantial form; but in the case of generation and destruction the original form does not remain in the thing that changes because generation is a path from what in a sense does not exist to what in a sense does exist (that is, from what exists potentially to what exists actually), and destruction is the path back from being to not being. Here however, because the book is introductory and logical rather than physical, he is not exact with regard to these matters but says that generation and destruction are motions. After all, he is not talking as a natural scientist here but as a logician who is asking what follows, or does not follow, upon what in these matters.[651]

> **15a15** In the case of the other motions it is clear that they are distinct from one another; for generation is not destruction, and nor of course is increase diminution, and nor is change of place, and the same goes for the others too.[652]

Having enumerated the species of motion he next goes on to distinguish them from one another and show how they are not the same. Generation, he says, is not destruction and increase is not diminution. For how could it be so when they are actually contraries? And nor yet is increase generation; it is what exists that grows, what does not exist that comes into being. And diminution is certainly not destruction. For the same goes for them: diminution means a certain reduction in the quantity of being (*on*), destruction the total obliteration of being. And nor again does change of place correspond (*sumbainein*) to any of the above-mentioned [forms of motion]. For a thing that changes from one place to another neither comes to be nor is destroyed, [and] neither grows nor diminishes [in size]. For even if Socrates moves from Athens to, say, Corinth, he will not suffer any of the aforesaid [changes] but, remaining the same in all respects, he undergoes only a change of location.[653]

> **15a18** But in the case of qualitative change there is a question as to whether it is perhaps necessary for the thing that is changing in quality (*alloiousthai*) to change (*alloiousthai*) as regards (*kata*) one of the other motions.

Nobody, he says, has disputed that the other motions are not the same as one another, but in the case of qualitative change one should pose the question

15   as to whether the thing that is changing in quality must change as regards generation or as regards destruction, or increase or diminution, or one of the other [types of motion].⁶⁵⁴ But this, he says, is not true. In the case of most affections (he means heating and cooling and the like) we certainly change yet are not subject to any one of the other motions; for the thing that is heated or
20   cooled does not have to grow or diminish or come into being or be destroyed or be subject to any of the other [motions]. Thus qualitative change is distinct from the other motions.⁶⁵⁵

> **15a25** [So qualitative change would be distinct from the other motions.] For if it were the same, the thing changing in quality would at once also have to grow, or diminish – or one of the other [forms of motion] would have to follow.

If, he says, qualitative change were the same thing as one of the other motions,
25   the thing that is changing would certainly also have to be subject to one of the other motions. But as it is this doesn't happen. Bodies change after spending time in the sun, becoming heated and tanned (*melainein*), but they do not on that account grow or diminish or undergo any of the other motions. And the same can be said of things that are changed by cold or in any other way.

201,1   **15a28** Equally, a thing that is growing, or undergoing some other motion, [would have to] be experiencing qualitative change.

[Here] he constructs the argument the other way round. For, he says, if qualitative change were indeed the same thing as the other motions, not only would the
5   thing changing in quality also have to at once move with (*kata*) one of the other motions, but conversely too, if something should move through (*kata*) increase or diminution or one of the other [motions], that thing must at once change in quality as well, [and that] whether qualitative change normally (*ta malista*) pre-exists the other motions or accompanies them. After all, a thing that is growing must certainly also become somewhat different in its qualities (*alloioteros*); for in things that are growing nourishment must first be changed
10   into blood and that into flesh, and growth (*auxêsis*)⁶⁵⁶ would not occur unless qualitative change preceded it. Indeed qualitative change precedes even the things that come into existence; for the sperm would be changed into blood and that into flesh, and [be further changed] however else the laws of nature may indicate (*agein*). And in the case of all the other motions one can observe qualitative change following or even preceding [them]. <For example>⁶⁵⁷
15   qualitative change follows [in the case of] things that undergo local motion, especially if they move to a greater degree and more rapidly, the things in motion

being, say, heated. So if, as I said, qualitative change accompanies the other motions, we do not on that account say that qualitative change is the same thing as the other changes, since local motion also accompanies all the rest. For something that comes to be certainly also undergoes local motion, and likewise something that is perishing, and also something that is growing or dwindling. Local [motion] must precede each of these, and if this is absent it is not possible for any of the other [forms of motion] to occur. At a general level (*koinôs*), [it is] as the sun approaches or moves away [that] generation and destruction in general (*katholou*) occur, but in the particular case (*idiâi*) the seed must clearly also fall to the earth, or into the womb, or the male come together with the female. And this is local motion. And in the case of destruction the elements that have come together evidently have to be separated from one another. And in the case of increase or diminution change of place is evident, for something that grows must occupy a larger space after [having occupied] a smaller one and something that dwindles, a smaller after a larger. And a thing that changes qualitatively also [undergoes local motion]. For a quality passes from the interior (*bathos*) to the surface, as in the case of people who blush or turn pale, and it is obvious[658] that the agent of qualitative change must approach the thing that changes. But even though local motion accompanies every [other kind of] motion, it is nevertheless evident that it is different from them, since a shadow also invariably accompanies a body in the light, yet the shadow is not on that account *ipso facto* (*êdê*) the same thing as the body in the light. In the same way, then, I say in the case of qualitative change too that, even if it accompanies all the other [kinds of motion], it is not on that account also the same thing as them, because (*hopote*) qualitative change does not even accompany every motion. After all, things that grow through an addition [of something] do [indeed] grow (for they get bigger after being smaller, as though water were being added to a receptacle), but they do not become any different qualitatively (*alloioteros*). In explaining this, [Aristotle] himself instances the square and[659] says that when a gnomon is placed around it, it grows but has not become any different qualitatively, for even after growing it remains a square.

But given that, wanting to show the difference of qualitative change from the other [types of] motion, Aristotle has made mention of the square and the gnomon, let us clarify what is said.

Geometers, then, call a gnomon one of the squares about the diameter when it is accompanied by both the complements at once. So as to make what we are saying clear, let us rehearse the argument using (*epi*) the appended (*auto touto*) diagram.

A square figure, then, means one that is bounded by four sides that are equal to one another and four right angles.

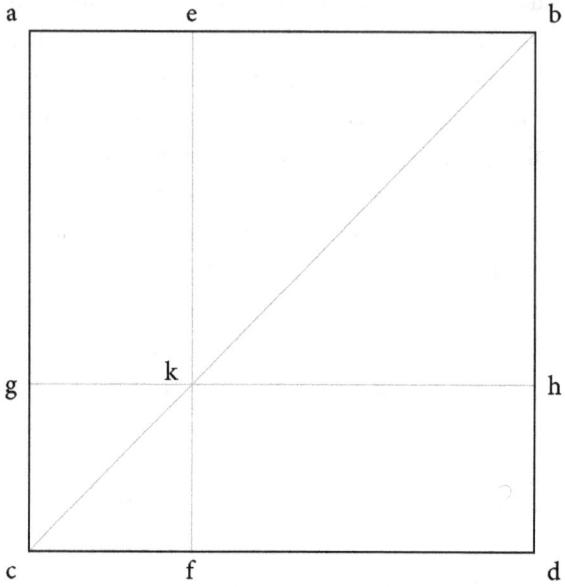

So let ABCD be a square figure whose four angles and four sides are equal and let its diameter BC be drawn. Let any point E be taken on the side AB, and from the same point E let a line EF, parallel to either of the lines AC [and] BD, be drawn, and from the line AC let AG, equal to EB, be subtracted, and from the point G let GH be drawn parallel to either AB or CD. There are, then, [now] four areas within the square ABCD, of which the two around the diameter, EBHK and KGCF, are squares, and the other two called complements. Either one of [these] two squares, say for instance GCFK,[660] along with the two complements AEKG and KHDF, is called a gnomon. The construction makes it clear that the square EBKH[661] is similar to the square ABCD.

Now observe that by placing the gnomon around the square EBHK I have made the whole larger (for the square ABCD has come into existence), but I have not changed its nature; for although it has been increased in size, the small square has nevertheless remained a square. And on the other hand if from the entire square ABCD you subtract the gnomon AEGHCD, the square EBKH is left, and the original whole has been decreased in size and has become smaller, but its nature has not been changed and the same square shape (*eidos*) has remained.

But if neither diminution nor increase, which are quantitative motion, has changed (*kinein*) the character of the square as far as shape goes, it is clear that qualitative motion is one thing and the motion of diminution and increase another. And if these are different, those of generation and destruction are much more so.⁶⁶²

15b1 Rest is the contrary of motion in general, but particular motions [are the contraries] of particular motions – destruction of generation, diminution of increase, rest in a place of change of place. (But especially opposed [to a change of place] would seem to be a change to the contrary place, upward movement to downward or downward to upward, for example.)

Now, lastly, [he reaches] the third of the questions we said⁶⁶³ he asks in the section on motion, I mean, which species of motion is opposed to which. Rest, he says, is opposed to all motion in general. For if motion is a kind of change of position (*metabasis*) and a path either from existing things (*onta*) to not existing or vice versa, or from the potential to the actual, or from place to place, or from lesser to greater and vice versa, or from being of such and such a quality (*toiosde*) to being of another (from being white to being black, for instance), and if rest is a kind of standing still, then rest is suitably opposed to all motion. More specifically, he says, the motions that are contradistinguished from one another are opposed – generation to destruction, and to diminution increase. To local motion rest is, on the one hand, most especially opposed, and reasonably so, since this type of motion above all is better known than the rest and the many apply the name 'motion' especially to it. On the other hand, it is possible, more specifically, to set this motion against itself by dividing it according to the different dimensions of space so that upward motion is opposed to downward, forwards motion to backwards, and motion to the right to motion to the left.

15b6 It is not easy to state exactly what is contrary to the other change that was listed.

In the differentiation of the motions too this one, I mean qualitative change, was again the one about which there was some question.⁶⁶⁴ So to this too should be opposed, he says, both stability (*êremia*) of qualification, as was also the case with local [motion],⁶⁶⁵ and change to the contrary qualification, for example, change from whiteness to blackness.⁶⁶⁶

On Having

15b17 Having is spoken of in several ways.

'Having' is an ambiguous (*homônumos*) word. It indicates (*dêloun*) not only one of the ten categories but a number of other things as well. We are, for example, said to have knowledge, or virtue, or each of the other things enumerated [by Aristotle]. But properly speaking, the category 'having' indicates the arrangement (*perithesis*) of one substance around another, as when we are said to be wearing (*perikeisthai*)⁶⁶⁷ a garment, or a ring, or shoes. Having a wife, or a field, or the like is something different. Accordingly, so that we won't be deceived by this ambiguity, he has outlined (*diarthroun*) for us here the number of senses in which 'having' is used. And perhaps [also], because earlier, after talking about substance and quantity and the relative and quality and acting and being-affected, he omitted the account of the other categories as being clear,⁶⁶⁸ but has [now] defined the category of 'having', stating that it is the arrangement of one substance around another, but 'having' is also used in other ways, on that account he now returns to discussion of it and says in how many ways we are said to 'have' a thing. Having is used (*legesthai*), he says, either in relation to quality (we are said to have⁶⁶⁹ a state, or a condition, or knowledge), or in relation to quantity, as if a piece of wood should be said to have [a length of], say, three cubits. These [so far] are things that are in body. We are also said to have [things] around the body, as a garment, or a place, or a length of time. And we are also said to have a part, a hand or a foot, for instance, and [a thing] as a possession, a house, say. And having is used as [when something is] in a container, as the wine jar is said to have wine [in it] – and in as many other ways as 'having' can be used.

It seems, he says, that to talk of having a wife is the oddest (*allotrios*) of the senses of having, because to have a wife is nothing other than to live in wedlock with a wife; he says 'very odd' because a man is no more said to have a wife than a woman is to have a husband.⁶⁷⁰ But to this one can say that in the case of possessions too we are not only said to have a field or a slave, but the field and the slave and the garment are also said to have an owner (*despotês*), and [moreover] in the case of the parts and the whole, not only is the whole said to have parts, but the parts are also said to have wholeness.

15b30 Perhaps yet other ways of having will come to light, but we have listed pretty much all of the commonly occurring ones.

Once again⁶⁷¹ not wanting us to rest content with his words, he says that there are perhaps yet other ways of having, but 'we have listed all the commonly occurring ones'.

Notes

1 At 49,8–22. (See Riin Sirkel, Martin Tweedale, and John Harris, *Philoponus, On Aristotle Categories 1–5*; with Daniel King, *Philoponus, A Treatise Concerning the Whole and the Parts*, London: Bloomsbury, 2015 in this series for a translation of the earlier part of Philoponus' commentary.)
2 3b28.
3 I would like to follow Ackrill in using 'chapter' for the major divisions of the *Categories*, but at 84,4 the *logos* on quantity is said to come second, which would leave everything before the section on substance homeless, so I have fallen back on 'section'.
4 In the present work, at 65,10 ff. (where Sirkel, Tweedale and Harris have a useful note).
5 cf. *GC* 329a34–5.
6 See the note at 133,5 for this translation of *poion*.
7 Literally 'plundered from them'.
8 cf. 56,24–6; 65,34.
9 cf. Ammonius 54,4–15. Ammonius has the second (4–12) and parts of the third (12–15) of Philoponus' three arguments – the third argument is in three parts, of which Ammonius has the first and, if rather obscurely, the third. Philoponus is at times verbally close to Ammonius and Philoponus 19–20 and Ammonius 10–12 are word for word the same.
10 At 5a33–6 it becomes apparent that Aristotle has spoken language in mind.
11 cf. Ammonius 54,16–18. (Ammonius goes on to deal briefly with quantities composed of parts with position in relation to one another and those not so composed, which Philoponus only discusses at 88,17 ff.)
12 Actually, only the first three. Nothing in Ammonius corresponds to the geometry lesson that follows (84,10–86,10) and nothing in his introductory section to the discussions (86,11–87,20) of the sense in which place and time can be said to have continuity that follows it. (He does use the wine jar illustration to explain the relation between body and place under a later lemma at 58,16–26.) On the other hand, at this point Ammonius tells us that some people argue that the species of quantity can be reduced to three – number, volume, and power – and Philoponus nowhere refers to this.
13 *Phys.* 204b3–206a8.
14 The Greek lacks a verb and perhaps *ên* has dropped out before the first *ê* at 84,16.

15 More literally, 'what was said'.
16 As Busse suggests, a case could be made for omitting the words between the dashes.
17 The phrase is a little difficult. Another possibility might be something like 'is conceived of in terms of both length and breadth'.
18 Euclid, *Elements* I, def. 2.
19 Euclid, *Elements* I, def. 1.
20 He presumably has, as Busse suggests, *Phys.* 241a2-6 in mind, although it isn't clear that what he says here is compatible with what Aristotle says there and elsewhere.
21 'Into breadth' and 'into depth' would be more literal than 'into the second dimension' and 'into the third'.
22 *Phys.* 214b30 ff., although the argument is not quite the same.
23 *sc.* flat. Actually the relevant arguments in the *Physics* (at 4.7-8) are based on the density of the medium and the weight of the moving object and shape (though not any specific shape) is mentioned almost as an afterthought at *Phys.* 216a19-20 in the words: 'For [a moving thing] divides [the medium] either by its shape, or by the impetus which the thing carried along or projected possesses'. Interestingly, however, Philoponus himself develops an argument from shape at *in Phys.* 646,23-647,8; 651,16 (where he sees an indirect reference to shape in the words 'if other aspects are the same' at *Phys.* 215a28) and 660,20-26 and actually uses the similar word *petalôdês*, which, like *petaloeidês* itself, does not occur in Aristotle or elsewhere in the commentators, at 660,22.
24 At 33,22-3. The definition of place that follows is basically Aristotle's at *Phys.* 212a5 ff. As Verrycken points out (Koenraad Verrycken, 'The Development of Philoponus' Thought and its Chronology', in Richard Sorabi (ed.), *Aristotle Transformed: The Ancient Commentators and Their Influence*, London: Duckworth, 1990, 246-7), Philoponus appears to accept it in his exposition of *Phys.* 3 and *Phys.* 4,1-4 but rejects it in the *Corollarium de loco* (*in Phys.* 557,8-585,4) and in his subsequent commentary on *Phys.* 4.4, 212a7 ff. Philoponus quotes it again at 165,1-2 and it also appears at *in Meteor.* 35,15-16; 134,3-4 and *in DA* 100,8-9 and at Ammonius *in Cat.* 58,17-18.
25 *sc.* like motion and time as was argued above.
26 There appears to be a pun on *atopos* (literally something like 'placeless') and *topos* ('place').
27 The translation assumes that one is to imagine that the container is split, down the middle, say, and that the wine remains in position with nothing surrounding the area where the container has been removed. Alternatively, one could translate: 'If you [notionally] separate the wine jar [from the wine] and hypothesize nothing outside the wine, neither air nor any other body, you will find that the portion of the wine at (*kata*) the [point of] separation appears not to be in a place ...'. This is perhaps a more plausible thing for Philoponus to have said, but the Greek favours the

rendering in the text. With the whole passage, cf. Ammonius 58,16-26 under the lemma 5a8.
28 Although the core meaning of *kinêsis* is 'motion', we would more normally call many of the 'motions' Philoponus goes on to mention here changes and *kinêsis* is often translated 'change' in contexts like this. However Philoponus can also describe these same 'motions' as *metabolai*, as he does in line 30, and I've opted to reserve 'change' for *metabolê* and use 'motion' for *kinêsis* – as do Sirkel, Tweedale and Harris in the passage Philoponus is referring back to in line 30.
29 For this and similar phrases, see the note at 166,6.
30 These first answers are close to Ammonius 55,10-13, some of the phrasing being identical. Ammonius doesn't have the alternative explanation.
31 48,14 ff.
32 Busse's suggestion of *kai* ('and') for *ê* ('or') at 87,31 is tempting, but there is a certain equivocation as to whether changes can be 'placed under' a category in the earlier passage and *ê* may well be correct here.
33 48,17-21.
34 Presumably he has in mind the long discussion of differentiae at 65,8, although the terminology 'substantial quality' and 'substantial quantity' is not used there. In fact the only places either designation has been used so far are 73,6 and 15 and 74,7 where 'substantial quality' is used. (Philoponus' fullest discussion of the terms is at *in Phys.* 38,25 ff.)
35 *ousiôdês* can also be translated 'essential' but 'substantial' seems to work better here and I've kept to that throughout.
36 cf. Ammonius 58,7-11 (under a later lemma and making the point differently).
37 84,9.
38 e.g. speak the first syllable of a two-syllable word but not the second.
39 As pointed out earlier (note at 84,9), Ammonius introduces this second division of quantity along with the first at 54,16-55,3. The nearest equivalent in Ammonius to what now follows at 88,19-28 is the material under the three short lemmas at 56,1-10.
40 *mora* in the Greek text is clearly a misprint for *moria*.
41 Since speech is obviously audible, he is presumably equating perceptibility with visibility.
42 Much of the remainder of this introductory material (*sc.* 88,28-89,17) is taken, largely verbatim, from under three short lemmas (5a25, 5a28, and 5a30), at Ammonius 59,11-60,8: (a) 88,28-30 ('the whole ... perishing') and 89,1-2 ('So how ... position?') from Ammonius 59,11-13; (b) 89,2-7 ('Or, rather ... first') from Ammonius 59,15-19; and (c) 89,10-17 ('And since ... no event') from Ammonius 59,21-60,8.
43 In reality *ou panu*, as often, amounts to 'certainly not' in the *Categories* passage.

44 These first few lines are close to Ammonius 57,3–5.
45 cf. Ammonius 57,8–9.
46 cf. Ammonius 57,11–17 (Ammonius, unlike Philoponus, explicitly rejects other ways in which language might be thought to qualify as a discrete quantity).
47 cf. Ammonius 57,22–4. Ammonius prefaces his remarks with an argument that *logos*, which I have been translating 'language', must be equivalent to *lexis* (presumably 'word'), since items in categories must be incomposite. However, unlike Philoponus, he doesn't go on to discuss the status of 'internal' language. (The Ammonian parallels adduced for material under the present lemma (4b25) are spread over three different lemmas.)
48 8b26–7.
49 cf. Ammonius 57,25–58,2. There are verbal echoes, but Philoponus considerably expands on Ammonius' briefer comments.
50 cf. Ammonius 58,5–7.
51 Euclid, *Elements* I, def. 2; cf. 85,2.
52 *sc.* just as the line is made up of extensionless points and thus of extensionless parts, so too is the surface made up of extensionless lines and thus of extensionless parts.
53 Literally, 'saying one instead of the other'.
54 Literally 'cut off'.
55 cf. Ammonius 58,4–5.
56 More literally 'with respect to depth', as in the next line.
57 cf. 90,15–16.
58 86,8, where the phrase is 'by moving into the second dimension'.
59 When we cut an apple, say, in half, we first penetrate its skin and then move the knife through the apple. The initial penetration of the skin is 'starting from a line', moving the knife though the apple is 'drawing it down' to create a surface, and the two halves of the divided apple can be said to be divided, or cut, by the surface.
60 There is nothing corresponding to any of this in Ammonius.
61 Ammonius (58,12–26) has two lemmas rather than one and deals briefly with time (which Philoponus has nothing to say about here) under the first and with body and soul under the second, using the case of wine in a container, which Philoponus used at 87,7–20, to illustrate the relationship between place and body.
62 cf. Ammonius 58,28–59,5, where neither the statement of Aristotle's procedure nor the three characteristics of things with parts that have position are the same.
63 89,10–16.
64 At this point (59,6 ff.) Ammonius has five lemmas with no equivalent in Philoponus, the material under three of which (5a23, 5a25, 5a28) has already been used by Philoponus (see the note at 88,28) under the long first lemma of the section on quantity.
65 *polus* can be translated 'many' when used of number, 'much' or 'great' when used of size or quantity, 'large' or 'wide' when used of space, and 'long' when used of time, and

its opposite *oligos* requires a similar range of translations. Rather confusingly most of these different renderings will be required at one time or another in what follows over the next ten or so pages and I shall translate as seems best on each occasion, signalling each change of rendering by adding the Greek in brackets. Philoponus, of course, would not have been conscious of any significant shift in the meaning of these words from one context to another. For him in each case they would simply have indicated a greater or lesser quantity.

66 Perhaps 'by participation of it' would be more literal.
67 cf. the first clause of the lemma.
68 Apart from 92,13–16, which are not represented in Ammonius, the material spread between this and the next two lemmas is for the most part verbally identical to the material under the single lemma 5b1 at Ammonius 60,14–61,5.
69 3a7–4b19.
70 This first sentence is almost word for word the same as Ammonius 61,7–9. However, the remaining material under the lemma is not paralleled in Ammonius.
71 At 63,14–17 – with reference to substance. He goes on to explain that a distinctive feature can substitute for a definition because it 'belongs to all and only that of which it is the distinctive feature, and they are convertible with one another' (63,20 in the translation of Sirkel, Tweedale, and Harris, whose note 151 on distinctive features is also useful).
72 6,3–11.
73 cf. 63,21 ff.
74 3b30–31. These first two sentences are for the most part word for word the same as Ammonius 62,2–4. However the continuation is different in Ammonius, who goes on to distinguish between definite quantities (which are quantities in the strict sense) and indefinite quanties and to state that large and small and many and few are of the latter kind.
75 As at 81,14 ff.
76 Philoponus explains objection and counter-objection for us as follows at 81,10–13: 'The counter-objection is to concede the difficulty but to show that even if things are this way, this does not invalidate what was said. The objection is not to accept the difficulty at all but to refute it [by showing] that things are not as stated.' (tr. Sirkel, Tweedale and Harris). cf. too 96,23–5.
77 'Rather' (*mallon*) is not present in Aristotle and the construction is changed at the end of the sentence.
78 Here the habitual sexism that Philoponus shares with most, if not all, Greek philosophers in cases like this has resulted in an obviously false statement!
79 Omitting *ti* at 94,16 as suggested by Busse.
80 With lines 20–25 cf. Ammonius 62,20–24.

81 With this paragraph cf. Ammonius 62,14–26. Ammonius, who divides his material between two lemmas (5b16 and 5b18), covers much the same ground as Philoponus, but is much briefer and not verbally close to him.
82 cf. Ammonius 63,2–9 (makes the same point but is not verbally close).
83 Ammonius, commenting on an earlier passage (at 62,4–13), accepted the existence of indefinite quantities, although he also says both there and at 63,3–9 that it is only definite quantities that are quantities in the strict sense. He has nothing corresponding to the present discussion.
84 Comparison with 96,7 ff. suggests that this means that there is no genus or species of 'three cubits'.
85 *sc.* in the case of 'animal' a few lines earlier.
86 The Greek rather oddly has 'which is individual'. In the other examples of less generic items only one example is given, so perhaps there was originally only one here.
87 Punctuating with a full stop after *ontos* at 95,24.
88 Emending *hoti* to *eti* at 96,16 (cf. the lemma).
89 Lines 7–11 above.
90 Ammonius 63,11–13, under the lemma 5b30, is similar in content, though not in wording.
91 For this warfare, compare 74,22–4.
92 96,30–32.
93 The material under this lemma is a transcription of Ammonius 63,15–25 with some expansion and some minor alterations.
94 The corresponding material in Ammonius is divided between three short lemmas (5b33, 6a1, and 6a4). With 16–23, cf. Ammonius 63,27–64,4 (shorter, but some verbal similarity); with 23–26, Ammonius 64,6–9 (verbally close); with 26–29, Ammonius 64,11–14 (some verbal similarity).
95 These first few lines are almost word for word the same as Ammonius 64,16–18. Ammonius then continues, 'But since, then, they are among the relatives, they must be in a different category, so as to take on the relation <appropriate to> relatives. And where would they be, if they are not included in the <category> of quantity and are not contraries?' (tr. Cohen and Matthews), the first part of which at least is pretty much the conclusion that Philoponus comes to at 99,3–15.
96 I've balked at 'long' and 'short' here for *polus* and *oligos* (for which see the note at 92,9) in view of the last part of the sentence. Although it will not have been Philoponus' intention, as I have translated one could think in terms of many or few hours, days, etc.
97 *gumnazein ton logon* is a favourite expression of Philoponus, both in the present work and elsewhere. Literally it should mean something like 'exercise the argument', but I have, depending on the context, used 'conducting', 'deploying', or 'rehearsing'.

98 Of course, long and short would be more normal and Philoponus in fact switches to long (*makron*) in line 19. However, the argument certainly requires *mikros* and *megas* and *makron* should perhaps be emended to *megan*.
99 The public speeches were speeches on public issues delivered in court, while the speeches against Philip, of which Dionysius of Halicarnassus identifies twelve (*ad Ammaeum* 10) were delivered before the Assembly.
100 Indeed, the phrase *pollên hodon* is commonly to be translated 'a long way'.
101 A unit of length equal to about 185 metres.
102 5a38-b2 (with minor deviations).
103 For the switches from 'many' to 'large' and from 'large' back to 'many' in this paragraph see the note at 92,9 above.
104 47,12 ff.
105 Or perhaps better, although the word order is against it, 'except for someone who accepts that the many and few is in quantity derivatively'.
106 More literally, 'are not in the nature of the things there are'.
107 Lines 19–25 ('he says ... a centre') are at times verbally very close to Ammonius 64,23–65,3, but the rest of the material under this lemma is not paralleled in Ammonius.
108 For *periphereia* in this sense see Lampe s.v. 2. (Actually, the phrase isn't easy and the translation is rather interpretative. The editor of the first printed edition, perhaps because he also found it difficult, printed *têi koilêi periphereiâi selêniakês sphairas* – something like 'the concave surface of the lunar sphere'.) In Aristotle's cosmology the natural place of fire is the uppermost layer of the sublunar region immediately below the heavens, which are the natural place of a fifth element, aether. Although Philoponus appears to accept this arrangement here, he rejects the existence of a fifth element in later works (e.g. in *Aet.* arg. 13) and argues that the heavens are predominantly fire.
109 Reading this in conjunction with lines 19–20 and 24–5, it looks as though Philoponus is actually talking about a radius, or half of the axis of the cosmos.
110 99,23–5.
111 Again, more literally 'in the nature of the things there are'.
112 3b24 ff.
113 With 3–5 cf. Ammonius 65,10–12, some of which is word for word the same (the continuation in Ammonius is paralleled under the next lemma).
114 77,25 ff., but there he is quite clear that being receptive of contraries is peculiar to substance.
115 At 94,5 ff.
116 75,16–17 (and cf. 110,10 ff.; 158,16 ff.; 167,2–3).
117 cf. Ammonius 65,12–17, some of which is word for word the same.

118 With this first phrase cf. Ammonius 65,22 and with 102,3-6 ('if ever . . . but qua bodies') Ammonius 65,23-6 (both almost word for word the same). Ammonius goes on to ask how it is that Aristotle previously placed body under substance but now puts it under quantity and provides an answer (65,26-66,3). Philoponus, on the other hand, is content to accept that body is a quantity (102,6).

119 This list of preliminary topics is reminiscent of the similar lists in the introductions to commentaries on the *Categories* and *Isagoge*, a number of the topics being identical or similar to topics in one or both of those lists. There is a very similar list at the start of the section on qualities in the present commentary and Ammonius has similar lists at the same points and Olympiodorus and David (Elias) also have them for other categories. Here Ammonius (66,5-8) has the same five topics as Philoponus but reverses the order of the last two.

120 Ammonius (66,7-10) gives a different reason for the claims of quality to come before the relatives.

121 The order of the clauses in the Greek doesn't work well in English and I have brought the words 'he does here as well' forward from later in the sentence.

122 5b14 ff.

123 With 22-29 cf. Ammonius 66,10-14 (at times with the same wording).

124 This paragraph is very close to Ammonius 66,14-21, but he has nothing that corresponds to the next.

125 Changing *ta peri tôn pros ti* at 103,6 to *ta pros ti* and *peri tou pros ti* at 103,7 to *to pros ti*. We need names for items in the category and for the category itself here rather than possible titles for the section and the difficult *ta* (which the first printed edition understandably omitted) points to what is probably the correct reading.

126 102,31-2.

127 This paragraph is close to Ammonius 66,21-6 but with the addition of (a) the suggestion that relatives are a mental construct, (b) the examples of father and son and slave and master, and (c) the examples of god and us and soul and body. Ammonius' examples of relatives and the whole thrust of his argument seem to suggest that by *thesei* he means 'by position' and Cohen and Matthews translate accordingly. However, as a reader reminds me, the *phusei* / *thesei* contrast is one that occurs in discussions of the origin of the names of things (see especially the commentaries on the *Cratylus* and the *de Interpretatione*) where *thesis* is the term for the giving of names to things by human beings and is to be rendered by something like 'imposition' or 'application', and the nature of Philoponus' additions to Ammonius' argument suggest that he understood it in some such sense here. To put it briefly, (1) if relativity is something we read into a situation rather than something that is present in the nature of things, it makes good sense to describe it as conceptual, while if the contention is that it depends on (variable) position, it is hard to see why it should follow that it is merely conceptual; and (2) while the

slave-master and father-son relationships could possibly be described as positional in some attenuated non-spatial sense, it is hard to see how it is relevant that the father is *also* a son and the slave can *at the same time* be a master if position is the point, whereas it might well be seen as bolstering the case for the view that relations are purely a matter of perspective. It seems, then, highly likely that Philoponus is construing the *phusei / thesei* contrast as being between natural occurrence and human attribution and so I have rendered *thesei* 'by imposition' rather than 'by position'. It also seems possible that, despite appearances to the contrary, Ammonius also construed the contrast that way, or at least that the people he is criticizing did.

128 It isn't clear who these people are. As a reader points out, Plotinus outlines a similar position in 6.1.6, although it isn't his own.

129 These last two examples are presumably meant to counter the earlier father – son and slave – master examples. (Notice that the master – slave relationship is construed as that of ruler and ruled at 105,6.)

130 Greek colour words are notoriously difficult to render. The word translated 'dark' can often be rendered 'black'; the one translated 'purple' literally means something like 'wrought in, or by the sea' and was normally used of cloth dyed purple with a dye obtained from various Mediterranean whelks; 'like gold' (*khrusoeidês*) presumably refers to the iridescent sheen of the necks of some pigeons in certain lights.

131 Actually the fourth as we number the books.

132 *Metaph.* 1007b18 ff.; 1009a6 ff.

133 *Theaetetus* 170C ff. (Although presented as such, not actually a direct quotation.) Ammonius also introduces Protagoras at this point, but much more briefly: he has, for instance, the example of the taste of honey, but not the others, and he gives Plato's refutation but not Aristotle's. Also, there are relatively few verbal echoes.

134 *sc.* besides those who say (103,18 ff.) that relatives do not exist in nature and those who say (18,31 ff.) that all things are relative.

135 These first sentences are for the most part word for word the same as Ammonius 67,7–10, but he does not have what follows, which, apart from the last sentence with its log parallel, is essentially a repetition of 47,12–20.

136 *sc.* relatives in other categories.

137 As a *TLG* search shows, the parallel is common enough, going back to Aristotle himself at *EN* 1096a21. (Philoponus has already used it himself at 47,16 and will do so again at 108,10.) However, only Asclepius (*in Metaph.* 76,1–2) goes on to invoke logs. (Both Philoponus and Asclepius were pupils of Ammonius and may have got the reference to the log parallel from his lectures. Alternatively, one of them may have taken it from the other, more probably, perhaps, Asclepius from Philoponus, since he mistakenly assumes that it, like the sucker parallel, goes back to Aristotle.)

138 The parallel to suckers is meant to illuminate the relationship of relatives to the other categories whereas this is presumably meant to illuminate that between a relative and its correlative.
139 *aithêton* at 105,7 is a typographical error for *aisthêton*.
140 All of this is close to Ammonius 67,16–25, much of it word for word the same.
141 *idion horismon autôn* could perhaps, especially in view of the relative clause, mean 'a definition proper to them', but later passages (and *eautou* in Ammonius), seem to fix its meaning here.
142 The phrasing is a little awkward and Ammonius (who is closely followed here) has a rather different text.
143 Again, all of this is very close to Ammonius 67,11–16. Most other commentators on the *Categories* (see Porphyry 111,27-9, Olympiodorus 112,19–20, David (Elias) 205,20–21; 215,21–2) attribute the first definition to Plato. According to Simplicius (159,12–15; cf. 163,7–8) this attribution went back to Boethus, perhaps the earliest commentator on the *Categories*, but Simplicius thinks it is wrong (159,15–22) – although he later (162,36) seems to waver. Philoponus, at 109,26–8, again following Ammonius (70,10–14), says this is to misrepresent Plato. Modern scholars of course assume that both definitions are Aristotle's. There is however disagreement as to the relationship between them. Does the second definition supersede the first or just supplement it in some way? For a recent treatment of the issue with discussions of earlier treatments see Matthew Duncombe, 'Aristotle's Two Accounts of Relatives in Categories 7', *Phronesis* 60, 2015, 436–61.
144 Actually, the statement of a relation between two entities.
145 I mostly translate *apodidonai* 'give' (as Ackrill does) and the cognate noun *apodosis* 'giving' in what follows. This often makes for rather awkward English, but none of the alternatives I could come up with worked better across all the relevant contexts and most were further from the base meanings of *apodidonai* and *apodosis*.
146 In the Greek the noun in the phrase 'by the striker' is in the genitive case. The topic of the cases in which relatives can reciprocate comes up again at 106,8–12 and 106,15–24, both of which are close to passages in Ammonius, but Ammonius has nothing corresponding to this paragraph at this point.
147 cf. Ammonius 67,28–30. (The words before the comma are verbatim transcription.) For criticism of this definition, 108,31–109,26; 114,13–14; 115,18–23; 124,17 ff.; for Aristotle's definition, 129,24–130,31.
148 Identical to Ammonius 68,2–3.
149 Close to Ammonius 68,5–7.
150 *sc.* things that are larger, double, etc. at 6a36 ff.
151 The word translated 'possessed' is a verbal adjective and with verbal adjectives the agent is normally expressed by a dative.

152 Although compound forms such as *endiathetos*, *adiathetos*, and *dusdiathetos* are reasonably common, *diathetos* only seems to appear in this and similar contexts in the commentaries on the *Categories*. Neither LSJ nor Lampe list it.

153 All close to Ammonius 68,9–19, which is split between two lemmas.

154 With this first paragraph, compare Ammonius 68,21–5 under the lemma 6b11 (the last sentence is almost word for word the same as Ammonius 68,23–5), with the second Ammonius 69,2–21 under the lemma 6b12. At first sight it is hard to see how the last sentence of the present paragraph relates to what precedes it, but it seems to be the justification of the statement that 'a position is the position of someone in [the] position'.

155 *keisthai* ('being-positioned') is the name of another category.

156 In the parallel passage Ammonius doesn't attempt an analysis of the difference between 'standing' and 'to be standing' and the like (or between 'time' and 'what is in time' and 'place' and 'what is in place') but merely says that things that are named paronymously can be subsumed under a different category from the things from which they are so named.

157 Aristotle has 'are named' (*legetai*).

158 More literally 'in the same column', i.e. in the same vertical hierarchy. (For two examples of such 'columns' see Philoponus *in An. Pr.* 189,11–13.)

159 Perhaps one should correct to 'relatives' (and to 'them' later in the sentence), as the editor of the first printed edition did.

160 For the manner of their reciprocation, cf. 105,19 ff. and 24 ff. above.

161 cf. 47,12 ff. and 104,28 ff.

162 This is awkwardly expressed. It is presumably individual relatives that are like suckers and the category that doesn't 'have separate things'. Ammonius (69,25) has simply 'and are (*estin*) not set things', which is easier.

163 Here Philoponus seems to leave nothing to belong to the category of relatives. However earlier, at 47,13 ff., he seems to suggest that, whereas the related items belong to other categories, the relationships themselves are located in the category of relatives.

164 Line 12 ff. above.

165 This presumably amounts to 'is related to *a thing in* a category that does not admit of contrariety'.

166 LSJ only gives 'imperceptibly' and 'secretly' for *lelêthotôs*, but something that contrasts with *dogmatizôn* ('stating doctrine') is required here.

167 6a36–7. Philoponus attributes the same behaviour to Aristotle in much the same words at 114,13 ff. There is nothing similar in Ammonius and such accusations would seem to be at variance with Philoponus' suggestion at 115,18–23 (and cf. 105,16) that Aristotle makes as strong a case as possible for the first definition so as to be seen to be giving it a fair hearing.

168 *sc.* items in other categories.
169 Adding *en* before *tôi* at 109,26.
170 476B.
171 Ammonius has simply 'that he characterizes them as *being*'.
172 The alternative statement would presumably be something like 'if there is something that acts, there must also be something that is said to be acted on', although something like 'if there is something that acts, there must also be something on which it is said to act' would be clearer.

Of the material under this lemma, 108,10–30 ('and this is reasonable . . . of all of them') is very close to Ammonius 69,24–70,8 and 109,26–31 ('One should be aware . . . is said [to be]') to Ammonius 70,10–14 (which is under its own lemma, 6b16). The rest of the material is not paralleled in Ammonius.
173 75,16–17.
174 110,7–15 ('And this concomitant . . . in all of them either') are close to Ammonius 70,17–22. The rest of the material under this lemma is not paralleled in Ammonius.
175 108,13–15.
176 *sc.* in which contrariety occurs.
177 Perhaps one should correct *dekhetai* to *epidekhetai* with the first printed edition.
178 'So if equal and unequal are relatives existing in quantity and nothing is contrary to a quantity, [then] the equal and the unequal are not contraries either' would be more natural.
179 The explanation that follows makes use of the circumstance that *antistrophê*, *strophê*, and *isostrophê* and the related verbs *antistrephein* and *strephesthai* all share the same root. Unfortunately, I've been unable to find English renderings of these words that are both similarly related and render them satisfactorily in the context.
180 More literally 'returning from the same and to the same [point]'.
181 I have borrowed the coinage 'equiversion' from Cohen and Matthews to translate *isostrophê*, which itself looks like a coinage of Ammonius', only occurring in related passages in Philoponus and David (Elias) outside of Ammonius himself.
182 Actually the word means something like 'opposed to the hand' (i.e. the other four digits).
183 cf. Ammonius 70,24–71 8 (very close at times, less so towards the end, where Ammonius is defective).
184 105,19–29, comparison with which should explain aspects of the translation of the present passage.
185 No equivalent in Ammonius.
186 Punctuating with a full stop after *pros ti* at 112,9 (cf. the parallel passage at Ammonius 71,15). Comparison with Ammonius also supports adding *de* after *hê*, but that is not strictly necessary.
187 *sc.* they respectively reciprocate with 'son of a father' and 'half of a double'.

188 *sc.* with feathered rather than membranous or sheath-like wings.
189 Presumably this means 'the ones we are talking about'.
190 *HA* 490a12, although Aristotle doesn't use the term 'split-winged' there.
191 This clause actually appears after the next but I've brought it forward to help the sense. (The equivalent clauses in Ammonius are in fact in the order I've adopted.) Philoponus should really say something like 'by substituting winged creature for bird'; the Greek as it stands suggests that the denotation would remain the same.
192 7a5.
193 7a12-13.
194 7a14-15.
195 112,5-113,2 ('Relatives should preserve … by [virtue of] a rudder') is often close to Ammonius 71,11-72,8 (chief divergences at 112,10-12 and 18-22 and towards the end). Also, cf. 113,9-11 with Ammonius 72,8-10 and 113,2-9 with Ammonius 72,13-19 under the next lemma.
196 Sometimes 'word' or 'noun' works better for *onoma*, but 'name' is usually best and I shall stick to it throughout the present discussion.
197 'He says to this' is mildly anacoluthic.
198 Changing *autous* to *auta* at 113,20; as the text stands, an object for *epinoein* needs to be understood from the first part of the sentence, which is awkward.
199 The Greek actually mentions them in the order 'equilateral', 'isosceles', 'scalene'.
200 More literally 'notes' or 'melodies'.
201 113,19-20.
202 Philoponus' commentary on this lemma is quite different from that of Ammonius (at 72,12-23).
203 This first sentence is identical to Ammonius 72,25-6, but Ammonius has nothing else under the present lemma and has no parallel to the criticism of Aristotle that follows here.
204 See 108,33 and the note there.
205 cf. lines 15 and 25.
206 Aristotle has the singular.
207 115,9-16 is fairly close to Ammonius 73,2-9 (under the lemma 7a22), though not verbally.
208 112,18.
209 *Propria* would work better here.
210 cf. 105,12-18.
211 Aristotle has 'it will *always* (*aei*) be spoken of'.
212 Since Philoponus is stating the rule that Aristotle is supposedly formulating, he actually uses the imperative 'know' (*isthi*) here.
213 Or, taking *to proteron* adverbially, something like, 'that [the predicate] was properly given earlier'. Either way, *to proteron* is a little awkward.

214 7a35-7.
215 *sc.* to the relationship between the master and the slave; 'the relationship *with* the slave' would be more natural.
216 104,28 ff.
217 The six lines (73,11-16) that Ammonius has under this lemma are fairly close, though not verbally, to 115,29-116,11 ('He says that . . . the master of a slave'). Ammonius 73,18-21 (under the lemma 7a32) is almost identical to 116,18-21 ('and there is nothing surprising . . . primarily and per se').
218 The words 'but for some not true' are not in Aristotle.
219 Lines 4-11 are at times verbally close to Ammonius 73,23-74,4, of which they are essentially a somewhat expanded version.
220 Literally 'Median'.
221 As Cohen and Matthews, commenting on the parallel passage in Ammonius, point out, LSJ don't list this sense for *suneispherein*, but cf. Lampe, s.v. 3.
222 If 'animal' is eliminated, 'human being' goes with it, but not vice versa, and the existence of 'human being' entails that of 'animal', but not vice versa.
223 For *ephistanai* in this sense, see Lampe s.v. 4.
224 *sunodos* can mean 'conjunction', but that doesn't seem to be what is needed here.
225 There is some doubt about the text, but the sense is clear enough.
226 cf. Ammonius 74,12-25. Philoponus 117,20-118,7 is very close to Ammonius 74,12-23 and 118,26-9 to 74,23-5, but Ammonius doesn't have the example of Thales and lunar eclipses (118,7-25).
227 To this point Philoponus is close to Ammonius 74,27-75,1. Ammonius goes on to give a single brief example, the invention of new written characters.
228 118,4 ff.
229 Reading *mêpote* for *ê mê tote* at 119,19 with the first printed edition and punctuating with a full stop after *sunakolouthêsei*.
230 All close to Ammonius 75,6-9.
231 For lines 12-17, cf. Euclid, *Elements* 1, def. 10-12 and the scholia on Euclid, 1.1.488-491 (Philoponus is verbally close to the scholia). 'Facing in the same direction' in line 12 translates *epi ta auta merê*, which also occurs in the scholia. In the definitions Euclid has *hexês*, which Heath translates 'adjacent'.
232 The core meaning of the Greek word is 'sharp' – and that of the word translated 'obtuse', 'blunt'.
233 Or perhaps 'suitable for cutting, like a knife'.
234 A paraphrase of the lemma rather than a direct quotation.
235 *all' ê* normally means 'except', but we seem to need 'than' here and LSJ *alla*, I.3 perhaps suggests that this could be the sense here.
236 120,24-121,5 follows Ammonius 75,11-19 closely, and sometimes verbally, but what precedes and what follows have no equivalent in Ammonius.

237 At this point Philoponus should be saying something like '... in the case of one example of a knowable and knowledge of it, he now shows this universally for all examples [of them]', but as the Greek stands he seems, although the wider context shows that this cannot really be his intention, to be saying that Aristotle now goes on to say that no pairs of relatives at all are simultaneous. There would seem to be a strong case for emendation, but since the same problem is present in the verbally similar, though not identical, parallel passage in Ammonius, we don't seem to be dealing with a simple scribal error and I have translated the passage as it stands.

238 cf. Ammonius 75,21–5, to which this is close in content and wording until the last clause.

239 Ammonius has only four lines under this lemma (75,27–76,3), of which the first two are close to 121,20–22.

240 cf. 15,5.

241 Of course, Aristotle doesn't actually say this and I am inclined to delete *legô* in line 18, giving. 'What, then, does he say?' (for which cf. Philoponus, *in An. Pr.* 201,14). If the text is correct, presumably Philoponus writes as he does to make it clear that what follows is a paraphrase of Aristotle rather than his own comment.

242 Punctuating with a question mark after *legô* and a full stop rather than a comma after *phêsin* in line 18 and a full stop rather than a question mark after *stoikheiôn* in line 20 (cf. 35,13; 47,22, etc.).

243 *epistêtos* ('knowable') being formed paronymously from *epistêmê* ('knowledge').

244 *grammatikos* could be translated 'grammatical' or 'a grammarian' and *tekhnê grammatikê* simply 'grammar' and I opt for such renderings in some contexts, at 157,4, for example, but the *grammatistês* was responsible for all aspects of elementary education and, on balance, the chosen translations seem to work better here.

245 cf. lines 9–10.

246 The three lines that Ammonius has under this lemma are not close to anything here, but 122,24–123,30 is often very close to Ammonius 76,10–30 under the lemma 8a11.

247 Not in so many words, but by implication in passages such as 49,5 ff., which Busse adduces.

248 The otherwise similar parallel text in Ammonius lacks *entautha* and Cohen and Matthews translate 'Now a division like this is traditional'. However, if *entautha* is sound, it suggests that Philoponus believes that the division that follows is implicit in Aristotle's text and I have translated accordingly.

249 'Once more' (*palin*) and 'as has often been stated' in the next line both look back to 28,20, and probably also to Philoponus' lost commentary on Porphyry's *Isagoge* (cf. Ammonius *in Isag.* 95,19; David *in Isag.* 186,5; Elias *in Isag.* 13,15).

250 Or 'subordinate'. A diagram similar to that following 28,23 is implied, the pairs linked by the vertical sides of the rectangle being 'subaltern' and those linked by the diagonal lines 'diagonal'.
251 Having introduced the first of the four possible pairings with 'either', Philoponus unexpectedly introduces the remaining three with 'again', 'and', and 'again'.
252 Taking up Busse's suggestion (made in the apparatus) that *merikon* ('particular') in line 14 and *meros* ('part') in line 15 should be transposed. (Philoponus has just (lines 5–8) said that the universal head or hand, which are universal *parts*, is predicated of every particular head or hand and (lines 11–13) that the head and hand of Socrates, which are *particular* parts, belong, qua particular, to him alone.)
253 124,17–22 is based on Ammonius 77,4–8 and 124,27–125,18 on Ammonius 77,8–14, but with a considerable amount of rewriting and expansion, especially in the case of the latter.
254 I translate *ousia*, the reading of all of the manuscripts, rather than *suzugia*, which is Busse's emendation, at 125,19. *suzugia* would give 'the first pairing' rather than 'primary substance', and also imply 'the second [pairing]' in line 23. The problem with this is that what is now the first combination was the third in the previous paragraph and what is now the second was the first. It seems to me that what has happened is that, after reporting that Aristotle says that three of the pairings that he (sc. Philoponus) has just identified are clearly not relatives, Philoponus goes on to specify two of the three using Aristotle's own terminology of primary and secondary substance in the passage he is paraphrasing rather than that he has been using himself. I suspect that Busse was encouraged to emend by line 27, where the reference can hardly be to anything but a pairing (Philoponus' second in fact), but it is understandable that Philoponus should go back to talk of 'pairings' given that Aristotle does not employ a specific term in this case in the *Categories* passage. All of this is, I think, quite comprehensible, if rather awkwardly handled.
255 'It' (*autê*) is actually a feminine pronoun referring back to 'hand' whereas we might have expected a neuter pronoun referring back to 'part'.
256 These first two paragraphs are based on Ammonius 77,4–19. There is however a considerable amount of rewriting and expansion.
257 *Cat.* 6a36-7.
258 Literally, 'with the hand of me'.
259 Homer, *Odyssey* 4,149.
260 Homer, *Iliad* 20,59.
261 Callimachus, *Hymns* 5,135 (with a different word for 'head').
262 As I have translated, the construction is anacoluthic. One possibility is that something has dropped out at the end of the previous clause. Another is to delete *de* in line 32 and translate: 'For if those things were said to be relatives that are said to be just what they are *of* other things, not only the universal part, as for instance the

hand *tout court* is said to be *of* the man *tout court*, but the individual hand too is said to be *of* the individual man; for we say that "this hand ... does not nod assent". And so, if the particular part too is the part *of* someone, then it too will be a relative.'
263 i.e. *Categories* 8a18–21.
264 *sc.* without adding 'individual' to the second 'hand'.
265 *proekkeimenou* could in fact mean something like 'included above' and a diagram similar to the one at 28,23 above have dropped out at, say, 125,15.
266 124,22.
267 This sentence and the paragraph that precedes it have no equivalent in Ammonius, who, in contrast, accepts Aristotle's position without demur.
268 'Impulse' works better than 'force' here because it is the rock's inbuilt propensity to move to its proper place, the sphere of earth, when unimpeded that causes it to roll down a slope.
269 *sc.* to public baths or a shrine.
270 Adding *mallon*, perhaps after *oikodomos* at 126,32 (cf. *mallon hugiazei* in line 33). Without some such addition, the sentence would translate 'The carpenter, or the builder, for instance, for the most part achieves his goal or fails to', which is not the required sense.
271 At 126,28–9.
272 *sc.* of those they deserve.
273 With 126,18–129,6 compare Ammonius 78,18–79,2, under the lemma 8a35, where Ammonius (followed by Philoponus at 131,5–6) uses essentially the same argument (though much more briefly expressed) for the immortality of the soul to illustrate the drawing of a corollary.
274 See 6a36–7.
275 Lines 10–13 are very close to Ammonius 77,21–6, but Ammonius has nothing corresponding to what follows and leaves the impression that he thinks that (or believes that Aristotle thinks that) the first definition of relatives may be defensible.
276 Oddly put, but the point must be that not everything that falls under the first definition necessarily also falls under the second.
277 *Iliad* 2.259–60.
278 This first paragraph is close in content, but not verbally, to Ammonius 77,28–78,16. Nothing in Ammonius corresponds to the next paragraph.
279 126,24 ff.
280 131,3–11 is close, occasionally identical, to Ammonius 78,18–79,2. Ammonius devotes nine lines to the proof of the immortality of the soul and its corollary, but unlike Philoponus (see 126,18–129,6 and the note at 129,6) he has not already used it to illustrate *reductio ad absurdum*.
281 We can see that we are dealing with a head or a hand but we cannot actually *see* that it is a part if we cannot see the body to which it is attached. Ammonius (at

79,17-23) is one of those who says that it is possible to know the hand definitely but not know whose it is, but he goes on to conclude that this means that a hand is not a relative. (There is nothing in Ammonius corresponding to the paragraph that follows.)

282 8a32.
283 117,15 ff. (for 'potential' and 'actual' see 123,11 ff.).
284 Busse punctuates with a full stop rather than a comma before this 'and' (i.e. after *eidenai* in line 17) but the clause seems to be part of the proviso.
285 8a35-6 and 131,7 ff.
286 With the first sentence compare Ammonius 79,10-11 under the lemma 8b10, with the second, Ammonius 79,5-8 under the lemma 8b7 and 79,13-14 under the lemma 8b13, and with the rest, Ammonius 79,16-23 under the lemma 8b15.
287 cf. Ammonius 79,25-80,13. Philoponus takes the first short sentence from Ammonius but thereafter isn't verbally close and is much briefer. (Ammonius, unlike Philoponus, suggests (80,9-13) that Aristotle himself believes that his first definition of relatives is defensible and further claims that it has often been defended by others; cf. Ammonius' comment at 77,22-3 and see the note at 129,20 above.)
288 In his discussion of this title at 133,21 ff. Philoponus first distinguishes *poion* and *poiotês* as respectively the qualified entity and the actual quality and then goes on to say that *poion* can also function as an umbrella term covering both *poion* and *poiotês* in those senses. It is presumably in this latter sense that Philoponus frequently uses *poion* as an alternative to *poiotês* to refer to the category 'quality'. Obviously 'the qualified' or the like isn't a satisfactory rendering of *poion* in such cases and a common expedient is to translate *poion* as well as *poiotês* 'quality'. This is not unreasonable, but one would like to be able to distinguish between the two terms in the translation. I considered adding the Greek after the English when 'quality' translated *poion*, but I have opted, when the umbrella term seems to be in question, for using 'qualification' for *poion*, which can, if rarely now, be a synonym of 'quality' and which Ackrill uses in some contexts in his translation of the *Categories*.
289 Although Aristotle uses masculine forms here, it is not only people that are 'qualified' in what follows and Ackrill actually translates 'things'.
290 *sc.* as we did in the case of the other categories.
291 In the corresponding passage (80,15-19) Ammonius has the rather different list: (1) position, (2) definition, (3) title, and (4) divisions. Both commentators have dropped 'mode of instruction', which was one of five topics discussed in the introductory remarks to the section on the relatives, although Ammonius may refer to it obliquely at 80,15-16. In Ammonius the discussion of the four topics takes up under four *CAG* pages, in Philoponus almost seven.

292 102,17 ff. (and cf. 83,17–19), but he doesn't mention the elimination argument there.
293 102,19–20.
294 102,26–9.
295 Ammonius (80,19–20) merely says that the position of the present section should be clear from what was said in the section on relatives.
296 Presumably this is equivalent to 'what is covered by the name of quality [*sc.* the category name] is twofold'. But it's hard to know what to make of the whole sentence. Perhaps Philoponus really wants to say something like 'Since, then, quality is twofold [this would be a new thought], either as it is just by itself and perceived by mind alone, like the genus of quality itself, or as grasped by sense-perception, on this account he has also made the title twofold.' Perhaps, on the other hand, all he wants to say is some version of 'Since, then, the things, and therefore their names, are twofold, he has made the title twofold.'
297 Or perhaps: 'Alternatively, it is possible to say'.
298 (1) Busse prints *koinoteron* <*ôn*>, which I have, with some misgivings, translated. One would expect an adverb paralleling *koinôs* later in the sentence, another *koinôs* say, and in fact *koinoteron* is a comparative adverb in virtually all the numerous passages in which it occurs elsewhere in Philoponus. The problem is that it isn't easy to make good sense of *koinoteron* as an adverb here. 'Fairly commonly' wouldn't provide the necessary parallelism with *koinôs* and something like 'more or less in common' would be stretching things too much. (2) I have left *poion* untranslated at various points in the sentence because to translate it by either 'qualified' or 'qualification' would obscure the point of the sentence. (3) If *poion* can cover both quality and the qualified (although 133,28–31 perhaps suggests that *poiotês* can too!) it is arguably a better name for the category than *poiotês* ('quality') and, as we have seen, Philoponus does in fact often use it. (4) At 140,20–21 and 143,3–9 Philoponus argues for a similar relationship between *hexis* ('state') and *diathesis* ('condition'), *diathesis* being the umbrella term, and again cites the case of *onoma* and *rhêma* as a parallel.
299 The central meaning of *onoma* is name, but once the Greeks began to discuss language it came to be used in contexts where the translations 'word' or 'noun' suggest themselves (for examples, see the passages at LSJ, *onoma*, VI). In the present sentence one could translate the first *onoma* 'word', the second 'noun', but that would obscure the point here.
300 cf. Ammonius 80,20–81,3. Ammonius' explanation of the title is actually contained within his discussion of the definition which ends with the words, 'It is also for this reason that he has placed the qualified first in the title, since that is what the quality is seen in' and some of the ideas in Philoponus' discussion of the title are present in Ammonius' discussion of the definition, notably the ideas that Aristotle proceeds

from the better known to the less known (Ammonius 80,24–81,1) and that the qualified thing partakes of the quality (Ammonius 81,1–2).

301 These introductory sentences are close to Ammonius 81,4–7 – the list of the four species almost word for word the same.

302 The division that follows is, with a few modifications that will be noted, essentially that of Ammonius. There is however a difference of presentation. Ammonius had begun by explaining each of Aristotle's four species of quality (81,7–31) then said that Aristotle's division can be criticized as incomplete (81,32–82,2) and gone on to complete it (82,2–84,5). Philoponus silently accepts Ammonius' elaborations (with some modifications of his own) and launches straight into a division of quality, adding (138,1 ff.), unlike Ammonius, a diagram to illustrate it.

303 Ammonius (82,2–3) groups capacity and incapacity under fitness (*epitêdeiotês*) and opposes that to actuality.

304 With 134,16–22 ('And should a quality ... virtue') compare Ammonius 82,5–11. Philoponus is close to Ammonius in content but has avoided verbatim transcription.

305 *sc.* they are not the kind of thing that can be perceived by any of the senses.

306 Ammonius makes this point about the concomitants of health and disease, at greater length, at 82,11–18.

307 For Aristotle sickness and health are in fact conditions rather than states (8b35–7).

308 The contention is that the fact that *euektein*, *hektikê*, and *kakhektein*, words used to describe states of health or sickness, are etymologically related to *hexis* ('state') goes to show that health and sickness are 'states'. Ammonius has nothing corresponding to these remarks about common usage.

309 'In good condition' would be the normal rendering, but we need 'state' here.

310 Something like 'intensified', 'heightened' would be more literal.

311 *euektein* and *kakhektein* describe contrary states.

312 The sentence is meant to illustrate the use of 'state' and 'condition' and bring out the difference between them, but unfortunately neither 'state' nor 'condition' (Philoponus actually uses the verb *diakeisthai*, the normal verb for 'being in a condition' rather than the noun *diathesis*) works well in the English. In the former case 'possesses the state of rhetoric' is scarcely acceptable and I have fallen back on 'possesses the skill', for which see LSJ, *hexis*, II.3; in the latter, I have not found a satisfactory alternative to 'condition', which is in any case perhaps not quite as awkward as 'state', and have retained it.

313 Or perhaps 'the rhetorical treatises' or 'the rhetorical methods'.

314 Presumably this means that he has not received the standard rhetorical training but has acquired some knowledge and skill outside the schools. In any case we are not, I think, to assume that he is anything like fully qualified.

315 He might, for example, be described as an amateur or as untrained. With this last paragraph, compare Ammonius 81,5–10. (Ammonius uses geometry rather than rhetoric in his examples.)
316 With this compare 140,20–21, 143,3–9, and Ammonius 84,6–11. Compare too the similar manoeuvre at 134,2 ff.
317 The normal meaning of *psuxis* is 'cooling' but in a number of passages in the present work (78,9; 79,23; 135,18; 148,2; 172,19) it needs to be rendered 'cold'. (It does have its normal sense at 200,17.)
318 Again (cf. the note at 134,29), there is nothing in Ammonius like this note on common usage.
319 I have borrowed 'an affection of our senses' from Cohen and Matthews. Something like 'an affection in the region of our sense-perception' would be more literal.
320 Ammonius doesn't offer an explanation of the terms 'perfective' and 'harmful'. (He does, however, invoke the distinction between substantial and accidental qualities at 83,21–3.)
321 Ammonius does so divide it (at 82,18–26) and the long explanation that follows is in effect a justification of Philoponus' departure from his teaching.
322 Treating the bracketed phrase as parenthetic and punctuating accordingly.
323 For *paralambanein* in this sense see Lampe s.v. 7.
324 More literally something like 'much-divided'.
325 *sc.* treating the two kinds of quality separately would lead to unnecessary and confusing repetition.
326 Or perhaps 'since we have more strictly speaking named it from …'.
327 This paragraph corresponds to Ammonius 82,28–83,2. The first few lines here (136,23–9) are close to Ammonius (although Philoponus doesn't give the steps of the division in quite the same order), but, unlike Philoponus, Ammonius doesn't tell us that affective qualities that arise from an affection also produce an affection of the senses or, more importantly, further divide qualities that are deep-seated and easy to lose.
328 On the status of the third, cf. 136,9–11.
329 Rather than anything corresponding to this paragraph Ammonius has a discussion of qualitative change and change in general taken from Aristotle's *Physics* at this point.
330 Perhaps the idea is that 'shape' does not extend to the soul and so can be present in even the lowest life forms. The corresponding passage in Ammonius is 83,24–30. The Ammonius passage is a little difficult to follow and I suspect that Philoponus' note here is an attempt to make sense of it. Ammonius goes on to discuss the status of colour rather than statues.
331 An *andrias* is strictly speaking a statue of a man and by extension a statue in general.

332 It is rather odd that he should choose examples of propensity involving inanimate things.
333 'Them' (*autas*) refers back to 'the affective qualities and the affections' and one would expect the neuter form *auta* rather than the feminine *autas*, as we in fact have in the pronominal adjective *ta toiauta* ('such [things]') at the end of the sentence, which has the same reference.
334 There is nothing like this paragraph in Ammonius.
335 cf. Ammonius 81,16-23.
336 133,31-134,1.
337 Taken, in large part word for word, from Ammonius 80,23-81,2, where it forms part of Ammonius' discussion of the definition of quality, one of the introductory topics to the present section.
338 As the text stands, one would expect something like 'meant' (and 'is meant' in the next line), but Busse's apparatus suggests that what Philoponus actually wrote is not entirely clear. Unfortunately there is no parallel text in Ammonius, but the comments of Simplicius and David (Elias) on the passage show that the correct interpretation of *pleonakhôs* ('in many ways') was an issue as early as Alexander of Aphrodisias.
339 Referring to the species as first and second (and later third and fourth) might suggest that we are dealing with a mere enumeration rather than a division. (cf. 55,1-2.)
340 It is Philoponus' view that quality is a summum genus that can be divided into precisely four species (or, alternatively, subaltern genera that can be further divided) and at 134,8 ff. he has provided a division that supposedly proves this. In this paragraph he combats two possible objections to this scheme of things and at 143,13 ff. (cf. too 147,9 and 151,13-14) and 156,5 ff. two others. (The last three sentences here are very close to Ammonius 84,13-16 under the lemma 9a14.)
341 With the last clause compare 135,9-14, 143,3-9, and Ammonius 84,8-10, where the same statement is made but in a different context and under a different lemma (9a10).
342 'Infallible' would do for *aptaistos* (more literally, 'not stumbling') here, but doesn't work well when it is used of the subject matter of a field of knowledge a few lines later.
343 Euclid, *Elements* I, defs. 1 and 2; for the former, cf. 34,32; 85,6.32, for the latter 85,2; 90,19.
344 First, or primary, philosophy is one of Aristotle's terms for the kind of philosophy he practices in what came to be called his *Metaphysics*, the 'first philosopher' one of its practitioners.
345 *Republic* 533C3-5 (close paraphrase rather than direct quotation).
346 *sc.* both what should be done and why it should be done.

347 Although the general sense is clear, this sentence (as I have punctuated) is clumsily expressed and there may even be something wrong with the text.
348 This is the standard Neoplatonic 'scale of virtues', which originated with Plotinus and was augmented and formalized by Porphyry and Iamblichus. (A further stage, the paradigmatic virtues, was normally added, but perhaps that is included in the contemplative virtues here.) There is a good brief account of this scale in Dominic J. O'Meara, *Platonopolis: Platonic Political Philosophy in Late Antiquity*, Oxford: Clarendon Press, 2003, 40-9.
349 141,23-4.
350 There is nothing in Ammonius resembling the material under this lemma or under the three that follow.
351 The Greek actually has the neuter plural of the relative pronoun ('those which'), but we are clearly talking about qualities.
352 I have been translating *hexis* 'state' (and will again), but that doesn't work here and I have fallen back on 'skill'.
353 cf. 135,4-9 and the note at 135,9.
354 cf. 135,9-12 and Ammonius 84,7-11, the first few lines of which are at times word for word the same.
355 *puktikos ê dromikos* would more often be rendered 'skilled in boxing or running', but the adjectival suffix *-ikos* can equally well express actual or potential fitness and Philoponus understands it in the second way here.
356 With lines 143,13-17, compare Ammonius 84,16-20; with lines 143,21-8, Ammonius 84,21-8; with 144,5-10, Ammonius 85,9-13 (under the lemma 9a21). (None of the three pairs of passages is verbally close.)
357 With 144,17-18 cf. Ammonius 85,2-3; with 144,17-22, Ammonius 85,6-9 and with the rest of the material under this lemma, Ammonius 85,9-27, which likewise discusses capacity and incapacity but much more briefly and for the most part along different lines.
358 22b36 ff.
359 It would arguably be better to use 'wish' for *boulêsis* and 'wish' / 'wish for' for *boulesthai* throughout, but 'will' and 'to will' are traditionally used in the case of the deity in English and I have opted for that here.
360 The antecedent of *auton* ('he') is the neuter noun *to theion* ('the divinity') and although the neuter accusative singular of *autos* can be *auton*, we would expect *auto* in Philoponus and Busse asks whether we should perhaps read *auto* rather than *auton* both here and later in line 18. In fact this question needs to be considered in conjunction with another. Busse's text is based on two manuscripts, C and F, and the first printed edition, a. In line 19, following C, Busse prints *ei gar dunamenos tis poiein touto mê bouletai poiein*, which gives either 'for if someone, being able to do this, does not wish to do [it]' or 'for if someone, being able to do [something], does

not wish to do this'. On both interpretations the sentence is rather awkward. On the former, it is difficult to see what the reference of 'this' could be, on the latter, we would expect *touto* to have an expressed antecedent such as *ti*. Further, the appearance of *tis* ('somebody') at this stage of the argument is most surprising. We would surely expect 'the divinity' to continue to be the subject at this point in the sentence, and in fact it is far from obvious that 'anyone at all' (which is presumably what *tis* amounts to) would in no case do something that he can do but does not want to do, whereas this makes good sense of god. It seems to me that that these awkwardnesses are avoided if we adopt the text of F, which has *ti* rather than *tis*, and render the clause as I have in the translation. Doing so does involve an apparent difficulty of its own: because the subject is still *to theion*, we would expect *dunamenon* rather than *dunamenos*. We could of course rectify this by emendation, but the occurrence of *auton* in lines 15 and 18 in conjunction with *dunamenos* here suggests another solution, namely that after writing *to theion* Philoponus inadvertently continues as though he had written *ho theos*, which he in fact switches to in line 21. All things considered, then, I would retain *auton*, which I would read as the masculine form, in lines 15 and 18, and accept the text of F (which I translate) in line 19. (It is perhaps worth mentioning that Busse himself (Praefatio, p. v) was of the opinion that F is a more reliable witness than C.) Finally, a prints *ti* rather than *tis*, but, presumably influenced by the masculine form, spoils things by adding *ho* before *dunamenos*.

361 Busse cites *EN* 1142a31 ff., where Aristotle says that people don't deliberate about what they know already, but in fact there is nothing verbally close in Aristotle. There are, however, parallels, some very close, in the commentators, including Philoponus himself, at Ammonius *in Int.* 134,12–13; Philoponus *in Phys.* 268,15–16; 321,2 and 18; Olympiodorus *in Alc. I*, sect. 146,22; Aspasius *in EN* 30,4 ff. (on *EN* 1098a20 ff.); Eustratius *in EN* 282,11–13; 286,6 ff. (on *EN* 1139a31 ff. and 1139a36 ff. respectively). Perhaps the original source was a commentary on *EN*.

362 Correcting *hê*, which is presumably a misprint, to *ê* at 145,29.

363 At *in Phys.* 268,15–16 he says that deliberation 'takes place on account of' a deficiency of wisdom, which makes rather better sense. (cf. too 146,2 above.)

364 145,8–10.

365 One manuscript has the tempting variant *antiphaseôn* ('opposing alternatives') here, but 'affirmation' and 'negation' in the diagram that follows tells against it.

366 *sc.* this species of quality that is based on capacity.

367 Busse's text is difficult and, with no great conviction, I have accepted his suggestion that *to* at 146,18 belongs after *touto*.

368 As at 143,13 ff. In what follows Philoponus adopts the overall structure, and at times (see especially 147,9–12 and Ammonius 86,2–5) echoes the language of the material under the same lemma in Ammonius (86,2–25), although, as often, he

frequently expands on Ammonius' comments. Philoponus discussed affective qualities and affections at some length from a rather different perspective in the introduction to the current section at 135,20–137,12 and there is some overlap between the two treatments.

369 Although it is not immediately clear in what follows in this and the next paragraph, the four types of affective quality envisioned are, as the diagram after 148,7 makes clear: (1) those present throughout an entire species and constitutive of that of which they are predicated, (2) those present throughout an entire species but not constitutive of that of which they are predicated, (3) those not present throughout an entire species but long-lasting, and (4) those not present throughout an entire species and not long-lasting. (Philoponus actually further subdivides (4) but says that one of the resulting kinds doesn't belong under quality.) Although Ammonius (86,2–11) also distinguishes four species of quality, Philoponus' division is rather different and he probably saw it as an improvement, or perhaps a correction, of Ammonius'.

370 Porphyry uses the blackness of the raven as an example of an inseparable accident at *Isag.* 12, and as a result ravens are rife in the commentators. Closest to the present passage in Philoponus himself are 64,29 ff. above and *in An. Post.* 63,8 ff.

371 The blackness of the raven and the whiteness of a swan are accidents, which can be used in a description (see Philoponus *in Cat.* 19,30–31 and the note ad loc.), but not in a definition, rather than differentiae, so I have translated *diaphora* 'difference' where it refers to them.

372 Ammonius has nothing like this here, but cf. Ammonius *in Isag.* 100,32 ff., where people are similarly said to use accidents (the blackness of the raven is again an example) or substantial properties in place of differentiae in division or definition when 'out of human weakness' they cannot discover the true differentiae. (At *in Cat.* 46,12–14 Ammonius actually classifies the raven's blackness as a kind of differentia.)

373 This division has some elements in common with the more complex one at 138,1.

374 cf. Ammonius 86,11–12. Unlike Philoponus, Ammonius doesn't go on to elaborate on this kind of affective quality.

375 For this sense of the phrase, cf. Lampe *sunarpagê* 4.

376 Much in the last two paragraphs in particular is very close, at times even verbally, to Ammonius 86,13–25.

377 There is a problem with the text at this point. As the text stands, *autas* must refer to the feminine form 'affective qualities' whereas the reference should be to the noun 'colours', as it is in Aristotle (at 9b,9–11), which is neuter here. One could either emend to *tauta*, the form of the pronoun required for a reference to 'colours' or, better, to *touto*, as in the otherwise identical sentence in Ammonius (at 87,3–4), where the reference is to neither affective qualities nor colours but to what it is that

Aristotle now establishes – in fact the missing 'this' in the lemma! (*autas* perhaps comes from Aristotle (9b11), where the word for colours is feminine rather than neuter as here.)

378 'Symptoms' is not an appropriate translation for *sumptômata* in Aristotle (Ackrill has 'circumstances'), but Philoponus' comment shows that that is how he reads it.

379 Ammonius merely says 'He has said that colours are symptoms because they supervene on other affections' under this lemma.

380 Almost word for word the same as Ammonius 87,8–9.

381 Almost word for word the same as Ammonius 87,11–12.

382 *ekstasis* is distraction of mind of whatever kind, but Aristotle actually writes *manikê ekstasis*, which shows that 'insanity' or the like is the appropriate translation.

383 Almost word for word the same as Ammonius 87,14–16.

384 Almost word for word the same as Ammonius 87,18–20. The six short lemmas and the material under them at 150,1–151,10, which are closely based on Ammonius, reappear, largely verbatim, at David (Elias) *in Cat.* 231,30–232,18, where I suspect they may be an interpolation. (It is clear that they are taken from Philoponus rather than from Ammonius in David (Elias) because several short sentences that occur in Philoponus but not in Ammonius are reproduced there.)

385 cf. 143,13 ff.; 147,9.

386 137,20 ff.

387 Up to this point Philoponus is close to Ammonius 87,22–88,4 (which is all that Ammonius has under this lemma).

388 'Named from' presumably covers the case where an object is said to be square as well as the case where a square is called a square.

389 This first sentence is very close to Ammonius 88,6–8, which is all that Ammonius has under this lemma.

390 The core meaning of *sôma* is 'body' but it is also used of a three-dimensional geometrical figure. Here the latter sense is the more appropriate while in line 19 the former is needed.

391 Euclid, *Elements* I, def. 6.

392 The Greek terms would normally be translated 'condensation' and 'rarefaction' (or 'making loose'), but, as Busse sees (cf. the entries in his Index verborum) they are here equivalent to *manotês* ('porosity') and *puknotês* ('denseness').

393 In contrast to Philoponus, Ammonius only has the equivalent of eight *CAG* lines under this lemma, but all of them are paralleled one way or another in Philoponus. Philoponus 152,24–7 is similar to Ammonius 88,10–14, 153,9–10 to 88,14, and 153,13–15 to 88,14–16, though none of them, especially the first pair, is verbally very close. Also, 153,25 ff. should be compared to Ammonius 88,16–17, where

Ammonius also refers to the *Physics*, though only to say that Aristotle defines porous and dense differently there.

394 'Uneven' would work better for a face, but 'rough' does more justice to *trakhus*. The problem is that Philoponus' example is not well-chosen.

395 Rather than indicating a certain qualification (cf. 152,27).

396 *sc.* things that are 'artificially' dense or porous.

397 216b30 ff.

398 Punctuating with a full stop rather than a question mark after *esti* at 154,4.

399 As his *in Phys.* 659, 12 ff. shows (see especially 696,5 ff.), Philoponus has in mind *Phys.* 217a21 ff. This is not the only passage in the *Categories* that suggests that Philoponus already has some knowledge of the *Physics*. (Other passages where he cites it are listed in the subject index.)

400 We would probably talk of closeness or separation here.

401 10a12-13.

402 The first of these two definitions = Euclid, *Elements* 1, def. 4 (the translation is Heath's). On its interpretation (it is obscure and appears to assume what it sets out to prove), see Heath's note, vol. 1, p.165 ff. The second is based on Plato *Parmenides* 137e3-4.

403 Philoponus is combining elements from each of the two definitions in lines 1-2 above. *isotêta* presumably takes up *ex isou* in line 1 above, but it isn't clear what picture Philoponus has in mind; perhaps *isotês* really amounts to 'straight-linedness'!

404 Presumably those of a line, but syntactically 'straightness' would be an easier antecedent.

405 Or perhaps 'move out of the species straight line', and 'species' for 'form' in lines 14, 15, 19, and 21.

406 I have opted for 'circular' rather than, say, 'rounded' for *peripherês* in view of 'every part of a circular line fits onto every other' (155,16-17). Philoponus wants Aristotle's *kampulos* to describe a line that forms the circumference, or at least an arc, of a circle, but this is not necessary to Aristotle's argument and is in fact unlikely, since (1) while *peripherês* is regularly used to describes circles and spheres in geometric contexts, *kampulos* is not, and (2) in other passages where Aristotle opposes *kampulos* to *euthus* ('straight') it need mean no more than curved, but when something circular or spherical is involved (*Cael.* 268b20; 270b34; 271a7,9; 294a2 ff.; *Phys.* 227b20; 265a32) he opposes *peripherês* rather than *kampulos* to straight.

407 *periphereia* is in fact the regular word for circumference.

408 Euclid, *Elements* 1, def. 15 in Heath's translation. The complete definition is: 'A circle is a plane figure contained by one line such that all the straight lines falling upon it from one point among those lying within the figure are equal to one another'.

409 cf. the similar words at 133,2–4.
410 These first two sentences are close to, in fact at times word for word the same as, Ammonius 88,19–23, but Ammonius doesn't go on to add anything like the last sentence, although his having 'said by the ancients' at 88,2 where Philoponus has 'he has said' perhaps prompted Philoponus' expansion.
411 By Aristotle at 10a27–8 and by Philoponus at 133,23 ff. – and cf. 136,35 ff.; 148,5–6.
412 Nothing in Ammonius corresponds to this first sentence but the rest of the material under this lemma is similar to, and initially close to, Ammonius 88,25–89,3.
413 133,23 ff.
414 Changing *ê hopôsoun* at 156,23 to *ê hopôsoun allôs* (the reading of the parallel text at Ammonius 89,3)). Aristotle actually writes *ê hopôsoun allôs ap' autôn* ('or in some other way from them'), as does Philoponus himself when he refers back to this passage at 157,18–20, and it is tempting to follow the editor of the first printed edition in restoring it here, but that wouldn't sit well with 'or not named from them at all' in the previous line. On the other hand, *ê hopôsoun*, which should mean something like 'or [called] in any way whatever' would misrepresent what Aristotle actually says and so, although it could nevertheless be what Philoponus wrote, I think the best solution is emendation to *ê hopôsoun allôs*.
415 A case could be made for deleting *poiotêtôn* ('qualities') here in lines 4–5, thereby establishing parallelism with *epi tôn pleistôn* ('in most cases') in line 2, and translating 'but in some cases'.
416 i.e. not from the capacity to, say, box but from the activity itself.
417 156,21–3.
418 Ammonius has nothing under the present lemma, but with 157,7–13 compare Ammonius 89,5–9, under the lemma 10a34, and with 157,13–16, Ammonius 89,11–13, under the lemma 10b5.
419 cf. 74,13 ff.
420 *sc.* as there is in the case of qualities.
421 cf. Ammonius 89,15–21. The second short sentence is almost identical to the second clause in the Ammonius passage and both commentators repeat Aristotle's example of intermediate colours, but that is the extent of the similarity between the two texts. In particular, Ammonius doesn't have anything like Philoponus' argument that contrariety is particularly associated with quality.
422 To determine whether they could contain the second member of the pair of contraries.
423 All but the last sentence, which isn't present in Ammonius, is almost word for word the same as Ammonius 89,18–21.
424 A number of times – for which see the note at 101,23.
425 Except for the second clause, this is all close to Ammonius 89,23–90,1, the first clause being almost word for word the same as the first sentence in Ammonius.

426 Or perhaps something like 'It might be questioned whether one justice is called more a justice than another', as Ackrill translates.
427 And as in fact defined at 8b27.
428 Busse, in the introduction to his edition of Ammonius *in Cat.* (*CAG* 4.4, p. v., n. 2), cites two passages where Philoponus, unlike Ammonius in parallel passages, refers to angels (49,26, where Philoponus gives angelic and psychic substance as examples of simple substances whereas Ammonius 35,21 has the substance of divine things; 52,10, where he gives angel as an example of intelligible substance whereas Ammonius 37,1 has divine substance) as evidence of Philoponus' Christianity. In addition, there are another six passages (apart from the present one, 30,4.19; 51,31; 68,6; and 196,26) where Philoponus mentions angels. Of course, angels appear often enough in Neoplatonic texts, but I think that it is significant that in all these passages angels are only cited *exempli gratia* and Philoponus could equally well have cited other forms of divine agency, *daimones*, for example, which would, I suspect, have been the choice of most Neoplatonists in similar circumstances. And the situation is much the same in Philoponus' other commentaries. *daimones* do appear in *in DA*, *in Meteor*, and *in Phys.*, but only when he is discussing the views of others. Angels, on the other hand, appear in *in An. Pr.*, *in An. Post.*, *in DA*, and *in Phys.* and always, apart from a number of occurrences at 535,6–537,3, where a position of Marinus' is being discussed (in a part of the commentary that has been attributed to Stephanus but which Pantelis Golitsis, 'John Philoponus' Commentary on the Third Book of Aristotle's *De Anima*, Wrongly Attributed to Stephanus', in Richard Sorabji (ed.), *Aristotle Re-Interpreted: New Findings on Seven Hundred Years of the Ancient Commentators*, London: Bloomsbury, 2016, 393–412, has reclaimed for Philoponus) as illustrative examples. It seems very likely, then, that angels owe their presence in Philoponus' commentaries to his Christian beliefs, their attraction probably being that their presence was inoffensive to both pagans and Christians.
429 One would expect something like 'that other thing'.
430 More literally just 'these qualified entities' (*sc.* things that are just, healthy, etc.).
431 See Lampe s.v. A.1 for other passages where *mignunai* is used of qualities.
432 Ammonius touches very briefly on the question of whether justice admits of more and less at 90,3–5 and 7–12 (under the lemmas 10b26 and 11a2 respectively), but he has nothing that corresponds to the lengthy argument under this lemma.
433 cf. Ammonius, 90,14–22. Philoponus is briefer because he takes up some of Ammonius' points at 160,17–24 under the next lemma.
434 'The above' is the whole of 11a5–14, not just the statement in the lemma.
435 'Healthy' things, including those mentioned here, are standard examples of things that are homonymous, i.e. described by the same term, because they contribute to the same goal, in the case of healthy things, health. In Philoponus, cf. 17,4 ff. and 21,25 ff. and, especially, *in DA* 206,6 ff., much of which parallels the present passage.

436 One would expect 'than a man'.
437 With 160,17-24, compare Ammonius 90,14-22 (under the lemma 11a5), and Ammonius 90,24-5. There is nothing corresponding to the rest of the material under this lemma in Ammonius.
438 *sc.* on account of all the arguments Philoponus has been outlining.
439 Perhaps *to* should be deleted.
440 Having used other examples in elucidating Aristotle's argument, Philoponus is at pains to point out in these last two sentences that the arguments he has outlined apply to the geometrical figures that Aristotle used as examples in stating his argument.
441 Aristotle is talking about quality (*poiotês*) and *poion* here should arguably be translated 'quality', but Philoponus goes on to draw a clear line between qualities and things that are qualified so I have opted for 'the qualified'.
442 With 161,6-11, compare Ammonius 90,27-91,2, where Ammonius makes the same point, though more briefly. Again, there is nothing corresponding to the rest of the material under this lemma in Ammonius.
443 *sc.* with respect to the amount of the quality they display.
444 78,34 ff.
445 The last three sentences are a recasting (with somewhat modified syntax) of a single, rather awkward, sentence in the Greek.
446 106,21-4.
447 Compare Ammonius 91,4-8, which is similar in content, though not verbally close.
448 With 162,7-11, compare Ammonius 91,10-14 (initially verbally close). Ammonius gives much less space to the first 'solution' and much more to the second and he deals with both under the present lemma.
449 cf. 106,21-24.
450 For Philoponus (134,27 ff.) health and sickness are states rather than conditions, but, in one sense of 'condition', 'state' is one species of 'condition' (135,9 ff.).
451 *sc.* categories.
452 Compare Ammonius 91,28-92,2, under 11a23.
453 Despite this section heading and the lemma that follows, Philoponus now launches into an introduction to all six of the categories not yet covered. The discussion of acting and being-affected actually begins with the repetition of the lemma at 165,20.
454 The structure, much of the content, and at times the wording (cf. especially 164,6-15 and Ammonius 92,12-22) of the material under this lemma derives from Ammonius 92,6-93,6, although Philoponus often greatly expands on Ammonius' comments.
455 The Greek actually has 'these', but the reference is clearly to the last three of the four mentioned.

456 Busse cites 84,6 and 47,29 ff. and 66,31 ff. are also perhaps relevant, but Philoponus nowhere calls divisibility a distinctive feature of quantity.
457 107,1–3.
458 'Having-on' would be a reasonable translation of *ekhein* here and at 165,17, but when the category is introduced at 204,22 ff. and the various senses of *ekhein* are listed it needs to be translated 'having' so I have used that here.
459 With these first three paragraphs, compare Ammonius 92,6–12. Ammonius is very much briefer and doesn't contain the formal division. Also, he here generates 'having' from substance and the relatives rather than from just substance, although later (at 93,5–6) he too says that it involves just substances.
460 For this sense of *epistêsai* + dative cf. Lampe *ephistêmi* 4.
461 I take it that this means that the exercise of its function is facilitated, or made possible, by them.
462 Presumably *anakekelisthai* (164,19) is a misprint for *anakeklisthai*.
463 107,4–6.
464 164,6–25 is very close to Ammonius 92,12–93,4, in fact often word for word the same, although Philoponus at times expands on Ammonius, notably at 164,16–18 and 164,18–22, which are not paralleled in Ammonius. Ammonius has no equivalent to the excursus on the reason for there being six species of 'where' that follows (164,25–165,17).
465 cf. 33,22–3; 87,7–8 (with note).
466 Changing *hôrismenôs* at 165,4 to *hôrismenê*.
467 In view of the measuring cord later in the sentence, I would like to translate, 'he will measure it with a plumb line (*kata katheton*), and a plumb line is a straight line', but 'with a plumb line' for *kata katheton* would be difficult.
468 This short sentence is very close to the first part of Ammonius 93,5.
469 The inflection of the pronoun suggests that 'these' means 'these categories'.
470 In Greek an infinitive can be turned into a type of noun by the addition of an article and the words being translated 'acting' and 'being-affected' are in fact present active infinitives functioning as nouns.
471 *poiêsis* is a noun formed from the same root as the verb *poiein*, whose articulated present active infinitive we have been translating 'acting'. The two most basic senses of *poiein* are 'make' and 'do', but the senses of *poiêsis* normally relate to making and not, as here, doing.
472 202a13 ff. (discussed by Philoponus at *in Phys*. 369,24 ff.), rather than 225b13, as Busse suggests.
473 For motion as a path in Philoponus (often, but not only, between the potential and the actual), see 87,3; 204,2–5; *in DA* 93,1–2; 296,26–7; *in Phys*. 211,34; 349,25.29–32; *Aet*. 60,32–6; 257,24–8. Although the idea originates with Aristotle, such phrases don't seem to.

474 A *hexis* in this context is an acquired habit, skill, or capacity which can be the basis for action and is thus a kind of potentiality. The usage is common enough in the commentators and already present in Aristotle (cf. *EN* 1098b31 ff.).

475 cf. 44,13 ff.

476 'Production' would work better in the example that follows and would be a more normal rendering of *poiêsis* (on which see the note at 165,30), but both Aristotle's own examples of *to poiein* and those provided by Philoponus before this suggest that he should have something like 'action' in mind. Perhaps Philoponus would argue that the category in fact embraces both making and doing, but if so his choice of an example of 'making' here suggests an awareness of the restricted range of meaning of *poiêsis*. (Philoponus may well have raised this question of terminology because Aristotle uses the terms *poiêsis* and *pathêsis* at *Phys.* 202a23 ff. in a passage he has just referred to at 166,3 ff.)

477 Despite what Philoponus says in line 31 below, Aristotle does not use section headings and those in the commentators seem to be their own.

478 To judge from LSJ, it is only in the case of poetry that *poiêsis* is used of the product as opposed to the process of production in earlier Greek, but Lampe (s.v. C) cites passages where it is used in the former sense.

479 75,16–17; 101,23–5; 110,10–12; 158,16–19.

480 Ammonius has nothing corresponding to the material under this lemma.

481 Normally I would not translate this *men* or the *de* in the next lemma, but Philoponus' argument at 168,5 ff. makes some acknowledgement of them necessary.

482 *DA* 402b7–8.

483 *An. Post.* 83a32–4.

484 cf. 9,4–12, where this is said to be Porphyry's position. Ammonius too ascribes it to Porphyry (though adducing different arguments) at 9,7–11, but has nothing to say about the matter at this point.

485 At 13,6–32 (with which compare Ammonius 14,2–15,2).

486 Known in Latin as the *praepraedicamenta*, the *praedicamenta*, and the *postpraedicamenta*.

487 With 167,27–168,3 ('in the third ... detailed one'), compare Ammonius 93,9–12. (Ammonius doesn't mention the tripartite division of the categories here but goes immediately to the present 'third' division.)

488 The 'aim' of the categories is discussed at 8,27–12,11.

489 These people, one of whom, according to Simplicius *in Cat.* 379,8–9, was Andronicus, felt, like some modern scholars (see, for example, Akrill, 70), that this last section was not originally part of the *Categories*. Ammonius mentions such doubts at 14,18 ff. in the section on the divisions of the *Categories* in his Prolegomena (though not here), but, rather surprisingly, Philoponus does not find a place for them in his own introductory material.

490 Modern grammarians describe *men* and *de* as particles rather than conjunctions. (The English phrases used to translate *men* and *de* are of course neither particles nor conjunctions.)
491 5b15 ff. Aristotle does not use the term 'opposites' there but does talk of 'contraries' and 'relatives', which he tells us here are types of opposites. (Philoponus, and Ammonius whom he is following closely here, could well have just said something like 'when he argued that quantities have no contraries', which is the point Aristotle is trying to make.)
492 Close to Ammonius 93,12-17, although Ammonius appears to refer back (incorrectly) to the section on relatives rather than to that on quantity.
493 Adding *kai* before *askheta* at 168,26 with the first printed edition
494 With 168,18-27, compare Ammonius 93,17-94,3. Ammonius has the same division but gives his examples on the way through it rather than after it and, although Philoponus uses all of Ammonius' examples, he adds a few of his own.
495 191b15-17 rather than 225a3 ff., as Busse suggests, as Philoponus *in Phys.* 174,7 ff. confirms.
496 It is hard to account for the neuter (or masculine) plural *ekeinois* and Busse may be right to suspect that Philoponus wrote *ekeinêi*.
497 There is nothing corresponding to 168,27-169,2 in Ammonius, but the remaining material under this lemma is an expanded version of Ammonius 94,4-29, sometimes verbally close and at times, for brief stretches, almost word for word the same. Philoponus' longest expansion of Ammonius is on the topic of things opposed as affirmation and negation, to which he devotes seventeen lines (169,20-170,3) as opposed to Ammonius' three (94,15-18), but there are others. Cases of strong verbal similarity are 169,6-8 (cf. Ammonius 94,4-5), 170,5-7 (cf. Ammonius 94,17-18), 170,8-9 (cf. Ammonius 94,19-20); of exact agreement, 170,12 (cf. Ammonius 94,21-2) and 170,13-15 (cf. Ammonius 94,27-9).
498 Busse (*CAG* 4, pt. 4, preface, v.) saw this last remark (which is repeated at 184,17-18) as evidence of Philoponus' Christianity.
499 These examples of *leukos* and *melas* and their different intermediates in the cases of sound and colour appear to be borrowed from the quite different context of Aristotle *Top.* 106b6 ff. (Aristotle, like Philoponus, goes on to use the phrase *opsin ekhein*, but this looks to be coincidental.)
500 '*to* a contrary' represents a dative, which is one of the ways in which relatives are 'completed' (see 106,8-11).
501 104,28 ff.
502 There is no parallel to the material under this lemma in Ammonius.
503 For two senses of 'good' elsewhere in Philoponus, cf. *in DA* 547,20-21; *Aet.* 594,23 ff. For the contrast between the good 'above being' and the good 'in us', see Proclus *in Remp.* 1.271,20 ff. (Proclus places a third kind of good, good as a form,

504 52,17–19; cf. *Aet.* 16,25 ff.
505 Just as light is accidentally (*kata sumbebêkos*) present in air, so too is darkness the accidental (*episumbainein*; cf. Lampe s.v. 3) consequence of the departure of light from air.
506 Busse has '*Theaet.* 151E sq. alias', and in fact no single passage seems to do duty.
507 *sc.* opposed to truth.
508 The slight oddity of expression here is also present in the Greek.
509 cf. *Metaph.* 1051b22 ff.
510 '*of* other things' translates *heterôn*, for which the Oxford Classical Texts edition (L. Minio-Paluello (ed.), *Aristotelis Categoriae et Liber de Interpretatione*, Oxonii: e typographeo Clarendoniano, 1949) prints the variant text *tôn antikeimenôn* ('of their opposites').
511 Much of this is word for word the same as Ammonius 95,2–7.
512 This first sentence is virtually identical to Ammonius 95,9–10.
513 At 12b16–25.
514 Deleting *eidôn* and accenting *diaphorôn* with a circumflex on the final syllable at 172,3 and at 172,7. The phrase *diaphora eidê*, (which can be translated 'different kinds') also occurs at 172,5, but while Aristotle could be said to instruct us in 'the different kinds of contraries', as Philoponus tells us there, he cannot be said to do anything similar in the case of things that are opposed as state and privation. This being so, it seems likely that somebody has misguidedly supplied *eidôn* in lines 3 and 7 under the influence of *eidê* in line 3. The occurrence of *diaphoras* in lines 4, 8, and 10 points in the same direction. (I have translated *diaphora* 'differentia' but 'difference', or even 'distinctive feature', might be better.)
515 At 12a26–34.
516 At 11b38–12a25.
517 At 12b26–13a36.
518 At 13a37 ff. (perhaps only a37-b3 strictly qualify).
519 At 13b3–35.
520 For *dunamei* in this sense, see Lampe *dunamis* X.c. For the 'division' see 12b27–13a3. With 172,1–13, compare Ammonius 95,10–11. (Ammonius merely says, 'Prior to this he gives a division of the contraries that is helpful to him along the following lines'.)
521 172,13–21 is often close to, at times even verbally identical to, Ammonius 95,11–19.
522 Presumably this division is based on 12a9–25.
523 Aristotle has *horizetai*.
524 With 172,21–7, compare Ammonius 95,27–96,4, under the later lemma 12a20.
525 *An. Post.* 73a34-b24.

526 There is no parallel to the material under this lemma, which in part duplicates the previous one, in Ammonius.
527 Adopting Busse's suggestions, both made in his apparatus, of emending *hina* to *ean* and adding *noson* before *pasan* at 174,3. (But the former change may not be strictly necessary since *hina* can amount to 'if' in later Greek (for examples, see Lampe s.v. 4)).
528 Again, there is no parallel to the material under this lemma in Ammonius.
529 Emending *rhêtheiê* to *heuretheiê* at 174,9, for which cf. Ammonius *in Cat.* 95,21. (Apart from *rhêtheiê*, Philoponus is almost word for word the same as Ammonius 95,21-2.)
530 Almost identical to the first half of Ammonius 95,24-5, which has 'horses' and adds 'and dogs and the like' at the end.
531 cf. 172,21-7. There, in contrast to the present passage where he refers to both divisions as subdivisions (*hupodiairesis, hupodiairein*), he refers to the earlier division as a 'division and subdivision' and uses the verb *epidiairein* ('re-divide', 'divide further') when introducing the second division. Ammonius (95,27-96,4) actually gives the division under this lemma rather than earlier.
532 172,2-4.
533 cf. Ammonius 96,6-9, which is not dissimilar at first but then diverges.
534 Emending *en tôi khronôi* to *ton khronon* at 175,4, one of two possible corrections mooted by Busse in the apparatus.
535 Actually, Aristotle is prepared to say that a thing that is incapable of having some attribute suffers privation of it (*Metaph.* 1055b4-5) and, commenting on the passage, Alexander uses a stone that lacks sight as an example (*in Metaph.* 621,31-2).
536 'Eyes' would have been a better choice of 'part'.
537 Compare Ammonius 96,12-28, under the lemma 12a29. The two passages are for the most part structured and phrased differently, but 175,6-7 is identical to 96,15. Also, 175,5-6 is almost identical to 96,8-9 under the lemma 12a26.
538 This first sentence is close to Ammonius 97,4-5, which is under the same lemma, but the arguments that follow are rather different, and in fact the material under this lemma in Ammonius is behind 176,18-24 below under the next lemma.
539 Changing *ê dia* to *kai* at 176,1 (cf. *tês opseôs kai tês tuphlotês* in the next line). But perhaps the whole of the phrase *ê dia tês sterêseôs kai tou tên sterêsin ekhontos*, which does not appear in the manuscripts C and F on which Busse's edition is based, should be omitted. In favour of such omission is the lack of any reference to privation in the previous parenthesis at 175,24-5 and the difficulty of *ê dia*; against it the mention of the privation 'blindness' in the parenthesis that follows at 176,2-3.
540 According to Greek grammarians, literally 'dividing the voice', 'articulate' and thence 'human'.

541 With 176,18-24, compare Ammonius 97,3-8 under the lemma 12a35 (and see the note at 175,20).
542 Busse casts doubt on the phrase *hôs sterêsis kai hexis* at 176,25-6 and it is indeed suspicious. One would expect *hôs hexis sterêsei* ('as state to privation') rather than *hôs sterêsis kai hexis* ('as privation and state'), and since the sentence construes well enough without the phrase it may well be an interpolation.
543 More literally, 'that which is under'.
544 The first sentence is very close to Ammonius 97,11-13 and the last two appear to be inspired by Ammonius 97,13-16.
545 cf. 175,24 ff.
546 *deiknunai* ('to show', 'to prove'; here translated 'to give, provide, a proof') without a direct object or dependent clause, as here and again in lines 25 and 27, is unusual (contrast the similar passage at 171,18 ff.).
547 cf. 171,19 ff.
548 The switch to the present tense is odd. Perhaps its occurrence is due to the similar present in the parallel text in Ammonius (who also has a present in the first part of the sentence).
549 With 177,15-17 cf. Ammonius 97,18-19, with 177,25-8 Ammonius 97,19-22. The material in between has no parallel in Ammonius.
550 'Sight' is not present in the text of Aristotle, which could be translated, 'nor is it ...'.
551 The sentence up to this point is close to Ammonius 97,24-5 (all that Ammonius has under this lemma). At first sight it seems that Philoponus has in mind cases where there is no existing term for the correlative of a relative and one has to be invented (for such cases, see *Cat.* 7a6 ff., where Aristotle uses *onomatopoiein* to describe the process). However, Aristotle is simply arguing that the relationship between sight and blindness is never expressed in any of the ways that the relationship between relatives is expressed and the continuation suggests that Philoponus understands the passage in the same way. This said, the passage is a difficult one and I'm not at all sure that I've got it right. In particular, my translation of *onomatopoiein* is rather forced, but Philoponus seems to have retained the word from the even more difficult parallel passage in Ammonius (on which see Cohen and Matthew's note) and may well be giving it a slightly unusual twist himself.
552 One possible translation of the Greek dative.
553 With this first sentence, compare the similar statement at Ammonius 98,3-5, which is all that Ammonius felt needed to be said under this lemma.
554 Translating *hê gar*, the text of the first printed edition rather than *ei gar hê*, the text of Busse and the manuscripts at 178,14. The sentence is unsatisfactory as it stands and Busse himself thought it possible that *hê gar* is the correct reading or that the words I have translated 'After all, the privation of vision is not absolute and

completely general privation but clearly a particular privation, i.e. blindness' are an interpolation.
555 All of Philoponus' examples are formed with the privative prefix *a* (the so-called alpha privative). Although this is often seen in English in words of Greek origin (e.g. atheist, aphasia), I haven't been able to find English equivalents for Philoponus' examples that use it and have fallen back on words using the Latin equivalent in-, and even then have had to translate rather loosely.
556 In both cases 'of' is equivalent to 'on the part of'.
557 *agnôsia*, for example, could in a sense be said to 'contain' *gnôsis*.
558 The best fit in Philoponus' extant works is *in DA* 341,10 ff., but *in Cat.* is probably condiderably earlier than *in DA* (see for example the suggested relative chronology for Philoponus' works at Richard Sorabji (ed.), *Aristotle Re-Interpreted: New Findings on Seven Hundred Years of the Ancient Commentators*, London: Bloomsbury, 2016, 391), so perhaps there was something in his *in Isag*. He returned to the topic briefly at *Aet.* 15,2 ff. and at greater length at *Opif.* 69,4 ff.
559 Deleting *onomaseien* at 179,23, which looks like a gloss on *kalêi* ('call'), as Busse suggests in the apparatus.
560 In what seems to be the only reference to Philoponus by name in later commentaries on the *Categories*, David (Elias) quarrels with this statement at *in Cat.* 246,14–18.
561 Herodian *Peri pathôn* fr. 673 (= *Grammatici graeci* 3.2, 380, 15–17; cf. fr. 672, ibid. 380,12–13. Simplicius, *in Cael.* 26,21–3, tells us that Philoponus came to Aristotle from the study of Menander and Herodian and the like and works on accents based wholly or in part on works of Herodian have survived (for these see Lloyd W. Daly, *Iohannis Philoponi de vocabulis quae diversum significatum exhibent secundum differentiam accentus / On the accent of homonyms*, Philadelphia: American Philosophical Society, 1983, and Georgios A. Xenis, *Iohannes Alexandrinus: Praecepta Tonica*, Berlin: de Gruyter, 2015.
562 *skhethein* was thought to be a collateral form of *ekhein* and *epekhein* is one of its compounds.
563 The clause *epekhei ... epikheirêsis* (180,21–2) makes little sense as it stands. *Faute de mieux*, I have translated *hêmas tou theasasthai* (a correction in the manuscript Laur. 72,1, which has Busse's approval) rather than *hêmôn to eidenai* (the reading of the manuscripts and Busse's text) and *epekhei* (the reading of F and the first printed edition) rather than *epikheirêsis* (the reading of C and Busse's text). The effect of this will be to have Philoponus suggest two possible explanations of the derivation of *skotos* from *skhethei*, but the Greek remains difficult and I'm not at all sure about the suggested solution.
564 Emending *tuphos* to *tuphlos* at 180,23.
565 cf. Apollonius, *Argonautica*, 2,445.

566 *pêthô* and *pêsô* appear to be alternative forms of *paskhô* and *peithomai* hypothesized for the present etymology (cf. LSJ, *pêthô*).
567 There is no parallel to this in Ammonius.
568 With 181,8–13 ('He now next … for the present'), compare Ammonius 98,7–10.
569 Adding *deixai* after *gar* at 181,15, as mooted by Busse in the apparatus.
570 cf. Ammonius 98,18–19 under the earlier lemma 12b26.
571 cf. Ammonius 98,22–3 under the lemma 12b33.
572 The closest thing to a parallel to this in Ammonius is 98,23–99,3.
573 The material under this and the next lemma is closely based on that under the same two lemmas in Ammonius, but not in a straightforward way. The first sentence under this lemma is based on Ammonius 99,5–7 under 13a3, the second on 99,13–14 under 13a4, while the first sentence under the next lemma as far as 'present to the subject' is almost word for word the same as Ammonius 99,7–9 under 13a3 and the rest of the material under the lemma is probably loosely based on Ammonius 99,14–17 under 13a4.
574 *Cat.* 11b38 ff.; 12b27 ff.
575 cf. Ammonius 99,13–17.
576 cf. Ammonius 99,19–22.
577 Which means that as far as their own nature goes, both could be absent from the subject at the same time. (Busse's suggested supplement seems unnecessary.) With 183,4–14, compare Ammonius 99,22–100,2 under the lemma 13a8.
578 Perhaps one should supply *têi* before *kat'* in line 14.
579 With this paragraph, compare Ammonius 100,4–9. The rest has no parallel in Ammonius.
580 Ammonius has nothing under this lemma.
581 The verb is more often translated 'restore' but that doesn't work very well here.
582 With this last sentence, compare Ammonius 100,11–12 under the lemma 13a18.
583 Compare the similar remark at 169,18–19 and the note there. No parallel in Ammonius.
584 cf. Porphyry *Isag.* 17,14 ff., and also Ammonius *in Isag.* 115,20 ff. and 122,22 ff., where the method is described in much the same terms as it is here, as it presumably was in Philoponus' own commentary on the *Isagoge*.
585 *Cat.* 13b2–3, with a minor difference of word order.
586 185,2–7 is close to Ammonius 100,14–17 under the lemma 13a37, but there is no parallel to the rest of the material under this lemma in Ammonius.
587 Both *egô peripatô* (finite verb plus pronoun) and *peripatô* (finite verb without pronoun) are equivalent to 'I walk', the only difference being that the former is normally more emphatic.
588 No equivalent in Ammonius.

589 Although I have translated Busse's text, *ouden* ('nothing'), which does not appear in the parallel passage at Ammonius 100,23–101,2 (which is otherwise almost word for word the same as this one), looks rather like an intrusion from the lemma, where it has a different reference, and a case could be made for deleting it both here and in line 5. However the Greek would then be slightly awkward ('express neither true nor false') and Philoponus may have added *ouden* for that reason.

590 This last statement (with which cf. Ammonius 110,10 ff.) isn't entirely accurate, since they never become examples of affirmation and denial in the sense intended by Aristotle. With 186,9–187,20, compare Ammonius 101,4–13. Unlike Philoponus, Ammonius is very brief, only dealing with the contrast between contraries and limiting himself to the single example of Socrates' state of health.

591 As Busse indicates, something has clearly dropped out here.

592 For this section title, cf. Ammonius 101,14. Philoponus normally uses the same section titles as Ammonius and it seems likely that this one was part of what was lost after 187,24.

593 Interestingly, in the parallel passage in Ammonius excess and defect are one example of opposed bad things rather than a description of the nature of the opposition involved. 187,27–188,4 is fairly close to Ammonius 101,16–21 but what follows has no parallel in Ammonius.

594 The thought is that opposites are constantly at war with one another and two against one isn't fair.

595 Reversing the positions of *huperbolê* ('excess') and *endeia* ('defect') at 188,13. In some ways reversing each of the pairs of opposed terms would be a better solution, but that would be rather radical surgery. (Of course, the reversal of 'excess' and 'defect' may be a slip on Philoponus' part, in which case emendation wouldn't really be warranted.)

596 For *panourgia* in the sense of 'cunning', 'craftiness', see Lampe s.v. 2.

597 Aristotle's ethical writings are behind these examples of mean, excess, and defect: for justice cf. *EN* 1129b1 ff. (different terminology, but same idea); for self-control, *EN* 1107b4 ff. (in Aristotle, the context is the degree to which a person indulges in pleasures and his term for the person exhibiting the defect is *anaisthêtos* ('insensible')) and *EE* 1221a2; for bravery, *EN* 1108b35 ff. and *EE* 1220b38; for practical wisdom, *EE* 1221a12 (*euêtheia* ('simplicity') replaces *anoia* ('folly'), but the passage is probably an interpolation).

598 With 188,23–9, compare Ammonius 102,2–5.

599 For *kataskeuê* in this sense, see Lampe s.v. D.

600 185,26–9; cf. 186,10 ff.

601 189,9–13 has some similarity to Ammonius 102,7–10.

602 Perhaps, in view of the occurrence of *eidei* and *genei* in the lemma and *tôi genei* in line 18 and *tôi eidei* in line 21, one should emend *genos* and *eidos* here in line 17 to

genei and *eidei*, which would give, 'to occur either in [something] one and the same in genus or in [something] one and the same in species'.

603 cf. 37,17 ff.

604 These are numerically the same because 'sword' and 'blade' are different names for the same thing.

605 In his brief comment under this lemma (102,12–14) Ammonius merely says that contraries are found in the same subject and that this is as one would expect since they are at war with one another.

606 For *telein* in this sense, cf. Lampe s.v. 6.

607 For the five kinds see *Sophist* 254C ff. The phrase 'genera of existing things' doesn't occur.

608 *posotês* only appears four times in *in Cat.* but not at all in the section on quantity. Aristotle uses it three times in the *Metaphysics* but not at all in the *Categories*.

609 Emending *khrômati* to *khrôma* at 190.27, although Busse may be right to suggest omitting the words *kai en poiôi to summetron hekastôi khrômati* (which without emendation would read 'and in quality, what is appropriate to each colour') with the manuscript Marc. 217.

610 Lines 190,28–191,5 reappear almost verbatim at David (Elias) *in Cat.* 250,19–27, where I suspect they may be an interpolation.

611 The words 'both from above and from below' (*anôthen te kai katôthen*) occur in both line 12 and line 13 and it seems clear that one of these occurrences should be deleted. The manuscript Paris. 2051, correctly in Busse's opinion, omits the first occurrence, but it seems palaeographically more likely that the second is the interpolation and I would omit that. (C does in fact omit the second, but along with other text.)

612 With 191,5–11 compare Ammonius 102,19–21 and with 191,11–14, Ammonius 102,12–14. The earlier material under this lemma is not paralleled in Ammonius.

613 7b23 ff. Ammonius (103,3) simply says 'during his teaching of the categories'. While Philoponus' commentary on this section is divided between this and the next five lemmas, the bulk of Ammonius' is confined to this one. Ammonius' comments are, as usual, briefer and largely consist of summary of Aristotle.

614 Aristotle actually calls this 'that which does not reciprocate with respect to implication of existence', as Philoponus does later at 192,5–6 (and Ammonius does at 103,9). It is at first sight a little odd that he should, without any explanation, choose to refer to it as the prior by nature here. The explanation will be that Ammonius (echoed by Philoponus himself at 192,16–17) ends his brief comments on this type of priority with the remark 'But this way of talking has to do with nature and not with time' (103,17–18; tr. Cohen and Matthews).

615 The sentence doesn't quite construe as it stands and I have translated *kuriôtaton*, the reading of C, at 191,24 rather than *kuriôtata*.

616 Ammonius (103,8) appears to claim that 'more ancient' is used *only* in the case of inanimate things.
617 Aristotle's only example of 'that which does not reciprocate with respect to implication of existence' is one and two. Philoponus gets the example of human being and animal – and the comment that this involves priority in nature rather than in time – from Ammonius 103,13-18.
618 Ancient rhetoricians normally distinguished four, sometimes five, parts of a speech. The terms for some of the parts, and the descriptions of their normal content and function, varied considerably. The noticeable absentee here is the *epilogos*, or peroration, with which a speech normally concluded. Also, *diêgêsis* would be more normal than *diêgêmata*.
619 Perhaps 'unskilled' is to be understood from its earlier occurrence in the sentence; or perhaps it has even dropped out here, as an anonymous reader suggests.
620 *grammatikê* also embraces the study of reading, writing, and literature and is probably synonymous with *ta grammata* in line 5 (which I translated 'writing', but which is more literally 'letters').
621 Clearly Philoponus wouldn't have approved of the Whole Word method of teaching reading. Ammonius (see 103,18-19), who has very little to say about this third type of priority (he merely mentions Aristotle's example of the introduction and the narrative in speeches), has no hint of the criticism of Aristotle in this last paragraph.
622 Philoponus doesn't at this point take up Ammonius' suggestion (at 103,23-4) that this fourth kind of priority is the most remote from the central meaning of prior because it is our invention but does later at 194,9-10. Also, Aristotle doesn't actually reject it, and Ammonius (103,23-4) hadn't claimed that he does.
623 At 193,30-31.
624 Ammonius also uses this example of father and son (it alone, in fact) in his brief treatment of this fifth sense of the prior (104,2-5). (Aristotle doesn't.) He has nothing like Philoponus' opposing of the second and fifth senses of the prior.
625 Much of this is word for word the same as Ammonius 104,8-12, of which it is a slightly expanded version. (Ammonius doesn't have the remark about relatives at the end.)
626 At 7b15.
627 *sc.* as well as the prior; Philoponus is looking back to 191,17 where he points out that the prior is mentioned in the section on the relatives. Ammonius (see 104,16-17) simply says 'in his teaching on the categories', as he also did in the case of the prior. Ammonius has just twelve *CAG* lines on the simultaneous, all of them under this lemma.
628 Aristotle, as Ammonius sees (104,18-19), really only distinguishes two senses of the simultaneous, the simultaneous in time and the simultaneous by nature – although his two examples of the latter are indeed rather different in kind.

629 Busse, seeing a reference to 193,30, emends the *ephthê* of the manuscripts to *ephthên* at 195,13, which would give 'I' rather than 'he'. My preference is to retain the manuscript reading and see a reference to *Cat.* 14b3 ff.

630 Aristotle himself doesn't match the senses of the simultaneous with those of the prior. Ammonius (104,19–20) opposes the first senses of each to one another and the second sense of the simultaneous to both the second and fifth senses of the prior, but of course has nothing to oppose to the third sense of the prior.

631 Changing *kuriôtata* to *kuriôtaton* at 195,17 with the first printed edition.

632 Although I have translated Busse's text, we would expect something like *kai to tôi khronôi hama kuriôtata an lekhtheiê hama* ('the simultaneous in time would also most properly be called simultaneous').

633 Changing *elegomen* ('we said') at 196,2 to *elegeto* ('was said'). Although Busse relates the reference to 192,5, Philoponus is clearly (as we would expect) citing what Aristotle said at 14a30 ff. rather than what he said himself there. Also, the fact that F has no verb at all at this point suggests that there may have been some doubt as to the correct reading. Compare too the similarly phrased citation of Aristotle at line 7 ff. below.

634 Deleting *to loipon* at 196,9. Retaining *to loipon* we would have to translate something like 'the cause of its existence the one for the other', which is not quite what is needed. (And we would surely expect *to heteron . . . tôi loipôi* anyway.) The present passage has perhaps been influenced by the similar locution at 194,13, which is more or less tolerable in that context.

635 14b11 ff.

636 *legô dê* ('I mean of course') is a little surprising since it makes it sound as though Aristotle only has in mind the double and the half whereas he is merely using them as an example – Aristotle has *hoion* ('as for instance').

637 The second sense of the simultaneous, then, is opposed to the second of the prior in that simultaneous things 'reciprocate with respect to implication of existence' and to the fifth in that 'neither [of two simultaneous things] is the cause of the existence of the other'. Although it isn't immediately clear, I think this must have been Ammonius' interpretation too (*pace* Cohen and Matthews I would translate 'for it both reciprocates with respect to implication of existence and neither [of the simultaneous items] is the cause of the existence of the other' at Ammonius 104,20–105,1, so that the reference is to the second sense of the simultaneous rather than to the second and fifth of the prior as they have it. Incidentally, it was careless of Ammonius to go on to give co-ordinate species, rather than double and half as Aristotle does, as an example of things involving a converse implication of existence.

638 See the note at 87,21 for the translation of *kinêsis* as 'motion' rather than 'change'.

639 The reference is probably, as Busse suggests, to *Phys.* 200b11, where Aristotle actually has 'the principle of motion and change'. Commenting on the passage in his commentary on the *Physics*, Philoponus writes 'Nature is the principle of motion and rest, but here, because he only has a need for motion, he has mentioned [only] it'.
640 Busse, not unreasonably, cites *Phys.* 200b11 ff., but, as 196,16–18 shows, Philoponus has in mind the last four books of the *Physics*.
641 cf. the similar statement at Simplicius *in Cat.* 427,12 ff., where Richard Gaskin (*Simplicius, On Aristotle Categories 9–15*, London: Duckworth, 2000, 242, n. 1032) identifies Plotinus as one of those in question.
642 48,23–7. (Busse's 8,23 is a misprint.)
643 48,25.
644 The reference is to 4a10-b19. Although Aristotle does not use the word *kinêsis* there (its only earlier occurrence is at 5b3), he does use the cognate words *kineisthai* ('to move') and *akinêtos* ('unmoving') as well as *metaballein* ('to change') and *metabolê* ('change'), which can be near synonyms for *kineisthai* and *kinêsis* in discussions of motion or change. Ammonius was content to say that motion is mentioned in 'what has preceded' (105,9–10). Pelletier (cited by Cohen and Matthews) suggested that Ammonius may be thinking of Aristotle's earlier references to action and affection and Cohen and Matthews themselves speculate that he may have in mind his own previous comments at 83,8 ff. on Aristotle's discussion of change in the *Physics*. If Ammonius did actually have a particular passage in mind, there must be a good chance that it was the one that Philoponus adduces here. (This paragraph is the only part of the material under the present lemma that is paralleled in Ammonius.)
645 197,12.
646 Or perhaps, in view of 199,23–4, rather less specifically, 'and what things follow, or don't follow, from what'. For the language, cf. Aristotle *An. Post.* 98a15–18.
647 Busse's '15a33' is a misprint.
648 163,4 ff.
649 With this paragraph, compare Ammonius 105,10–19 under the same lemma. The details of the division are different, the result the same. The other material under this lemma has no parallel in Ammonius.
650 224b35 ff., especially 225a34 ff.
651 cf. 198,20.
652 The text, which is also that of the Oxford Classical Texts edition (L. Minio-Paluello (ed.), *Aristotelis Categoriae et Liber de Interpretatione*, Oxonii: e typographeo Clarendoniano, 1949), is unsatisfactory and Minio-Paluello indicates as much by placing a dagger after *kata topon metabolê* ('change of place'). As things stand, we would expect something to follow 'nor change of place' – 'any of the others',

say – but the text could be emended in various ways. Ackrill adds *ê* ('or') before *meiôsis* ('diminution') and translates 'for generation is not destruction, nor yet is increase or diminution, nor is change of place'. (For what it's worth, my guess is that Aristotle wrote something like 'for generation is not destruction, nor indeed [is it] increase or diminution, or change of place', which would involve a number of changes.) Nothing in Philoponus' comments suggests that he saw any problem with the text, but then we can't be sure that what he read was what we have.

653 Ammonius covers the same ground as the material under this and the next lemma with the remark 'He now does what he did in the case of the opposites: he distinguishes the species of motion from one another' (105,19–20, under the lemma 15a23).

654 This is odd since the only remaining candidate is change of place.

655 In seeking to establish the independent nature of qualitative change, Aristotle argues (1) that qualitative change does not involve one of the other motions, and (2) that none of the other motions involves qualitative change (15a20–33). Philoponus sees this and deals with (1) under this lemma (supplying his own cases, since Aristotle has none) and with (2) under the next, where Aristotle's example of the square and the gnomon is prominent. Ammonius, on the other hand, writes as though he doesn't appreciate the structure of Aristotle's argument, going straight from a repetition of Aristotle's statement that it is clear that the motions other than qualitative change are distinct, to a discussion of (2) and the square and gnomon, all under the present lemma.

656 I normally opt for 'increase' for *auxêsis* but 'growth' is clearly better in the present passage.

657 This sentence (or clause in the Greek) lacks a connective and Busse suggests supplying *amelei* before *tois* at 201,14 or deleting the whole clause. For purposes of translation I've adopted the former course.

658 Adding *dêlon* before *hoti* at 201,32, as suggested by Busse in the apparatus.

659 The text is awkward as it stands and the first printed edition deletes the second *kai* in 202,7 and Busse (in the apparatus) suggests emending it to *hoion*. For purposes of translation, I have, without much conviction, placed it before *phêsi* in the next line.

660 Previously referred to as KGCF.

661 Previously referred to as EBHK.

662 With 202,10–203,21, compare Ammonius' much briefer explanation of the square and gnomon at 105,24–106,5. Ammonius' commentary ends at this point, providing no parallel to the material under the next two lemmas on motion or the two on 'having'.

663 At 198,23–5.

664 At 15a14 ff.

665 Of course in the case of local motion it was remaining in the same *place* or change to the contrary *place* that was in question.
666 'From white to black' would be more consistent with what he says at 133,23–7. Ammonius has nothing corresponding to this paragraph.
667 *perikeimai* is used as the passive of the verb *peritithêmi*, the verb corresponding to *perithesis*, and could, in the present passage be, less idiomatically, translated 'to have around [us]'.
668 *sc.* because it was clear what it would contain.
669 'Have' isn't always the most idiomatic translation of *ekhein* in what follows, but it has seemed best to stick to it throughout.
670 In reality Aristotle probably means that it is the least central of the senses he has identified.
671 cf. the similar comments at 133,3 ff. and 156,8 ff.

English–Greek Glossary

above being: *huperousios*
absence: *apousia*
absurd: *atopos*
absurdity: *to atopon*
accident: *sumbebêkos*
accidental: *ek tautomatou*
accidental, be: *sumbainein*
accidentally: *kata sumbebêkos*
accompany: *parakolouthein*
account: *logos*
acted on, be: *paskhein*
action: *energeia*
activity: *energeia*
actuality: *energeia*
actualization: *energeia*
actually: *energeiâi*
admit of: *epidekhesthai*
admixture: *epimixia, epimixis, mixis*
affected, be: *paskhein*
affection: *pathêsis, pathos*
affective: *pathêtikos*
affirmation: *kataphasis*
agree: *homologein*
aim: *skopos*
alter: *metaballein*
ambiguity: *homônumia*
ambiguous: *homônumos*
ancient: *arkhaios, palaios*
angel: *angelos*
animal: *zôion*
animate (adj.): *empsukhos*
area: *topos*
argue: *kataskeuazein*
argument: *epikheirêsis*

art: *tekhnê*
assume: *hupotithenai*

bad: *kakos, phaulos*
beautiful: *kalos*
beginning: *arkhê*
being-affected (the category): *to paskhein*
being mutual causes: *sunaitios*
being-positioned (the category): *to keisthai*
belong: *huparkhein*
birth: *genesis*
bodily: *sômatikos, sômatoeidês*
body: *sôma*
boundary: *horos*
bring together: *sunagein*
by accident: *ek tautomatou*
by-product: *parakolouthêma*
by-product, be a: *parakolouthein*

call: *onomazein*
capacity: *dunamis, epitêdeiotês*
case ending: *ptôsis*
category: *katêgoria*
cause (n.): *aitia, aition*
cause, without: *ek tautomatou*
chance: *tukhaios*
change (n.): *metabolê*
change (v.): *alloioun, kinein, metaballein*
characteristic, be: *huparkhein*
choice: *proairesis*
civic: *politikos*
classify with: *suntattein*
coexist: *sunistanai, sunuphistasthai*
coextensive, be: *exisazein*

coherence: *sunekheia*
combination: *sumplokê*
combine: *sumplekein*
come under: *telein*
commentator: *exêgêtês*
common practice: *sunêtheia*
common usage: *sunêtheia*
compare: *sunkrinein*
comparison: *sunkrisis*
completed: *teleios*
composed, be: *sunistanai, sunkeisthai*
comprehension: *gnôsis*
conceive of: *noein*
concept: *noêma*
conception: *ennoia*
conceptual: *ennoêmatikos*
conclude: *sunagein*
conclusion: *sumperasma*
concomitant: *parakolouthêma*
concomitant, be: *parakolouthein*
condition, be in a: *diakeimai*
condition: *diathesis*
conditioned: *diathetos*
congenital: *ek genetês*
consider: *theôrein*
consist of: *sunistanai*
constitutive: *sumplêrôtikos*
constitutive, be: *sumplêroun*
contemplative: *theôrêtikos*
continuity: *sunekheia, to sunekhes*
continuous: *sunekhês*
contradistinction: *antidiastolê*
contrariety: *enantiôsis, enantiotês*
contrary (n.): *to enantion*
contrary (adj.): *enantios*
contribute to: *sumplêroun*
co-ordinate: *antidiêirêmena*
copy: *mimêma*
corollary: *porisma*
cosmos: *kosmos*
count with: *suntattein*

counter-objection: *antiparastasis*
create a name: *onomatopoiein*

death: *thanatos*
decision: *proairesis*
decrease (v.): *meioun*
defect (n.): *endeia*
deficiency: *endeia*
deficient: *endeês*
definable: *horistos*
define: *aphorizein, horizein*
defined, to be: *horistos*
definite: *hôrismenos*
definitely: *aphôrismenôs*
definition: *horismos, horos, logos*
demarcation: *to horizon*
demonstrative: *apodeiktikos*
deprive: *sterein*
derivatively: *kata sumbebêkos*
destroy: *phtheirein*
destruction: *phthora*
destructive: *phthartikos*
diatonic: *diatonikos*
differ: *diapherein*
difference: *diaphora*
different: *diaphoros*
differentia: *diaphora*
differentiation: *diaphora*
difficulty: *aporia, to aporon*
dimension: *diastasis*
dimensional: *diastatos*
diminish: *meiousthai*
diminution: *meiôsis, phthisis*
discourse (n.): *logos*
discrete: *diôrismenos*
disposed, be: *diakeimai*
disproportion: *ametria*
dissimilar: *anomoios*
dissimilarity: *to anomoion*
distance: *diastasis*
distinct, be: *diakrinesthai*
distinction: *diakrisis*

English–Greek Glossary   185

distinctive: *idios*
distinctive feature: *idion*
distinguish: *antidiastellein, diakrinein*
distinguished: *diôrismenos*
distinguishing: *diakrisis*
divide: *diairein, epidiairein*
divine: *theios*
divinity: *to theion*
divisible: *meristos*
division: *diairesis, tmêma*
do away with: *aphanizein*
draw conclusions: *sumperainein*

easily lost: *euapoblêtos*
element: *stoikheion*
eliminate: *anairein*
eliminate along with: *sunanairein*
end (n.): *telos*
end-product: *telos*
endow with form: *eidopoiein*
engage in philosophy: *philosophein*
ensouled: *empsukhos*
entail: *suneispherein*
enumerate: *aparithmeisthai*
enumeration: *aparithmêsis*
equal, be: *exisazein*
eradication: *phthora*
essence: *ousia*
essentially: *ousiôdôs*
establish: *kataskeuazein*
ethical: *êthikos*
everyday usage: *sunêtheia*
exist: *huphistanai, sunistanai*
existence: *huparxis, hupostasis*
explain: *exêgeisthai*
extended: *diastatos*
extension: *diastasis*

faculty: *dunamis*
false: *pseudês*
falsehood: *pseudos*
falsity: *pseudos*

figure: *skhêma*
fine: *kalos*
finite, be: *perainesthai*
follow: *akolouthein, sumbainein*
follow (from): *parakolouthein*
force (n.): *hormê*
foresee: *pronoein*
form (n.): *eidos, idea*
formative: *eidopoios*
formulate a term: *onomatopoiein*
from birth: *ek genetês*
further divide: *epidiairein*

general (adj.): *katholikos*
generation: *genesis*
generic: *genikos*
genitive [case]: *hê genikê*
genus: *genos*
genus, highest: *genikôtaton genos*
geometer: *geômetrês*
geometry: *geômetria*
give: *apodidonai*
giving: *apodosis*
gnomon: *gnômôn*
goal: *telos*
god: *theos*
godlike: *theios*
good: *agathos, kalos, spoudaios*
grow: *auxanein*
growth: *auxêsis*

happen: *sumbainein*
hard to lose: *dusapoblêtos*
harmful: *kakôtikos*
heaven: *ouranos*
heavenly: *ouranios*
heteronymy: *heterônumia*
homonymous: *homônumos*
homonymy: *homônumia*
hypothesize: *hupotithenai*

idea: *ennoia, epinoia*

illumination: *ellampsis*
immortal: *athanatos*
immortality: *athanasia*
implication: *akolouthêsis*
imply along with: *suneisagein*
impulse: *hormê*
inactive: *anenergêtos*
inanimate: *apsukhos*
incapacity: *adunamia*
incidentally: *kata sumbebêkos*
include under: *anagein*
incorporeal: *asômatos*
increase (n.): *auxêsis*
increase (v.): *auxanein*
indefinite: *aoristos*
indefiniteness: *aoristia*
indeterminate: *aoristos*
indeterminateness: *aoristia*
indicate: *sêmainein*
individual: *atomos*
indivisible: *ameristos*
induction: *epagôgê*
infima species: *eidikôtaton eidos*
infinite: *apeiros*
injustice: *adikia*
instruction: *didaskalia*
intellect: *dianoia, nous*
intellective: *dianoiêtikos, noeros*
intelligible: *noêtos*
intelligize: *noein*
intensification: *epitasis*
intermediaries, without: *amesos*
intermediates, with: *emmesos*
internal speech: *endiathetos logos*
invent: *epinoein*
irrational: *alogos*

just (adj.): *dikaios*
justice: *dikaiosunê*

kind (n.): *eidos*
knowable: *epistêtos*

knowledge: *gnôsis*

lack: *endeia*
lacking: *endeês*
later in origin: *husterogenês*
learning: *mathêsis*
letter: *stoikheion*
lie: *keisthai*
light (n.): *phôs*
likeness: *eikôn*
limit (n.): *peras*
local: *kata topon*
location: *topos*
locomotion: *phora*
logical: *logikos*
logician: *logikos*
long-lasting: *polukhronios*
lost with difficulty: *dusapoblêtos*

made up, be: *sunkeisthai*
make coextensive: *exisoun*
mathematical objects: *ta mathêmatika*
matter (n.): *hulê*
mean (adj.): *phaulos*
mean (v.): *sêmainein*
meaning: *sêmainomenon*
mental representation: *phantasia, to phantaston*
method: *methodos*
mind (n.): *nous, psukhê*
mixture: *epimixia, mixis*
more recent: *neôteros*
mortal: *thnêtos*
mortality: *to thnêton*
motion: *kinêsis*
move (intrans.): *kineisthai*
move (trans.): *kinein*
movement: *kinêma*

name (n.): *onoma, onomasia*
name (v.): *onomazein*
narrow (v.): *meioun*

natural: *kata phusin, phusikos*
natural scientist: *ho phusikos, phusiologos*
natural sequence: *akolouthia*
nature: *phusis*
negation: *apophasis*
noble: *kalos*
not in a relation: *askhetos*
not overseen by providence: *apronoêtos*
not subject to change: *ametablêtos*
notion: *ennoia*
noun: *onoma*
number: *arithmos*

objection: *enstasis*
obliteration: *aphanismos*
observe: *theôrein*
occur: *sumbainein*
old: *palaios*
operation: *energeia*
oppose: *antidiairein, antidiastellein, antitattein, antitithenai*
opposed: *enantios*
opposed, be: *antikeisthai*
opposite (n.): *to antikeimenon*
opposite (adj.): *enantios*
opposition: *antidiastolê, antithesis*
orator: *rhêtôr*
order (n.): *taxis*
origin: *genesis*
own (adj.): *idios*

paronymous: *parônumos*
paronymous name: *parônumia*
part (n.): *meros, morion*
partake: *metekhein*
participate: *metekhein*
particle: *morion*
particular: *merikos*
parts, without: *amerês*
patient (n.): *to paskhon*
peculiar: *idios*
perceive: *noein*

perceptible: *aisthêtos*
perception: *aisthêsis, antilêpsis*
perceptive: *aisthêtikos*
perfect (adj.): *teleios*
perfect (v.): *teleioun*
perfection: *teleiotês*
perfective: *teleiôtikos*
perish: *phtheiresthai*
perish along with: *sumphtheiresthai, sunapollusthai*
philosopher: *philosophos*
philosophy: *philosophia*
physical: *phusikos*
place (n.): *taxis, topos*
portion: *meros, morion*
position (n.): *taxis, thesis*
position, be in (a): *keisthai*
posterior, the: *to husteron*
potential: *dunamis*
potentiality: *to dunamei*
potentially: *dunamei*
practical wisdom: *phronêsis*
predicate (n.): *to katêgoroumenon*
predicate (v.): *katêgorein*
predicated, be: *huparkhein*
predication: *katêgoria*
pre-exist: *prouparkhein*
premiss (n.): *protasis*
premiss (v.): *hupotithenai*
principle: *arkhê*
prior: *proteros*
priority: *to proteron*
privation: *sterêsis*
privative: *sterêtikos*
proof: *apodeixis*
propensity: *epitêdeiotês*
property of, be a: *huparkhein*
prove: *apodeiknunai, kataskeuazein*
providence: *pronoia*
pupil: *mathêtês*
purificatory: *kathartikos*
purposive: *proairetikos*

puzzle (n.): *aporia, to aporon*
puzzle (v.): *aporein*

qualification: *to poion*
qualified: *poios, to poion*
qualitative change: *alloiôsis*
quality: *poiotês*
quantity: *posotês, to poson*

raise a difficulty: *aporein*
rational: *logikos, logoeidês*
rationality: *to logikon*
ready: *epitêdeios*
reason: *aitia, logos*
reason, to: *dianoeisthai*
reasoning: *logos*
receptive, be: *epidekhesthai*
reciprocate: *antistrephein*
reciprocation: *antistrophê*
rectilinear motion: *euthuphoria*
reductio ad absurdum: *eis atopon apagôgê*
reductio ad impossibile: *eis adunaton apagôgê*
regard as: *theôrein*
relation: *skhesis*
relationship: *skhesis*
relative: *pros ti*
remove: *anairein*
response: *apantêsis*
result: *akolouthein*
rhetoric: *rhêtorikê*

sameness: *tautotês*
section: *logos, tmêma*
see: *theôrein*
self-warranting: *autopistos*
sense (n.): *sêmainomenon*
sense-perception: *aisthêsis*
separate (v.): *diairein, diakhôrizein, diorizein, merizein*
separation: *diakrisis*
set against: *antitattein, antitithenai*

shape (n.): *morphê, onkos*
share in: *metekhein*
short-lived: *oligokhronios*
show: *apodeiknunai*
showing scant movement: *oligokinêtos*
signify: *sêmainein*
situated, be: *keisthai*
skill: *tekhnê*
skilled speaker: *rhêtorikos*
solid: *sôma*
solution: *epilusis*
solve: *epiluesthai*
sophist: *sophistês*
soul: *psukhê*
sound: *phônê*
space: *topos*
species: *eidos*
specific: *eidikos*
speech: *logos*
spoken speech: *prophorikos logos*
squaring: *tetragônismos*
state (n.): *hexis*
student: *mathêtês*
subaltern: *hupallêlos*
subdivide: *hupodiairein*
subdivision: *hupodiairesis*
subject (n.): *hupokeimenon, skopos*
subject matter: *hupokeimenon*
subsist: *huphistanai*
substance: *ousia*
substantial: *ousiôdês*
substratum: *hupokeimenon*
suffer: *paskhein*
suitable: *epitêdeios*
suited: *epitêdeios*
supervene: *episumbainein*
syllogism: *sullogismos*
symmetry: *summetria*
synthesis: *sunthesis*

take away as well: *sunanairein*
take away from: *aphairein*

teach: *didaskein*
teacher: *didaskalos*
teaching: *didaskalia, didaxis*
temperance: *sôphrosunê*
text: *lexis*
theorem: *theôrêma*
think of: *noein*
think up, of: *epinoein*
thought: *dianoia, epinoia*
three-dimensional, the: *trikhêi diastaton*
time: *khronos*
topic: *theôrêma*
true: *alêthês*
truth: *alêtheia, to alêthes*

unbounded: *apeiros*
uncaused: *automatos, ek tautomatou*
uncaused, the: *tautomaton*
unchanging: *ametablêtos*
unequal: *anisos*
unhypothetical: *anupothetos*
universal: *katholikos, katholou*
universally: *katholou*

universe: *to pan*
unlike: *anomoios*
utterance: *logos*

various: *diaphoros*
verb: *rhêma*
vice: *kakia*
virtue: *aretê*
virtued: *enaretos*
visible: *horatos*
vision: *horasis*
visualization: *phantasia*
volume: *sôma*

wane: *meiousthai*
want: *boulesthai*
when (the category): *pote*
where (the category): *pou*
will (n.): *boulêsis, thelêma*
will (v.): *boulesthai*
wisdom: *phronêsis*
wish (n.): *boulêsis*
wish (v.): *boulesthai*
word: *lexis, logos, onoma, phônê*

Greek–English Index

Note: References are to the page and line numbers of the *CAG* edition of the Greek text (indicated in the margins of the translation).

abebaios, insecure, 132,8
adespotos, masterless, 124,5.8
adiastatos, dimensionless, 85,5; extensionless, without extension, 85,31; 86,6.7; 90,13; 91,6; *adiastatôs*, extensionlessly, 90,13.20; 91,7
adikia, injustice, 108,6; 157,22; 188,2; 189,24; 190,10; 191,8
adikos, unfair, 188,4
adunamia, incapacity, 134,9–15; 138, fig.; 139,4–9; 143,13–144,26; 146,12–147,6; 157,7
agathos, good, 126,29–127,7; 145,11; 170,30–171,14; 187,25–188,16; 190,12–28
agnoein, be ignorant, in ignorance, 83,12; 102,25.28; 109,2; 132,13; 133,20; 193,27; not know, 145,28; 193,24.26; be at a loss, 145,31
agnoia, ignorance, 107,33–109,2
agnôsia, ignorance, 179,1
agnôstos, not known, 167,26
agônes, argument, 193,9
agorazein, buy, 127,27.28
aidôs, shame, 137,4.6.17; 138, fig.; 148, fig.; 148,4
aigokerôs, Capricorn, 128,5
aisthanesthai, perceive, 149,2; 162,2
aisthêsis, perception, 88,23.28; 105,6.23–26; 118,27.28; 121,21–123,31; 131,23; 134,18; 139,24; 191,19; sense-perception, 133,28.30; senses, 134,24.27; 135,21.22.27; 136,28.31; 138, fig.; 139,32; 147,24; 148, fig.; 148,11.13; 149,3.13.22.29
aisthêtikos, perceptive, 95,19; 122,10–18
aisthêtos, perceptible, 105,6.7.23–6; 118,27.28; 121,19–123,31; 130,30; 131,23; 134,1; 191,18

aitia, reason, 83,9.21; 86,16; 89,32; 93,18; 102,14.17; 133,8; 153,9; 168,17; 197,18; cause, 118,8; 128,11; 179,16
aitiatikos, accusative, 105,26; 106,11
aitiatos, caused, 105,9
aition, cause, 105,9; 194,6–24; 195,26; 196,9–16
akhroia, loss of colour, 151,8
akinêtos, motionless, 166,10
akolasia, licentiousness, 188,2.13
akolouthein, follow, 84,19; 112,7.8; 126,20–26; 128,25.26; 192,7–16; 193,7; 194,15.20; 196,3.7.11; 197,7.8; 200,23; result, 106,3
akolouthêsis, implication, 192,6–13; 194,6–18; 195,26; 196,2–14; 197,7
akolouthia, natural sequence, 181,10
akroasis; *hê phusikê akroasis*, the physics course, 84,13; 153,25; 166,3; 168,31; 197,15; 198,17; 199,11
akroatês, reader, 102,25
aktis, ray, 118,21
alêtheia, truth, 185,8–27; 186,13.15; 187,16; 198,10–16; *têi alêtheiâi*, truly, 187,11; *kata alêtheian*, in truth, in reality, 92,12; 99,23; 108,2; 156,12
alêthês, true, 104,9–23; 117,2.10; 126,22.24; 128,14–28; 129,13; 131,7; 152,26; 157,2; 169,22–31; 179,37; 180,3; 185,6.7; 186,3–29; 187,1–24; 194,17–25; 200,17; *to alêthes*, truth, 97,33; 171,9
alloiôsis, qualitative change, 87,27; 197,11; 198,22; 199,6; 200,14–202,10; 204,19
alloios, different in qualities, qualitatively, 201,8; 202,7.9
alloioun, change, change (in) quality, qualities, qualitatively, 154,15; 164,13; 200,11–201,32; 203,12.16; *to alloioun*, agent of qualitative change, 201,32

alogos, irrational, 141,26; 159,8
amathia, illiteracy, 179,1.4
amblus, obtuse, 120,15.19.20
amerês, without parts, 90,12; 141,14; 152,7
ameristos, indivisible, 163,15
amesos, without intermediaries, 172,13; 173,27; 182,10.13.19
ametablêtos, unchanging, 183,27; not subject to change, 184,5
ametria, disproportion, 188,8–16; 190,31.32
amianton, asbestos, 139,13
amoibê, retribution, 126,29
amphibolos, doubtful, 177,27; *to amphibolon*, ambiguity, 119,24; doubtful case, 178,6
amudros, vague, 132,8
amuêtos, not initiated, 84,10
anabasis, way up, 103,11
anablepein, see again, 169,19; recover sight, 184,17
anagein, include under, 88,8; 136,35; 92,16; 100,26; 107,7–18; 108,22; 144,7–14; 149,10; 152,27; 153,9.11.19; 158,8.9; 161,32; 162,1.21–32; 165,23; 197,24
anairein, eliminate, 94,14.16; 117,6.17.18; 121,15–122,2.4; 133,14; 169,10; 193,19.20; remove, 104,35
anakampsis, conversion, 106,19
anakamptein, be reversible, 89,4.5
anakeisthai, be lying, 107,19
anaklinesthai, be lying, 107,8–27; 164,19.20
anaklisis, lying, 106,27; 107,5.8.10.23
analogein, be analogous, 86,4
analuein, decompose, 154,8
analusis, analysis, 85,33
anamartêtos, not subject to error, 171,14
ananetos, not admitting of abatement, 159,22
anapherein, compare, 94,13.17.22; refer, 96,28; 158,10; classify, 136,11.34; 137,3.10; 138, fig.; 139,27.29; 148,1.4; 148, fig.; 149,6.8; 162,8.11; 166,2
anaphora, reference, 94,19
anaplasma, construct, 85,8; creation, 103,19
anaplêroun, fill in, 155,32

anapologêtos; *to anapologêton*, indefensibility, 129,20
anatolai, rising point, 86,18; the east, 118,12.17
anatolikôteros, more to the east, 118,17
andrias, statue, 137,28
aneideos, formless, 83,15
anendeês, in need of nothing, 166,10
anenergêtos, inactive, 145,21
anepidektos, in such a way that it does not admit, 160,29.30
anepistreptos, indifferent, 141,34
anepitatos, not admitting of intensification, 159,22
anêr, man, 111,21; 121,1; 156,13; 184,9.13; 197,12; 205,19; husband, 205,19; *phusikos anêr*, natural scientist, 198,15; *logikos anêr*, logician, 198,19
angelos, angel, 159,8; 196,26
aniatos, inveterate, 142,14
anisos, unequal, 102,1.4.5; 110,3.19–111,7; 112,6–25; 113,25; 153,3.5
anô, up, 99,17–100,26; 164,25; 199,8; 204,13; upper, 165,15; *anôtaton genos*, most generic genus, 197,1
anoêtos, senseless, 145,16; devoid of intellect, 171,12
anoia, folly, 188,15
anomoios, unlike, 102,7.8; dissimilar, 110,2; 161,10.15.18.26; *to anomoion*, dissimilarity, 161,12.15
anopherês, borne upwards, 128,7
antereidein, support, 104,35
anthrôpeios, human, 189,24
anthrôpos, man, human (being), person, people, 94,26; 95,16; 98,12; etc.
antidiairein, oppose, 199,12; 204,7; *antidiêirêmena allêlois eidê*, co-ordinate species, 196,18
antidiastellein, distinguish, 135,12.13; oppose, 143,5.7
antidiastolê, opposition, 143,9; contradistinction, 171,3
antikeisthai, be opposed, 126,23; 128,27; 167,19; 168,8–23, etc.; *to antikeimenon*, opposite, 104,10; 126,20; 144,5; 168,8–18; 169,2; 177,23; 179,2–12; 187,27.29; opposition, 168,13
antikinein, move in return, 103,31

antilêpsis, perception, 149,14
antiparastasis, counter-objection, 94,9; 96,24.25; 98,2
antiphasis, opposed, opposing, alternative, 146,7.9
antistrephein, reciprocate, 105,21.23.25; 106,17; 108,9; 111,13-112,27; 114,5.10; 115,2-20; 116,4.6; 117,5; 122,1; 181,1.3; 192,3-13; 194,11-23; 195,25; 196,2-15; 197,6; reciprocation, 113,3; reverse, 193,16; turn around, 116,14
antistrophê, reciprocation, 105,28; 106,16.20.21; 111,14.19; 113,7; 115,6.14; 116,10.14; 192,10
antitattein, oppose, 146,10; 188,5; set against, 194,2
antithesis, opposition, 169,4.7.11.12.16.17.21.31.32.34; 170,5.15; 171,18.19.28; 172,2.10.11; 176,25; 177,8.11.15; 181,7; 182,7.9.19; 183,15.19; 185,22
antitithenai, oppose, 194,2; 195,11.13; set against, 204,11
antônumia, pronoun, 185,14.16.19
anupothetos, unhypothetical, 141,8
aoristia, indefiniteness, 95,13; indeterminateness, 111,5
aoristos, indeterminate, 87,22; indefinite, 95,8-21; 96,22; 11,5; *aoristôs*, indeterminately, 131,9.18.19; 132,24; in an indefinite way, 132,9
apagôgê: eis adunaton apagôgê, *reductio ad impossibile*, 97,16; *eis atopon apagôgê*, *reductio ad absurdum*, 126,18.19; 128,29
apantêsis, response, 130,2
aparallaktôs, in every detail, 159,9; exactly, 160,2.8.18.24.26; without some variation, 160,12
aparemphatos, infinitive, 165,26.29; 185,17
aparithmeisthai, enumerate, 86,13; 89,10; 92,13; 191,19; 193,33; 198,26; 199,28
aparithmêsis, enumeration, 172,3.7; 181,14
apartan, be foreign to, 168,3
apeinai, be absent, 172,16; 173,25; 174,18; 182,2.15.23
apeiros, infinite, 84,12.13.14.31; unbounded, 85,29

aphairein, eliminate, 97,7; take away, from, 114,22-28; strip away, 116,8; rob of, 147,16; subtract, 203,3.14
aphanismos, obliteration, 200,5
aphanizein, do away with, 113,16
aphôrismenôs, definitely, 132,2.15.16; 183,6-30; in particular, 172,18
aphorizein, define, 95,12.17.21; 96,2.4.21; *aphôrismenos*, discrete, 94,1; separate, 99,5; 108,11
aphôtistos, unilluminated, 118,12.17
aplatês, without breadth, 85,2.9.13.23; 90,19; 141,13.15
apodeiknunai, prove, 91,21; 99,18; 126,19; 131,5; 132,13; 141,17; show, 93,20
apodeiktikos, demonstrative, 192,21
apodeixis, proof, 86,27; 104,19; 141,10.14.16; 193,4; proving, 131,5
apodidonai, give, 83,8; 93,17.19.24; 105,15, etc.; formulate, 109,21; describe as, 112,23; assign, 161,21
apodokimazein, reject, 101,25; 161,6.8
apodosis, giving, 105,24.26; 106,8.11.21; 115,9.14.15; statement, 113,4
apokatastasis, return, 86,18; return to original position, 93,1; returning, 111,16
apokathistanai (intransitive forms), return, 111,18; give way, 136,33; 137,2; 138, fig.; 147,30; 148,3; (transitive forms), bring over, 184,11
apophainesthai, make statements, state, 104,2; 132,26; 157,1; 184,26; talk, 156,28
apophasis, negation, 68,15.22; 146,13.17; 169,6.20; 170,4.15; 172,8.24.27; 177,3.4.12; 180,11.14; 181,10.12.13; 185,4.20.22; 186,6.16; 187,12.15.22.23
aporein, raise a difficulty, puzzle, question, 98,25; 117,11; 133,1; 154,32; 158,23; 186,9; 198,7
aporia, difficulty, problem, puzzle, 122,24; 124,10; 129,29; 131,21; 135,5; 155,10; 162,3.7; 198,10; puzzlement, 133,1; want, 147,19
aporon, to, puzzle, 124,4; difficulty, 142,23
apostasis, separation, 117,22.24; 118,1; 196,25.28; 197,2; departure, 118,10; 128,5; 171,8
apotelein, produce, 155,21; render, 161,18
apotelesma, outcome, 119,15

apotunkhanein, fail, 127,33
apousia, absence, 169,2; 180,8.15.16.18; 191,1.3
apronoêtos, not overseen by providence, 127,11
apsukhos, inanimate, 136,1; 137,20.23.24; 138, fig.; 139,2; 151,18.19; 189,20; 192,1; 196,27
aptaistos, well-grounded, 132,9; absolutely stable, 140,23; stable, 141,3
araios, open-textured, 153,17.20
araiousthai, become rarefied, 153,28
aretê, virtue, 108,5.7.24.26.28.31.35; 134,22.23.29; 138, fig.; 141,23.25.28; 142,2.3; 146,1; 157,15; 184,6.9.15; 188,9.15; 190,11; 191,3.9; 204,26
argos, idle, 156,9
aristeros, left, on the left, 89,7; 103,1.21.26.27; 104,27; 105,11; 108,20; 164,25; 165,16; 168,24; 169,27; 170,7.8; 171,21; 177,21; 187,6; 192,9; 204,15
arithmein, count, 92,5; list, 205,28
arithmêta, ta, things that are, can be, counted, 89,11.14
arithmêtikê, arithmetic, 141,5
arithmos, number, 83,22; 84,2.3.9; 87,32; 88,1.11.15; 89,9–31; 92,4.6; 95,10.23; 96,9; 98,9.12.13.29; 102,3; 124,3; 161,23; 173,12–16; 174,9.10; 181,20; 182,17; 184,25.26; 189,26.27.29; 190,1; 191,20; 198,6.9
arkhaios, ancient, 126,2
arkhê, principle, 86,2.5.7; 141,7.10.11.17.19; 197,14; beginning, start, 86,14; 106,18; 133,1; 156,26; 167,22; 168,8; 197,22.23; *ex arkhês*, original, 199,16.17; 203,16
arkhein, rule, 103,29; 105,5; *arkhesthai*, start, begin, 86,19; 89,5.7; 91,12; 96,25; 103,13; 105,19; 111,18; 118,15; 124,20; 134,2; 166,18.19; 167,21; 169,7; 170,15; 184,14
artios, even, 172,13; 173,10–28; 174,9; 181,20; 182,17
artiotês, symmetry, 179,22
asebês, impious, 127,10
askhêmatistos, shapeless, 83,15
askhetos, not in a relation, 163,13; 168,20.26

asômatos, incorporeal, 83,14; 121,30; 170,1.7; 189,25; 196,25
astron, star, 123,3
astronomia, astronomy, 141,5.9
asummetria, asymmetry, 188,7.8
asustatos, cannot occur, 124,30
ataktos, disorderly, 127,8.11
atelês, imperfect, 166,8
athanasia, immortality, 131,6
athanatos, immortal, 126,24; 128,18.22.24.27; 145,17
athetein, rule out, 129,5; reject, 193,31
atomos, individual, 95,22–96,21; 125,4; 161,22.26
atopia, absurdity, 127,10; 129,18.20; 130,2
atopos, absurd, 87,19; 97,28; 105,14, etc.; *to atopon*, absurdity, 106,2; 115,23; 124,20.21, etc.; *eis atopon apagôgê*, reductio ad absurdum, 126,18.19; 128,29
automatos, uncaused, 127,14; *ek tautomatou*, without cause, 127,12.13.18; 128,10; by accident, accidental, 127,23.29
autophronêsis, absolute wisdom, 146,1
autopistos, self-warranting, 141,7.10.18
auxanein / auxein (transitive forms), increase, 112,19.20; 203,12; broaden, 113,9; (intransitive forms), wax, 118,10; 128,4; grow, 200,2.7.19.27; 201,8.9.21.28; 202,5.6.8.9
auxêsis, increase, 87,27; 199,6.26; 200,1.2.16; 201,6; 203,17.20.23; 204,8; growth, 201,10.27
axiôma, mark of appreciation, 127,5; worth, 140,15

badisis, act of walking, 98,23
banausos, manual, 141,1.22
barus, heavy, 99,8.27; 119,7; 179,30; 182,3; 188,6
bathos, depth, 84,12; 85,29; 88,9; 91,7; 101,15.16; 152,16; 165,8; interior, 84,27; 137,14; 139,21; 201,30; third dimension, 86,8; 91,6; *dia bathous*, deep, 136,23.24; 137,12; 138, fig.; *kata bathos*, internal, 137,18
biblion, book, 127,8.26.28.29; 167,22.23; 199,21

bios, life, 126,28.30.31; 127,1.13; 128,15.16.17.20
bioun: *ta bebiômena*, conduct during one's lifetime, 127,1.9; 128,17
boulê, deliberation, 145,25.26.27.29.30; 146,2
boulêsis, wish, 145,13; will, 145,15.25; willing, 145,16
boulesthai, want, wish, 86,24; 89,23; 93,16; 99,19, etc.; be bent on, 99,19; please, 113,15; see fit, 113,16; mean, 160,6; will, 145,15–24
bouleuein, deliberate, 145,25.27.31
brakhus, brief, 84,10; short, 88,13; 92,18.22; 98,5.7; *brakhutatos*, least, 159,6

daktulios, ring, 165,19; 205,1
daktulos, digit, 111,22; finger, 165,19
deiknunai, show, 85,9; 86,1.23; 94,8, etc.; give, provide, a proof, 177,19.25.27; display, 123,13
deiktikos, such as to prove, 121,10
deiktos, can be, capable of being, pointed to, 88,21.23.26.27; 92,2
dekhesthai, receive, 83,16.17; 175,4; 182,28; 183,7; admit, admit of, 110,22; 152,28; 153,1; get, 118,9; take on, in, 154,20; 139,6; absorb, 134,15; 144,1
dektikos, receptive, able to, capable of, receiving, that can receive, 97,22.23; 101,10.11; 116,8.18; 154,17; 157,28; 161,23; 182,25; 183,6.26; 185,27; 186,13; 187,18; 198,6–12; capable of, 122,1; *ho dektikos*, recipient, 179,2; 180,17; 181,29; 182,2; *to dektikon*, receptivity, 159,7
desmoun, bind, 122,30
despoteia, ownership, 103,14
despotês, master, 103,12.14.23; 105,5.6, etc.
deuteros, second, 83,8–22, etc.; later, 84,1; latter, 123,20; 174,4; secondary, 125,23; 129,3
dexamenê, receptacle, 202,6
dexios, right, on the right, to the right, 89,5.6; 102,32; 103,1.21.26.28; 104,27; 105,11; 106,5.6; 108,20; 164,25; 165,16; 168,23; 169,23–170,8; 171,21; 177,21; 186,23; 192,9; 204,14
diagônios, diagonal, 125,2

diagramma, diagram, 126,13; 193,2.5; 202,14
diairein, divide, 83,21; 84,5; 86,31–33; 87,16; 90,14.18.19.28; 91,6.11; 98,23.24; 134,8; 135,34; 136,18; 147,4–6; 167,23; 169,22; 170,4; 173,14; 183,18; 186,11.14.17; 187,13.14.20.24; 197,3; 198,19; 199,2.10; separate, 84,7; 89,25; 154,11.12
diairesis, division, 87,18; 88,17; 90,15; 91,8.28; 92,4; 93,15; 96,6; 102,16; 105,1; 124,27; 133,8.9; 134,12; 136,21; 137,32; 138,2; 140,11.12; 148,7; 156,12; 163,10; 164,8.10; 169,3.23.25; 172,12.21; 196,24; 197,4.5; 198,28
diakeimai, be in a condition, 135,8.10; 142,11.25; 143,29; 144,1.15; 146,20; be disposed, 137,25; 151,21; 152,24
diakhôrizein, separate, 113,31
diakrinein, distinguish, 170,20; 172,1.6.9, etc.; *diakrinesthai*, be distinct, 109,11
diakrisis, separation, 96,6; distinguishing, 174,23.24; distinction, 177,15
dialambanein, intersperse, 154,10
dialegesthai, address, 153,20; carry on conversations, 193,25; discuss, 107,34; talk, 134,6; 156,16; 166,31; 167,25; 199,23; say, 198,18
dialogos, dialogue, 104,19
dialuein, dissolve, 154,6
diametros, diameter, 99,26.30; 100,1.19.26; 202,13.18; 203,6; *ek diametrou*, diametrical, 103,31; *kata diametron*, diametrically, 118,13
dianoeisthai, reason to, 171,11
dianoia, intellect, 85,8; thought, 103,19
dianoiêtikos, intellective, 171,10
diapherein, differ, 97,2; 111,27; 125,14; 140,15.18; 141,31; 155,6.19.27.28; 156,4; 166,21.22; 186,15; 187,12
diaphora, difference, 105,11; 132,4.12; 172,11; different kind, 137,26; 165,1; differentia, 147,19.21; 172,4.8.10; differentiation, 195,11
diaphoros, different, 95,28.29; 100,9; 104,8; 140,10; 155,26; 166,25; 172,5; 176,6–24; 182,7; 204,12; various, 113,26; 174,21; 191,19; 193,33; *diaphorôs*, in different ways, 140,8.9.11

diaskedannunai, disperse, 154,2
diastasis, dimension, 83,16; 84,11.24.32; 85,1.4.30; 152,8.10.16; 165,3–15; 204,13; extension, 90,21; 101,15.16; distance, 99,26; 100,20.25
diastatos, dimensional, 83,16; 84,3; 88,6; 95,27; extended, 85,31; 95,26; 96,4
diathêkê, will, 124,6
diathesis, condition, 90,6.7; 106,22.23; 134,9.21; 135,2.3.9.11.13.15; 138, fig.; 139,1; 140,18.19.20; 142,16; 143,5–8.28; 149,9; 160,17; 161,31; 162,2.12–15.27; 191,10; 205,10
diathetos, conditioned, 106,23; 162,2.13.14
diatonikos, diatonic, 113,28
diaxainein, card, 153,17
didaskalia, instruction, 87,24; 102,16; 105,12; 130,31; 134,2; 198,2; teaching, 102,13; 133,20; 139,31; 140,5; 167,26; 168,2; 174,23; 194,29; 198,3; exposition, 102,23; presentation, 157,23
didaskalos, teacher, 103,14; 133,15; 141,29; 164,17
didaskein, teach, 120,26; 130,15; 168,9.12; 174,21; 177,15
didaxis, teaching, 166,20
diistanai (intransitive forms), be separated, 99,30; 100,1.25; be apart, 99,20.23.31; 100,22; 153,1
dikaios, just, 126,30; 159,15
dikaiosunê, justice, 108,6; 141,27.28; 158,24; 159,2–10; 188,1.3.11; 189,24; 190,10; 191,8
dikaiotêrion, place of correction, 126,27
diorismos, boundary, 85,10.21.22
diorizein, separate, 85,17.18.19; state an opinion, 197,21; *diôrismenos*, discrete, 84,5.7.9; 88,11.12.13.15; 89,23.26.31; 92,4; 95,25; 96,6; 98,13.14.28; distinguished, 94,30; *to horizon*, demarcation, 85,12
dipêkhus, two cubits [long], 93,8.12.21; 94,2; 95,6; 96,16; 103,5; 109,5.17.18
diplous, twofold, 133,21.29.31
dipous, bipedal, 116,8.13.17
dogmatizein, state a doctrine, 108,32
dokêsis, opinion, 132,9
dotikê, dative, 105,25; 106,10.17.20.23; 178,1

doulos, slave, 103,12.13.22; 105,5; 111,25.26; 115,9; 116,6.7.11.12.15.20; 117,8; 124,5.7.8.10.13; 205,21
doxazein, opine, 171,11
dromeus, boxer, 143,24.25.27
dromikê, running, 157,13
dromikos, suited to boxing, 143,19.20.24.25; 146,19; 157,7.12
dunamis, strength, 111,22; power, 169,19; capacity, 134,9.13.14; 138, fig.; 139,4–18; 143,12–147,6; 157,7.9.10.13; potential, 123,25.26; 166,12; 168,31; 169,1; faculty, 179,27.31.34.36; value, 193,24.26; *dunamei*, potentially, 90,16.21; 91,8; 123,11–124,11; 134,14; 143,21.23.25; 166,13; 185,15.19; 199,19; as a potentiality, 123,23; potential, 131,27.28; in effect, 172,12; 180,30; *to dunamei*, potentiality, 87,22; the potential, 124,9; 166,6; 204,3
dusapoblêtos, lost with difficulty, hard to lose, 134,19.20.28; 135,3.31; 136,24.25; 138, fig.; 140,20; 148, fig.
duskinêtos, hard to shift, 142,14; 151,2
dusmai, the west, 118,11.18
dutikos, to the west, 118,11

eidikos, specific, 135,12.13; 180,10; 204,7; *eidikôtaton eidos*, *infima species*, 143,15; 196,26; 197,2
eidopoiein, endow with form, 135,25; 180,5; 190,30; 199,14
eidopoios, formative, 149,17.20
eidos, species, 84,8; 87,20.21; 88,3.10.11, etc.; kind, 88,10; 164,24; 168,16; 172,5; 181,14; 183,18; form, 102,18; 155,13–29; 168,30; 190,32; 199,16.17
eikôn, likeness, 84,19.20
eisagein, introduce, 196,16; *eisagesthai*, follow, 128,23; *eisagomenos*, beginner, 87,24; 153,19
eisagôgikos, introductory, 199,20
ekbasis, departure, 174,4
ekhein (the category), having, 164,4.5; 165,17; 204,22.26; 205,6
ekleipsis, eclipse, 118,8.18.21.23.24; 123,20.24.28.30
ekpheugein, escape, 91,23; 129,18; elude, 121,30

ekstasis, insanity, 151,4; mental disorder, 151,9
ektisis, retribution, 126,29
ektropê, deviation, 188,15
elattoun, narrow, 112,26
elenkhein, find fault, 93,26; refute, 104,13.18.19
êlithiotês, insentience, 188,14
ellampsis, illumination, 184,18
ellattôn, less, 111,4; 117,24; 120,15; 128,2; 159,12; 168,17; lesser, 105,5; 112,19; 120,17; 159,24; fewer, 134,11; 138,2; 198,28; smaller, 201,29; 202,6; 203,16; narrower, 112,20; 113,9; minus, 184,25.28
elleipein, have less, 84,29; fall short, 96,1; 190,26; *to elleipon*, defect, 191,5
elleipsis, inferiority, 105,3; defect, 191,3
emmesos, with intermediates, 172,14.15.22; 174,16; 182,22; 183,4.9.14
empoiein, produce, 134,18.19.21.24; 135,21.22.27; 136,14.19.27.28.32; 137,9; 138, fig.; 139,24; 147,23; 148, fig.; 148,11; 149,24.25.29
empsukhos, animate, 95,19; 135,16.18.32; 136,16; 137,21.26.30; 138, fig.; 139,1.2.9; 151,18.20; 152,19; 165,15; 189,19; 192,2; 196,27; ensouled, 121,24.26; 122,3.4
enantios, to enantion, contrary, 83,11; 93,14; 94,1, etc.; opposite, 110,10; 128,9; 158,1.2.8; 160,29; opposed, 157,31
enantiôsis, contrariety, 157,28; 188,24
enantiotês, contrariety, 99,16.19; 101,24; 107,32; 108,9.14.15.18.29; 110,11.12.13.14; 157,21.25.30.31; 158,3.17.18; 161,9; 163,2; 165,20; 166,33.34; 167,3.4.6.9; 170,24.26.27; 188,24
enaretos, virtued, 157,16
enargeia, evident fact, 154,13
endeês, lacking, 145,32; deficient, 166,7
endeia, deficiency, 145,27; lack, 146,2; defect, 188,4.8.10.12.13.17
endiathetos logos, internal language, 90,3.5
energeia, activity, 87,26.29; 166,29.32; 177,7; 180,22; action, 165,26.27.29; 166,6; actuality, 123,24.29; 134,14.16.21; 135,20; 137,19; 138, fig.; 166,13; 169,2;
actualization, 145,20; operation, 164,17; *kat' energeian*, in operation, 157,11; actual, 157,12; *energeiâi*, actual, 90,16.22; 123,29.30; 124,9.12; 131,28; 166,6; 204,4; actually, 123,11–27; 124,10; 143,25.27; 144,17; 166,14; 199,19; as an actuality, 143,22; in actuality, 143,24
energein, practice, 141,34; operate, 164,10
energês, in actuality, 123,13
enginesthai, occur, 136,7; arise, 136,19.26.29; 137,9; 138, fig.; 139,25; 147,25.28; 148,12; 148, fig.; 149,5; come to be (in), 149,12.15.16.23; 150,4; result, 148,2
eniausiaios, a year long, 93,3
eniautos, year, 86,21; 93,1
enistanai, counter, 135,6; *enestôs khronos*, the present, 164,23
ennoêmatikos, conceptual, 167,14
ennoia, notion, 85,23.25.28; 140,1.2.4; 168,2; conception, 141,8; idea, 170,19
enstasis, objection, 94,9.11; 96,23; 98,2; 117,15; 122,24
enudros, aquatic, 196,29
epagein, add, 86,14; 107,19; 111,28; 129,19; 130,2; 168,7; 198,10; supply, 122,24; come to, 156,7
epagôgê, induction, 187,26
epamphoterizein, go either way, 145,3.4.12; 146,4
epanapauesthai, rest content, 133,2; 156,9; 205,26
epanerkhesthai, return back, 86,19
epexerkhesthai, look into, 92,13
epharmozein, fit, 155,17.18; 160,3; apply (to), 159,5.7; 160,7.8.10; 161,20.27
ephistanai (transitive forms), understand, 118,7.18.23; gather, 164,9; (intransitive forms), stand, 120,13.14.16
epibolê, glance, 127,7
epidekhesthai, admit, admit of, 97,24.26; 99,21, etc.; accept, 99,14; be receptive of, 108,5.9.13.15; 157,25.28; receive, 152,19; take in, 139,7; take on, 198,13
epidiairein, divide, 88,18; further divide, 172,22
epigraphê, title, 102,14.30; 103,9.17; 133,8.22.31; 156,17

epigraphein, give a title, 102,29; 166,27; use a title, 102,32; 166,31
epikheirêsis, argument, 115,5; 122,15
epiluesthai, solve, 124,4; 131,20; 162,3; hold the solution, 124,9; say, add, in resolution of, 131,25; 198,10; resolve, 142,23; 155,10; 186,9; explain, 180,1
epilusis, solution, 162,4.7
epimixia, mixture, 110,26; admixture, 161,17
epimixis, admixture, 159,24
epinoein, think up, 113,20; invent, 119,5; think of, 119,17; 120,23; have an idea, 119,21
epinoia, thought, 116,27; idea, 119,14.15.18
epipedon, plane, 90,25.26.27.29; 155,25
epiphaneia, surface, 84,8.30; 85,25, etc.
epipolaios, superficial, 162,19; *epipolaioteron*, somewhat superficially, 162,3
epipolês, superficially, 108,3; superficial, 136,24; 137,20; 138, fig.
epiprosthêsis, blocking, 180,19
episêmainesthai, indicate, 90,4
epistasthai, know, 131,9; 141,24; 184,9
epistêmê, knowledge, 92,11; 105,7.8.9, etc.; science, 157,12; 192,19.21
epistêmôn, scholar, 92,11; knowledgeable, knowledgeable person, 105,8.9; 108,8; 109,1; 162,17; *epistêmonôs*, with [real] knowledge, 132,10
epistêmonikos, scientific, 148,10; *epistêmonikôs*, scientifically, 198,26
epistêtos, knowable, 105,7; 106,23.24; 108,8, etc.
episumbainein, supervene, 109,4; 133,18; 150,7; 171,8; 180,18; 187,17
epitasis, intensification, 135,15
epitêdeios, suitable, 120,19.21; 127,17.18.20; ready, 139,19; suited, 143,20
epitêdeiotês, propensity, 139,5.11.12.14; capacity, 143,26; 157,8
epiteinesthai, extend, 85,17; be at a high pitch, 134,30; intensify, 159,23
epitekhnêsis: *ex epitekhnêseôs*, artificially, 153,10; through an artificial process, 160,29
êremia, rest, 197,14
erêmê, by default, 115,21

ergon, job, 92,11; fruition, 119,20.22; deed, 126,29; *ergôi*, actually, 154,3
eruthêma, redness, 137,13; ruddiness, 147,29
eruthrian, turn red, 137,6; blush, 201,31
eruthrias, red-complexioned, 137,6
eruthriotês, blushing, 138, fig.
eruthros, red, 137,4.17; ruddy-complexioned, 137,15; 150,8
eruthrotês, redness, 148,5; 148, fig.
êthikos, ethical, 141,28
euapoblêtos, easily lost, 134,19.20; 135,1.4.31; 136,25.32; 138, fig.; 140,19; 147,30; 148,2; 148, fig.; 150,12
eudiairetos, readily divided, 98,21
eudoxia, great repute, 126,31
euektein, be in a good state, 134,29; 135,17
euexia, good state, 135,15.16
eukhroia, good complexion, 134,25; bloom, 136,5
eukinêtos, easily changed, 142,8
euôdia, perfume, 136,5
euporia, affluence, 126,31; finding the way, 133,1
euruthmôs, in an orderly fashion, 128,12
euthugrammos, rectilinear, 120,21.22.24.26; 155,22
euthuphoria, rectilinear motion, 199,8.10
euthus, to euthu, straightness, the straight, 154,32; 155,10; *eutheia ptôsis*, nominative case, 105,19; *eutheia, eutheia grammê*, straight line, 120,12.14.16; 152,3.9; 155,1.3.12.13.14. 15.17.18.19.20.21.23.26; 165,4.7.9.11
euthutês, straightness, 152,3.4; 154,29; 155,6; 156,2; 179,22
exallassein, differ, 155,15.21.28; depart from, 155,33
exameibein, change, 156,1
exaploun, disperse, 154,1
exêgeisthai, explain, 118,32
exêgêtês, commentator, 167,12
exelenkhein, find fault with, 93,27
exetasis, scrutiny, 127,1.9; 128,17
exetazein, examine, 89,19; 94,5; look at, 188,24
exisazein, be coextensive, 112,17; be equal, 115,16.18
exisoun, make coextensive, 112,18.19

exokhê, protuberance, 127,17; projection, 153,3
exonkousthai, acquire extension, 83,15

gê, earth, 96,1; 99,28; 100,3.7.12.19.20.24; 113,6; 118,19.20.28; 122,5; 126,27; 127,16; 182,4; 201,25
gelastikos, capable of laughter, 112,2
genesis, generation, 87,27; 171,15; 195,6; 197,10; 198,21; 199,5-29; 200,2.15; 201,24; 203,20; 204,8; origin, 199,3; birth, 151,1; *genesin ekhein*, be born, 195,16
genetê: *ek genetês*, congenital, 136,27; 138, fig.; 148, fig.; 151,3.4; from birth, 137,15; 147,11.29
genikos, generic, 93,19; 95,21.23; 135,13; 135,11; *genikôteron, genikôtaton genos*, higher, highest genus, 93,24; 143,14.15; 191,6.11; *hê genikê*, genitive [case], 105,24.25.27; 106,8-21; 111,28.29
genos, genus, 90,28; 93,19.22.24; 95,14; 96,10.12; 99,22; 100,23.26; 107,1-26; 133,30; 140,12; 143,4-144,13; 147,7; 151,11.13; 158,10; 162,5-24; 167,10.14; 168,8; 175,25.28; 176,7.14; 178,9-25; 179,6; 180,1.4.6.14; 189,14-191,14; 196,8.24; 197,1-19; 199,11
geômetrês, geometer, 84,11; 85,6; 113,24; 120,9.24; 131,4; 141,12.15; 193,3.12; 202,12
geômetria, geometry, 84,10; 141,4.6; 162,10; 193,2
glukus, sweet, 99,8; 104,5.11; 122,5; 149,21
glukutês, sweetness, 135,23; 136,26; 138, fig.; 140,4; 147,28; 149,16.28
gnômôn, gnomon, 202,8; 202,11.12; 203,9.11.15
gnôsis, comprehension, 132,8.9.11; 171,8; knowledge, 178,23-179,3
gônia, angle, 120,10.11.13.14.15.16.23; 155,13; 202,16.18
grammata, ta, writing, 193,5.15; *grammatôn anepistêmôn*, illiterate, 193,23
grammatikos, literate, 123,13.15.26.27; 134,14; 162,16; grammarian, 157,4; *grammatikê*, grammar, 134,15; 138, fig.; 139,6; 140,24; 142,21.22.24; 157,4.17; 162,18; 193,22; (female) grammarian, 157,17; *grammatikê tekhnê*, literacy, 123,14
grammê, line, 84,8; 85,2-86,14; 88,25; 90,8-91,29; 95,5-96,8; 98,28; 102,1; 141,11.15; 152,3-15; 155,1-25; 165,4-11; 193,3; 203,3
graphein, write, 126,3; draw, 203,2
grupotês, hookedness, 173,11.17.18
gumnasion, gymnasium, 160,10.12.14
gumnazein, conduct, 98,9; 170,20; deploy, 121,20.21; 177,18; rehearse, 202,15
gumnos, uncovered, 131,13
gunê, woman, 157,18; 205,19; wife, 205,1.16.17.19

haima, blood, 150,9; 201,10.12
haireisthai, choose, 145,30
hairesis, choosing, 145,30
hama, at once, 88,22-30; 92,3; 100,3; 202,13; at the same time, 97,14; 100,12; 119,1.3.4; 190,4; simultaneous, simultaneously, 117,2-20; 118,26; 119,6.9.22.24; 122,30; 123,1.5; 124,14; 131,22; 193,33; 194,1.29; 195,8-197,4
hamartôlos, wrongdoer, 126,30
haplous, single, 133,22; 155,23; simple, 163,4.5; 189,6.7; *haplôs*, simply, 88,7.9; 140,23; 162,17; 175,13; 176,23; 180,20; *tout court*, 93,23; 96,19, etc.; just, 90,25; 95,16; 120,9; even, 96,10; in a word, 189,19.22; without qualification, 195,6
hêdonê, pleasure, 141,33; 142,1
hektikos, hectic, 134,30
hektos, possessed, 106,21.22; 162,12.13
hêliakos, of the sun, 118,21
hêliokaia, exposure to the sun, 136,34; 138, fig.; 144,21
hêlios, sun, 85,11; 86,18.20.22; 93,2; 104,6; 118,8-19; 128,4.5; 138, fig.; 171,5.6; 200,27; 201,23
hêmisphairion, hemisphere, 100,8; 118,20
henikos, in the singular, 102,30; *henikôs*, in the singular, 103,7.8
henôsis, unity, 96,5
henoun, unite, 84,6; 86,12; 90,14; *to hênômenon*, unity, 98,17
hêpar, liver, 103,26.27

heterogenês, of another kind, 152,28; 153,1
heterokinêtos, moved to action by others, 133,4; 156,9
heterônumia, heteronymy, 105,2.3
heterotês, difference, 189,28; 190,18; 202,10
heurêma, discovery, 119,7
heuretis, discoverer, 113,22
hexadaktulos, with six fingers, 128,3
hexagônos, hexagonal, 120,23
hexis, state, 90,7; 106,21.22; 134,9.20, etc.
hippos, horse, 89,15; 95,16; 123,26, etc.
histanai (intransitive forms), stop, 92,15; stand, be standing, 104,7; 107,8.10.20.23.27; 164,19.22; be upright, 107,6
hodopoiêtikos, practical, 141,21
hodos, road, 85,24; 98,22; 133,2; path, 87,22; 166,6.28.33; 198,1; 199,18.19; route, 87,31
holos, whole, 84,26.27; 87,9, etc.
holotês, wholeness, 125,5.13; 205,23
homoios, same, 102,7.8; 153,24; 154,6.8; identical, 154,7; like, 105,2; 110,6.7.8; similar, 161,10.14.17.26; 203,10; *to homoion*, similarity, 161,12.15
homologein, agree, 84,22; be a matter of general agreement, 177,25; *to homologoumenon*, the agreed case, 178,5
homônumia, homonymy, 105,1; ambiguity, 166,30; 205,2
homônumos, homonymous, 95,16; ambiguous, 204,24; *homônumôs*, homonymously, 140,8.9.10; 156,22; 157,16; by the same name, 179,28
horasis, vision, 164,15.16
horatos, visible, 164,15.16
hôrismenôs, definitely, 131,8-18; 132,24; 183,5
horismos, definition, 85,2; 93,17.19.22.24; 99,21; 100,21.27; 105,13-106,3; 108,33; 109,13.21; 114,14; 115,19.20; 124,17-22; 125,18.28.31; 126,17.19; 129,7-131,7; 147,18; 159,4-9; 160,7-161,2; 164,7.9; 173,7.9.10; 190,32
horistos, to be defined, 130,23; definable, 159,1
horizein, define, 85,6.32; 93,3; 94,20; 95,15.19.28; 104,12; 109,14-27; 141,12; 173,11.14.17; 190,30.31; 197,14; 205,6; *hôrismenos*, definite, 94,20; 95,8.19; 103,33; 104,2.12; 190,32; 191,2
hormasthai, start out, 141.7.8.10.18
hormê, force, impulse, 127,15.16.19.25
horos, definition, 84,2; 105,18; 164,6; boundary, 89,24; 90,1-23; 91,2.4.19; 95,25
hugeia, health, 134,22-30; 138, fig.; 142,9; 158,24; 159,2-16; 160,10-16; 162,14; 174,2; 188,22; 189,21
hugiainein, be in good health, healthy, well, 181,21; 182,18; 185,27.28; 186,11.25.26; 187,18; 188,21; 189,10.12; *hoi hugiainontes*, healthy people, 104,5
hugiazein, heal, 127,33; 128,1.2; 145,6
hugieinos, healthy, 143,11.19; 144,21; 146,21.26.27; 159,16; 160,9.15.16.17; 162,16
hugiês, sound, 105,12; 124,13
hugrotês, fluidity, 154,12
hulê, matter, 83,14; 122,21; 128,4; 132,12
humenopteros, membrane-winged, 112,15
hupallêlos, subaltern, 125,2; 143,16; 191,7
huparkhein, belong, 101,4.25.29; 105,16; 116,9; 125,15; 149,24; 160,18; 161,9; 169,31; 171,2.27; 173,3-20; 183,30; be present, 95,17; 110,13-16; 147,22-9; 148, fig.; 149,15-24; 173,23.26.28; 174,19; 181,19.22.27; 182,1.12.21.27; 183,25.30; be a property of, 92,3; 101,5.7.8; 198,8; apply, 117,16; 167,8; be predicated, 115,29; be characteristic, 136,29; be, 85,19; 99,17; 107,32; 110,8; 117,11.17.20; 137,20; 157,21; 158,3; 167,8; 194,30; 196,9; 203,13; exist, with existence, 119,13; 159,27; 180,7.9; be the case, 189,2; originate, 195,18
huparxis, existence, 96,17.19; 99,8; 129,27; 178,20
huperbolê, excess, 188,4-17; 191,3
huperekhein, overtop, 95,30.31
huperokhê, superiority, 105,3
huperousios, above being, 170,31
huphesis, reduction, 200,4
huphistanai (intransitive forms), exist, have existence, 88,29.30; 92,3; 97,9; 102,20; 116,22; 123,2; 133,13; 163,11;

Greek–English Index

180,5; 190,16.20; subsist, 108,17; 133,14; be present, 103,16;
hupodeigma, example, 96,15; 98,9; 121,6.13
hupodiairein, subdivide, 135,30; 174,17
hupodiairesis, subdivision, 88,17; 136,13; 172,21; 174,17
hupokeimenon, substratum, 83,17; subject, 87,29; 95,15; 116,3; 134,17, etc.; subject matter, 141,3.6
hupolambanein, think, 104,15.17; imagine, 106,9; 170,21; take [to be], 143,15; suppose, 167,12
hupolêpsis, conjecture, 132,7.8
hupomenein, wait for, 88,31; last, 89,1; meet with, 128,15; remain, 128,19; hold its ground, 169,14; undergo, 183,28; 200,28; be subject to, 200,19.20.25
huponoein, consider, 100,24; 125,16; suppose, 170,22
hupostasis, existence, 96,31; 97,11; 102,15.19; 103,18; 104,12.29.33; 108,11; 109,28; 133,17; 170,29; nature, 190,31
hupostatikos, responsible for [a thing's] existence, 169,11
hupotithenai, hypothesize, 87,17; 97,32.33; 129,1; 154,4; premiss, 100,3; imagine, 116,9; assume, 128,22; 188,21
husterogenês, later in origin, 167,14
husteron, to, the posterior, 194,28–195,3

iatrikos, of medicine, 184,17; **iatrikê**, medicine, 141,5.22
iatros, doctor, 127,33; 145,5
idea, form, 155,26
idios, distinctive, 101,27.29; 110,4; 117,4; 137,1; peculiar, 83,10; 101,4.7.8; 111,13; 161,4; 198,7; own, 88,14.16; 89,30; 95,15; 97,11; 102,19; 104,33; 105,15; 124,19; 129,24; 131,3; 133,17; 170,29; **idion**, distinctive feature, 93,17–28; 94,14; 101,3.22.26; 108,1.2.4; 115,17.18; 157,23.24; 161,4–24; 163,14; 198,15; **idiâi**, separately, 170,20; 177,15; in the particular case, 201,24
idiotês, character, 203,18
isoonkos, having the same mass, 86,26
isopleuros, equilateral, 113,25
isos, equal, 101,27; 102,4.5, etc.
isoskelês, isosceles, 113,26

isostrophê, equiversion, 111,19.22
isotês, equality, 112,5.9; evenness, 155,5
isousthai, equal, 111,21

kaiein, burn, 104,16.17; 139,14.15.16; 164,14
kainotomein, invent, 113,14.16.19
kakia, vice, 107,33–109,1; 134,22.29; 138, fig.; 188,9; 190,11; 191,1.2.4.9
kakizein, discredit, 108,33; 114,14
kakos, bad, 108,8.27.28; 109,1; 171,1.4.15; 187,25–188,16; 190,12–31
kakôtikos, harmful, 134,16.17.22.26; 135,20.23.26.32; 136,2.6.12.14.20.23; 137,19; 138, fig.
kalos, noble, 104,10; beautiful, 132,1–13; fine, 141,28.29; good, 184,5–9
kampulos, curved, 152,4.9; 154,32; 155,5.10.11.14
kampulotês, curvedness, 152,1.4.5; 154,29; 155,7; 156,2
kanôn, rule, 112,9; 114,7; 115,28; model, 157,23
kantharos, beetle, 112,16
karkinos, crab, 113,6; 128,6
karpos, fruit, 103,11; 135,24; 136,8
karuon, nut, 153,13.15
katabasis, way down, 103,12
kataginôskein, reject, 110,4
katakhrasthai, be mistaken, 111,6; misuse, 149,8
katakhrêstikôs, incorrectly, 98,14; 151,20; loosely, 137,30
katalambanein, take up, 153,31; occupy, 201,29
katalêgein, end up, 111,19
kataleipein, leave, 115,26; 116,3.9; 203,15; bequeath, 124,12
kataluein, live out, 126,31
katametrein, measure out, 88,12
katanoein, recognize, 118,8
kataphasis, affirmation, 146,17; 168,14.21; 169,6.20; 170,3.14; 172,8; 177,1.2.3.4.11; 181,10.11.13; 184,19; 185,4.20.22; 186,6.15.16; 187,12.15.17.19.22.23
kataskeuastikos, such as to establish, 121,7
kataskeuazein, prove, produce a proof, 89,22.24; argue, 107,1; 184,4; establish,

122,6; 128,24; 150,4; 159,27; construct, 201,3
kataskeuê, confirmation, 189,5; construction, 203,9
katastasis, pleading, 193,8
katatrekhein, run down, 105,16
katêgorein, predicate, 93,20; 111,23; 114,9.10.11; 116,1.2.5.20; 125,3.8.10; 134,3.5; 135,11; 143,3.5.6; 171,26; 173,2.5; 174,8.11; 176,16.19.20.21; 178,9.10.24.25.26; 179,5; 180,4.16; 181,18 *katêgoroumenon, to*, predicate, 116,2.4
katêgoria, category, 83,7.8; 87,31, etc.; predication, 167,6
kathartikos, purificatory, 141,31; 142,3
kathedra, sitting, 106,25.27; 107,6.9.10.24; seat, 127,17.18.20
kathêsthai, be sitting, seated, 107,9.11; 164,19.21; 177,6.7.9.10.11; 185,6.7
kathetos, perpendicular, 120,14; 165,6.7; *kata katheton*, vertically, 118,20
kathezesthai, be sitting, 107,20.24.27
katholikos, universal, 151,17; general, 183,19; *katholikôs*, universally, 121,14
katholou, as a whole, 84,25; in general, 87,30; 201,23; generally, 175,1; universal, 124,28.31; 125,2-32; 126,11.14; 133,24.25; 167,14; 169,32; universally, 178,15
keisthai, form, 86,1; be situated, 88,21.26; 89,15; 92,2; have, be in, (a) position, 88,22; 107,2.5; 152,28; recline, 107,6; lie, 155,2; be, 114,4; 115,2.8; 157,5.9.13; exist, 113,13; 174,15; 180,15; *to keisthai* (the category), being-positioned, 107,7.15.26.28; 152,26; 153,9.10.19; 164,3.18
kenkhros, grain of millet, 94,21.23.25; 97,19; 98,10
kenos, empty, 154,9; *to kenon*, void, 86,23.24
kephalê, head, 100,13; 113,2-114,27; 125,7-126,7; 129,12-132,25
kephalôtos, headed, 113,7.8.9.18; 114,12
keramos, wine jar, 87,9.17; 205,15
keratoeidês, horn shaped, 118,11.18
kharakhtêristikos, characteristic, 149,28
kharakhtêrizein, characterize, 92,1; 108,34;
109,30; 129,1.2.17; 135,30; 136,19.30; 147,22; mark off, 165,11
kheimerinos, winter, 128,5
kheimôn, wintry weather, 148,2
kheir, hand, 114,20; 125,7-126,12; 131,13.17.14; 132,14.23.25; 153,13.30
khiôn, snow, 110,7; 135,17; 140,20, etc.
khôrein, go, 136,24; 137,12; 138, fig.; move, 137,17
khôrizein, separate, 106,15; *khôrizesthai*, be distinct, 200,21
khrasthai, employ, 88,17; 157,24; 177,19; use, 96,15; 105,12; 106,2; 128,30; 141,23; 167,25; 171,19; deal with, 193,11
khrêsis, usage, 126,3
khrôma, colour, 150,2.3.6.7; 170,10; 172,15; 190,9.27
khrômatikos, chromatic, 113,27
khronos, time, period of time, 83,20; 84,9; 86,3-32, etc.
kinein, move (transitive), 103,30; 119,8; 166,13; 197,24; 198,13; change, 203,18; *kineisthai*, move (transitive), 86,8.9; 87,26; 111,17; 166,7.11; 198,12.13; 199,15; 201,5.15; undergo motion, 201,15.20; be in motion, 201,16; other translations, 166,9; 201,2
kinêma, movement, 86,3.5.7
kinêsis, motion, 86,3-88,1; 92,27.28; 100,9; 166,4-24; 190,19; 197,9-199,28; 200,11-202,11; 203,17-204,18
klinein, recline, 164,20.21
koilainein, excavate, 155,31
koilos, concave, 87,10; 99,29; sunken, 153,7
koilotês, cavity, 155,32; concavity, 173,18
koinônein, share, 136,15
koinônia, association, 159,15
koinos, common, 85,23; 89,20.24; 90,1.8.12.17.23; 91,2.4.19; 95,25; 114,8; 126,2; 141,8; 191,9.14; general, 134,3; 185,4.5; *koinôs*, in common, 95,17; 103,9; 134,5; at a general level, 201,23
koleopteros, sheath-winged, 112,16
korax, raven, 147,15.16; 148, fig.
korônê, crow, 141,27
kosmos, cosmos, 100,17.19.25; 128,10
kouphos, light, 179,30; 182,4; 188,6
krasis, constitution, 137,16; 149,3

kratunein, validate, 105,18; 126,26; 129,5; strengthen, 115,21
ktêma, possession, 125,25; 205,20
kuamos, bean, 97,19
kubikos, cubic, 152,18
kuklophoria, rotation, 199,10
kuklos, circle, 111,17; 120,7.24.27; 121,4.8; 123,32; 137,22; 155,24; 158,3; 159,30; 160,1; 161,1.2.3; *zôdiakos kuklos*, zodiac, 86,21
kulindrikos, cylindrical, 90,29; 152,18
kunê, dog, 160,21
kurios, proper, 195,15.23; 191,24; 195,17 (last two by emendation); important, 151,17; significant, 149,25.26; *kuriôs*, properly, 87,25; 92,7.18, etc.; strictly, strictly speaking, in the strict sense, 88,1; 100,11; 111,12, etc.
kurtotês, convexity, 173,19

legein, call, say, speak of, name, refer to as, mean, etc.; 83,10; 84,7; 86,27, etc.
leios, smooth, 152,20; 153,2.4.8; 154,31; 155,8.27.30.33; 156,3
leiotês, smoothness, 152,25; 154,30
leptos, thin, 101,12.16; small, 154,3; *to lepton*, thinness, 152,17
leukainein, colour white, 179,29
leukos, white, 92,9–93,13; 96,32, etc.
leukotês, whiteness, 109,5; 133,25; 140,3; 147,13.15; 149,18.19; 156,18; 157,3.22; 175,22; 179,29; 183,12.32; 188,23; 189,18; paleness, 159,13.14
lexis, text, 126,9; word, 193,6; 196,22; *epi tês lexeôs*, textually, 89,19; *kata tên lexin*, verbally, 111,27
logikos, rational, 125,5; 148,10; 149,1; 173,8; logical, 199,21; a logician, 198,18; 199,23; *to logikon*, rationality, 159,7
logoeidês, rational, 145,4.5.11; 146,3
logos, account, 83,13; 87,25; 92,6; 102,29, etc.; statement, 106,2; 124,13; 157,2, etc.; utterance, 102,3; 193,26; discourse, 197,12; discussion, 205,8; argument, 84,32; 85,3; 98,10, etc.; sentence, 193,16.23; word, 89,8; 133,3; 149,2; 205,26; speech, 98,16.19; 192,19; 193,7; 196,22; language, 84,9; 88,11.27.30; 89,7.31.32; 90,2.3.5; 98,29; story, 157,1;

section, 83,10; 84,4; 94,6, etc.; book, 104,14; 198,17; topic, 161,31; subject, 198,16.18; question, 94,5; definition, 159,1.30; 160,1.2.10.25; 172,23; 180,9; status, 99,27; form, 190,25.26; law, 169,19; 184,17; relation, 86,5.6; reasoning, 121,20; reason, 86,5; 161,3; *poieisthai logon*, address, 87,24; speak, 134,6; 197,19; *logôi*, mentally, 154,4
luein, resolve, 126,9.17; let go, 128,19; instance, 137,28
lusis, solution, 122,24; 162,19

makhê, strife, 97,1
makhesthai, war, 97,5.12.29
makros, long, 88,13; 92,18.22.24.25; 98,5.7.19; 136,34; 142,6; 148,1; 148, fig.; 150,7; 151,8
malakos, soft, 147,3.5; mild, 169,7; 170,15
manikos, mad, 149,3
manos, porous, 152,20–153,22; open-textured, 153,18
manôsis, porosity, 152,24; 153,18.21.24.26; 154,23
manotês, porosity, 154,19.22.26
manoun, make porous, 153,12; *manousthai*, become porous, 154,22
mathêmatika, ta, mathematical objects, 137,21
mathêsis, learning, 133,2; 166,21
mathêtês, student, 103,14; pupil, 133,15; 164,17
megas, large, 94,4–99,18; 101,14.17; 102,27; 105,4; 111,22; 168,11; 199,1.2; great, 142,4
megethos, magnitude, 86,23–32; 95,27; 96,20
meionexia, taking less than one's due, 188,4.12
meiôsis, diminution, 87,27; 197,11; 198,22; 199,6.26; 200,1.3.4.16; 201,6; 203,17
meioun, decrease, 112,19; 203,16; narrow, 113,6.10; *meiousthai*, wane, 118,15; 128,4; diminish, 200,7.20.23.28; dwindle, 201,21.29
mêkhanikê, mechanics, 119,7
mêkos, length, 84,11.28–85,28; 88,9; 90,19; 141,13.15; 152,10.16; *kata mêkos*, longitudinal, 86,20; vertical, 165,5.15

melainein, darken, 164,2; tan, 200,27
melania, blackness, 133,26;147,15.16; 148, fig.; 151,3; 156,18; 157,22; 183,32; 188,23; 189,18; darkness, 159,14
melansis, darkening, 136,35; 138, fig.
melas, black, 96,32; 97,3.4.26, etc.; dark, 104,6; 111,2; 170,10; indiscernible, 170,9
meli, honey, 104,4; 135,23.25; 138, fig.; 140,3; 149,17.27
mellein: *mellôn khronos*, future time, 91,17; *to mellon*, the future, 89,3; 117,24; 164,23
menein, remain, 135,34; 155,29.31; 156,9; 161,23; 193,20; 198,9; 199,17; 200,9; 202,9; 203,13.16; be lasting, 199,13
merikos, particular, 96,7; 124,29–126,14; 180,13
meristos, divisible, 163,14
merizein, separate, 154,9
meros, part, 85,7.11.32; 86,33, etc.; portion, 87,18; 153,30; *para meros*, by turns, 161,23; 198,6.9; *kata meros*, particular, 162,18; 169,32; separately, 183,18
mesos, in the middle, 169,27; middle, 187,21; between, 172,14; *to meson*, centre, 99,24.25; 100,2.16.17; intermediate, 172,23; intermediate step, 141,19; mid-point, 155,2.5; *ta en mesôi*, intermediate, 172,24; *ana meson*, between, 171,27; 173,21–174,15; 181,17–28; 182,20; intermediate, 172,26
metabainein, move, move on, 101,22.26; 110,4; 111,12; 200,8
metaballein, change, 200,6; 154,17.20; 166,8; 168,20–169,18; 183,20–184,15; 199,17; undergo a change, 200,9; alter, 142,8; convert, 142,17; switch, 154,21
metabolê, change, 87,30; 142,4; 150,1; 183,17.26.28; 197,11; 198,22; 199,7.11.14.27; 200,6; 201,28; *tên metabolên poeisthai*, change, 183,29
metalambanein, partake of, 133,26; get a share of, 159,18
metalêpsis, transference, 92,21
metapherein, derive, 107,25.26
metekhein, partake, 105,7.8; 110,28; 122,17; 137,2; 140,5.6; 148,6; 151,22; 152,25; 156,18.20; 159,12.13.14.16; 162,17.18; 176,6; participate, 133,25; 156,27;

157,3.6.15.16.17; share in, 137,5; have to do with, 160,17; have, 179,26
methodos, method, 120,26; 135,5.7; 184,24 organization, 137,33
metokhê, participle, 165,28
metrein, measure, 85,24.26.27; 89,12; 165,6.9
metrion, to, due measure, 191,4; *metriôs*, 142,25
metron, measure, 86,17.22; 87,3.32; 88,1; 92,28
mikros, small, 94,4–99,18; 101,14.17; 102,27; 105,4; 153,29; 154,1; 168,11; 203,13
mimeisthai, mimic, 108,12
mimêma, copy, 137,30; 151,20
mixis, mixture, 101,24; mingling, 110,17; 158,17.18; admixture, 161,19
mnêmê, mention, 168,10; *kata mnêmên*, retrospectively, 187,11
mnêmoneuein, mention, 87,23; 94,7; 102,24; 109,14.17; 173,11.14.18; 191,17; 194,28; 195,8; 198,3.4; 202,11
mokhthêros, wicked, 184,9
monas, unit, 88,16; 89,27.29; 173,15; one, 184,25; 185,1
monimos, established, 141,2
morion, part, 84,6.7; 86,11; 88,19–92,3; 95,25; 103,24; 126,13; 152,23–156,4; 179,26; 205,13; portion, 153,30; particle, 154,1
morphê, shape, 134,10; 137,21–32; 138, fig.; 139,19; 151,12–19; 152,8.17.19
mousikos, musician, 113,26; musical, 157,18; *mousikê*, music, 157,18; 162,19
muthos, story, 119,20

neôteros, more recent, 90,27
nôdos, toothless, 175,13.15; 180,12; 182,17; 186,29; 187,3
noein, conceive of, 122,25; 123,4; think of, 122,27.29; 123,1.3; 153,15; perceive, 133,30; intelligize, 171,12
noêma, concept, 167,13
noeros, intellective, 171,9
noêtos, intelligible, 89,14; object of intellection, 171,13
nosein, be sick, ill, 181,20; 182,18; 186,12.25.27; 189,1.9.13

nosôdês, sickly, 143,11.19; 144,20; 146,23.25; 147,1
nosos, illness, 134,22–34; 138, fig.; 142,4.6.9; 148,1; 148, fig.; 149,5; 150,7; 151,8; 162,14; 174,1; 184,12; 188,22.23; 189,21
nous, mind, 133,28.29; intellect, 171,12.13
nukteris, bat, 112,16
nun, the now (the present moment), 83,3.4.6

oikeios, own, 89,26; 104,29; 105,18; 108,11; 114,22.28; 125,4.10; 128,14; 160,28; 164,16; particular, 127,32; *oikeiôs*, fittingly, 94,5; appropriately, 112,4; 113,13; 114,8.9; 115,24.26.28; 116,2.5.6.15
ôkhrian, turn pale, 137,3.6; 201,31
ôkhrias, pale complexioned, 137,7
ôkhriasis, pallor, 134,26; 136,27.34; 137,13; 138, fig.; 147,29; 148,2.fig.; 150,7
ôkhros, white, 137,18; yellow, 158,1; off-white, 170,11; 172,25
ôkhrotês, pallor, 148,4
oligodeês, with scant deficiency, 166,9
oligokhronios, short-lived, 135,1.34; 136,9.18.32; 147,26.30; 148, fig.
oligokinêtos, showing scant movement, 166,9
onkos, shape, 120,18.20
onoma, name, 113,13–116,3; 133,25.27.29, etc.; word, 95,21; 135,11–18; 143,3; 151,19; 179,35; 193,16.17.24; noun, 143,3.4
onomasia, name, 114,22.25.28
onomatopoiein, create a name, 113,12; 114,1.7; formulate a term, 177,30
onomazein, name, 113,31; 133,5.27; 137,2.5; 151,22; 152,25; 156,22.27; 157,3.13; 178,27.30; 179,7.28; call, 136,11; 180,15
ophthalmos, eye, 144,12; 153,6; 179,25–33
opsis, sight, 144,13; 168,27–170,12; 175,5–183,24; 185,9; 186,12.22; 187,5
organon, organ, 179,31.35; 180,26
ornis, bird, 112,11–20; 113,9.10; 114,27; 197,3.5
oros, mountain, 94,20.23.24; 95,31; 98,10
orthodoxastikos, guided by right opinion, 184,7; *orthodoxastikôs*, as matters of right opinion, 141,29

orthos, upright, 107,4; 164,21; right, 120,11; *orthê*, *orthê gônia*, right angle, 120,13.14.15.16; 202,16
orthotês, straightness, 179,22
ouranios, heavenly, 87,1
ouranos, heaven, 100,4.7; 199,9
ousia, substance, 83,7–23; 84,3, etc.; essence, 160,23
ousiôdês, substantial, 88,5.6; 135,29; 147,19.21; 150,8; 199,16; of substance, 171,6; *ousiôdôs*, essentially, 149,16.20; substantially, 171,2
oxus, acute, 120,15.17; sharp, 120,18
oxutês, sourness, 135,24; 136,8

palaios, old, 90,25; ancient, 105,16; 107,34; 111,20; 124,17; 129,26; 156,13; 191,23.26
pan, to, universe, 99,27.28.30; 111,17
panselênos, full moon, 118,22
paraballein, compare, 94,26; 96,1; 97,20
parabolê, comparison, 94,22
paradeigma, example, 106,18; 170,19; 173,27; 174,4
paradidonai, give, 93,15.26.28; 105,12; 114,7; 115,28; 124,28; 143,18; 156,7.12; 157,19; 161,7; 170,19; 172,4.5.12; 184,23; 185,3.4; 187,28; 195,10; teach, 106,19; pass down, 129,26; present, 146,18
parakolouthein, be (a) concomitant, 108,30; 110,9; 156,28; 158,16; 161,10; follow (from), 128,23; 129,3; result from, 115,23; be attendant upon, 124,19; be a by-product, 127,25; hold good for, 130,3.13; 167,6; accompany, 201,8.19.33; 202,1.4.5; *ta parakolouthenta*, consequences, 105,17
parakolouthêma, concomitant, 110,4.8; 111,12; 117,4; 121,14; 124,18; 130,19; 134,25; 137,1; 158,14; 161,8.24.27; 164,7; 172,10; by-product, 127,14
paralambanein, use, 85,29; 98,10; 135,13; 147,8; 168,1; invoke, 97,3; include, 109,13; 130,22.24.30; 136,14; 173,9.10; link, 144,27.28;
paralêllos, parallel, 203,3.4
paralogizesthai, lead astray, 184,8
paraphuas, sucker, 104,33; 108,10
paraplêrôma, complement, 202,13; 203,7.8

paratropê, deviation, 191,4
parepesthai, accompany, 201,17
parônumia, paronymous name, 123,8
parônumos, paronymous, 114,9;
  parônumôs, paronymously, 107,20.21; 123,6; 133,25.26; 137,1.5; 148,6; 152,3; 156,15–157,15; 162,16; 175,22.23
paskhein, be affected, 144,3–27; 146,10–147,2, etc.; be acted on, 109,31; suffer, 118,20; *to paskhon*, patient, 105,10; *to paskhein*, (the category) being-affected, 109,6; 137,3.10; 138, fig.; 139,29; 148,4. fig.; 149,8; 163,1.24.25, etc.
pathêsis, affection, 165,30; 166,20.27
pathêtikos, affective, 134,9; 135,21; 136,25; 137,8.11; 138, fig.; 139,17–25; 147,7–27; 148,fig.8.10; 149,4–29; 150,3.13.15; 151,3–10
pathos, affection, 134,10–138, fig.; 139,17–28; 147,8.23–150,16; 151,1; 152,2–17; 165,26.27.29; 175,15; 180,17.26; 200,17
pêdalion, rudder, 112,23–114,27
pêdaliôtos, ruddered, 112,27; 113,1.2.18.30; 114,11
pêkhuaios, cubit long, 93,11
pêkhus, cubit, 205,11
pentadaktulos, with five fingers, 128,2
pentagônon, pentagon, 120,25
perainesthai, be finite, 84,12.14.15; 85,3.30
peras, limit, 84,15–85,31; 87,8.13; 91,14, etc.
peratoun, bound, 84,16–30
periairein, strip away, 115,25; 116,2.12.16
periekhein, surround, 84,27; 165,13.14.18; contain, 87,8–15; 155,23.25; 165,2; 185,16.19; encompass, 91,22; embrace, 125,4; bound, 152,13; 202,16
periektikos, embracing, 125,11
perigraphê, boundary, 88,14.16; 89,26.30
perigraphein, circumscribe, 84,30; 90,2
periodos, circuit, 86,22
periorizein, limit, 128,16
peripatein, walk, 168,22; 185,15.18.19
peripatos, walking, 144,20
periphereia, sphere, 99,30; circular line, 155,15–26; circularity, 156,2
peripherês, circular, 155,14; circumference, 155,24
peripherogrammos, curvilinear, 120,22.23

periphora, rotation, 199,8
perithesis, arrangement, 164,5; 165,18; 205,7
peritithenai, place around, 203,11
perittos, odd, 172,13; 173,10.11.13.16.28; 174,8.9; 181,20; 182,18
petaloeidês, leaf-shaped, 86,26
phainesthai, appear, 104,1.5.7; 126,27; seem, 152,22; 153,7; come to light, 156,11; be seen, 190,29; *to phainomenon*, appearance, 128,15
phaios, grey, 170,11; 172,14.17.25; 174,7; 181,25
phantasia, visualization, 119,19; mental representation, 137,23
phantaston, to, mental representation, 137,20.21.24; 138, fig.; 151,18
phaulos, mean, 104,10; bad, 172,27; 174,13; 184,3.4.8.13
philosophein, engage in philosophy, 184,14
philosophia, philosophy, 141,8
philosophos, philosopher, 84,13; 128,30; 141,16.23; 165,23; 175,19.24; 194,19.21.22.23; 197,22
phônê, word, 95,16.18; 167,25; 168,1; 198,2; sound, 169,29; 170,8; 193,25.26; *meta phônês*, voiced, 90,2
phora, locomotion, 199,7.10
phôs, light, 118,9; 171,4.8; 179,18.19.24; 180,16.19; 202,1.2
phôtizein, illuminate, 85,10–22; 118,9–16
phronêsis, wisdom, practical wisdom, 145,27.32; 146,2; 188,14
phthartikos, destructive, 135,26
phtheirein, destroy, 169,8.13; 164,18; 200,7.20; *phtheiresthai*, perish, 88,30; 89,1; 128,20; 136,5; 201,20
phthisis, diminution, 201,28
phthora, destruction, 164,14; 197,10–201,24; eradication, 168,30; 169,1
phulaktikos, protective, 160,12
phulattein, preserve, 114,25; 160,15; retain, 199,16
phusikos, natural, 89,2.4.8; 119,4.10.11, etc.; of nature, 127,30; 169,19; 184,17; physical, 180,7; 199,21; inborn, 151,6; *ta phusika*, products of nature, 128,8; *ho phusikos*, natural scientist, 198,15;

199,23; *phusikôs*, in the nature of things, 85,23; naturally, 147,11; 149,15
phusiologos, natural scientist, 197,12
phusis, nature, 83,12.13; 85,9; 93,22, etc.; entity, 95,19; *kata phusin*, natural, 174,4; 179,23
platos, breadth, 84,11–86,8; 88,9; 90,20.21; 152,10.16; width, 101,15.16; *kata platos*, horizontal, 165,7.16
platus, wide, 101,12.15; *to platu*, wideness, 152,12
pleonazein, become excessive, 137,16; exceed, 190,25; *to pleonazon*, excess, 191,5
pleonexia, surplus, 128,3; taking more than one's due, 188,3.11
plêroun, complete, 124,17; 167,21; 187,27; fill, 153,13.31; round out, 193,32
pleura, side, 113,24; 120,10.11; 202,16.18; 203,1.2.3
poiein, act, 144,19.25.26.28; 145,1.2; 163,25; 164,10.11.12; 165,29.31; 166,1.2.4.23; 197,20.25; do, 92,13; 93,17; 101,5, etc.; perform, 124,11; make, 94,28; 103,17; 105,28; 106,20, etc.; create, 83,18; 86,2.8,9; 91,11.12; 128,5; 155,3.13; 191,4; produce, 112,21; 128,3; 148,13; 154,15; 155,24; 163,18.19.21; 164,3.4; 174,17; provide, 102,29; 198,2; present, 139,31; 140,5; give, 195,10; cause, 137,25; 106,8; deliver, 133,20; put, 84,4; proceed, 93,27; base, 130,31; carry out, 134,12; undergo, 183,29; *to poiein* (the category), acting, 109,6; 163,1.2.24; 165,20.22; 166,32.33; 167,1.5; 197,17.22.24; 205,5; *ho poiôn*, *to poioun*, agent, 105,10; 164,11; 165,24; 166,3.5.12.16.18.20; *poieisthai logon*, write, 83,13; 197,19; address, 87,24; speak, 134,6
poios, qualified, 133,6; 139,30; 144,16; 150,10.11; 156,14; 162,15.23; *to poion*, the qualified, qualified thing, qualified entity, 133,5.14.22.23.25.28.31; 134,3.4.5; 139,31.32; 140,1.4.5; 156,16.18.20; 157,21; 158,3.12.14.26; 159,11; 161,8.10.12; 162,8.11; 175,22.23; qualification, 83,18; 88,5.6; 99,7.8.10; 102,18; 104,32; 106,14; 108,25; 116,23; 144,9; 152,21.22; 157,29; 158,5.6; 163,6.18.23; 190,23.27; 199,2.16; 204,20
poiotês, quality, 83,17; 88,7.8; 90,6.7, etc.
politikos, civic, 141,30.32; 142,3
pollaplasiazein, multiply, 184,24.27
polugônon, polygon, 160,31; 161,3
polukhronios, long-lasting, 134,27; 135,34; 136,18; 147,26.27; 148, fig.
polus, large, 92,9–21; 93,10; 98,31; 99,9.11; 101,14; many, 94,3–27; 95,8.29; 96,9.21; 97,8–99,15, etc.; long, 92,27.28; 98,22; 148,2; much, 98,21; 136,34; 152,7; most, 180,21; *hoi polloi*, the many, 204,10; *epi polu*, (too) long, 83,11; 102,24.28; 133,20; *epi to polu*, mostly, for the most part, 118,30.32; 120,3; 127,31; 128,2.8; 131,23
ponêros, wrongdoer, 126,29; 127,6
porisma, corollary, 131,3.4
poson, to, quantity, 83,5–84,6; 87,25–88,18, etc.
posotês, quantity, 190,27; 199,6; 205,10
pote (the category), when, 107,18.29.30; 109,6.7.8; 130,26; 163,19.20; 164,22
pou (the category), where, 107,18.31; 109,6; 130,26; 163,19.21.23
pous, foot, 98,23; 100,4; 126,5.6; 175,8; 205,13
pragma, thing, 83,14; 85,9; 87,22, etc.; reality, 119,19; entity, 122,25.29.31; 123,3.9; 124,12; 162,27; 173,7; 180,5; 188,25; object, 139,10; matter, 142,7; concern, 184,12; fact, 194,17.24.25
praxis, activity, 92,17.22.24; 93,4; action, 128,15
presbuteros, older, 191,23.26; 192,1
proairesis, choice, 145,29; decision, 194,9
proairetikos, purposive, 127,15
proapodidonai, give earlier, previously, 125,31; 126,17; 129,16
proêgeisthai, come first, 192,21; 193,7; precede, 201,10.11.22
proêgoumenôs, in the first place, 137,28; primarily, 149,24
proepinoein, conceive of before, in advance, 123,21.23
prokatastasis, introduction to the pleading, 193,8
prokathezesthai, preside over, 128,11

prolambanein, assume in advance, 141,21; 193,4; anticipate, 186,9; precede, 198,2
pronoein, foresee, 127,8
pronoia, providence, 127,3.9.10.28.30; 128,8.12.17.24; 131,6
proodos, getting out, 180,21
prooimia, ta, preliminaries, 193,7.11; 196,22
prophorikos logos, spoken speech, 90,3.5
pros ti, relative, 83,19; 94,8-31; 95,3; 97,2.5.10; 98.1-25, etc.
prosdiorismos, qualification, 126,13
prosôpon, face, 153,5; 175,11; [grammatical] person, 185,16.17
protasis, premiss, 126,22.23.25; 128,22.25; 193,1
protattein, place before, 83,7; 133,10
proteros, earlier, 84,1; 116,6; 130,3.14; first, 86,13; 137,11; before, 89,3.4.10; previous, 91,28; 110,5; 189,5; preceding, 106,14; prior, 117,13-118,5; 121,5-123,3; 191,15-197,6; former, 123,20; 173,28; *to proteron*, priority, 120,3.5; 193,9.13; 193,5; *ta protera*, what precedes, *proteron*, first, 83,15; 93,25.27.28; 97,11.32; 105,13.17; 108,1; 111,14; 119,13; 124,19; 139,11; 161,6; 162,1; 172,1.4; 182,9.23; 193,12; previously, 96,32; 98,32; 121,13; earlier, 123,25; 131,5; 174,17; 189,27
prouparkhein, pre-exist, already exist, exist in advance, 118,25.30; 119,2.4.11.17; 120,4; 122,18; 123,1; 131,22.24; 139,12.18; 201,7
pseudês, false, 104,9; 126,22.23; 128,26.27; 129,4; 186,26.28.29; 187,1.2.5.7.8.9; wrongly, 104,24
pseudesthai, make a false statement, 104,22.24; state a falsehood, 186,23
pseudos, false statement, 104,1; 169,22; falsehood, 171,10.11.12; 185,10-21.27; 186,13.15; 187,16; 198,10.13; falsity, 185,8; false, 154,13; 185,6.7.25; 186,2-25; 187,13.15.20
psilos, bare, 130,28; empty, 185,18
psukhê, soul, 89,11.12; 90,4.6; 103,29, etc.; mind, 119,17
psukhein, chill, 145,9.10; cool, 164,1; 200,19
psukhos, cold, 200,29

psukhros, cold, 97,25; 168,26; 169,15; 170,25; 179,29; 181,25; 182,3; 183,21; 190,4
psukhrotês, coldness, 147,13; 172,20; 174,5; 183,13.31.32
psuxis, cold, 135,18; 172,19; 183,12; chill, 148,2; cooling, 200,17
ptênos, aerial, 196,29; 197,3.4.5; *to ptênon*, winged creature, 112,13
pteron, wing, 112,11-22; 114,15.18.27; 147,16
pterôton, to, winged creature, 112,21.22
pteroun, give wings, 119,21
ptôsis, case, 105,20; 106,16; 111,29; 178,1; ending, 111,27
puknos, dense, 152,20-153,27
puknôsis, density, 152,24; 153,19.22.26; 154,23
puknotês, density, 153,27; 154,19.20.21.26
puknoun, compress, 153,17; 154,21
puktês, boxer, 143,23.24.27
puktikê, boxing, 157,12
puktikos, suited to boxing, 143,10-25; 146,19; 157,8.11
pur, fire, 88,5.7.8; 99,29; 104,15.16, etc.
puraktein, harden by fire, 139,26
puretos, fever, 139,25
purros, red, 158,1

rhein, flow, 91,10; 128,7
rhêma, verb, 134,5; 143,3.4; 165,26.28.30; 185,11.12.13.19
rhêseidion, brief remark, 167,12
rhêtôr, orator, 193,10
rhêtorikê, rhetoric, 135,4.5.7.8.9; 139,6; 142,21.22.24
rhêtorikos, skilled speaker, 162,16
rheustos, fluctuating, 141,6

saphênizein, make clear, 138,2; clarify, 202,12
selênê, moon, 86,19; 93,1; 99,30; 118,8; 128,4
selêniakos, lunar, 118,8.18.23.24; 123,21.24.28.30
sêmainein, indicate, 95,2-20; 107,13; 130,26.28; 140,8; 143,16; 152,27; 155,9; 160,17; 163,20; 164,5; 165,27.28; 172,27; 177,4.5; 185,8-21; convey, 96,13; mean,

111,20; 155,15; 169,27; 179,26; 200,4; signify, 152,21; *to sêmainomenon*, sense, 140,10.24; 141,4.22.23; 174,21; 190,15; 193,31; 194,3; 196,1; 205,17; meaning, 191,19.24; 192,5.20; 193,25.33; 194,1.3; 195,14.19; 196,21

sêmantikos, indicative, 160,13; 165,27; 185,12

sêmasia, reference, 113,23

sêmeion, point, 85,6–86,21; 90,12–15; 111,17; 141,11.13.14; 152,6.7; 155,2; 193,3; 203,1.2.4

skalênos, scalene, 113,26

skazein, be defective, 121,14

skhêma, figure, 120,21; 134,10; 137,20–32; 138, fig.; 139,19; 151,11–152,18; 155,9–25; 158,2; 159,26.28; 171,20; 177,20; shape, 167,5

skhesis, relationship, relation, 83,19; 95,29; 97,9; 100,10; 102,21.22.31; 103,10.12.25; 104,3; 107,10–15; 116,20.21.26; 122,26.30; 123,1; 129,28; 130,25.27.28.29; 133,12; 162,28; 163,12.13; 165,28; 166,25; 168,20.23.24; 188,28

skhizopteros, split-winged, 112,13.15

skia, shadow, 180,19; 202,2

skiasma, shadow, 118,19

skiazein, shadow, 85,13–22; 180,19

skopein, view, 88,7; investigate, 92,12; observe, 128,21; 203,10

skopos, subject, 98,16.18.20; 167,12; aim, 168,3.9

skotos, darkness, 171,6.7; 179,18.19.23.24; 180,16.18

skulakion, pup, 175,9.15; 182,15; 187,4

sôma, body, 84,2–32; 86,9.10.14.25, etc.; volume, 85,28; solid, 152,6; corporeal thing, 169,34

sômatikos, bodily, 149,3

sômatoeidês, bodily, 149,1

somphos, muted, 170,9

sophistês, sophist, 103,32

sôphrosunê, temperance, 141,25.27; 188,2.13

sôzein, preserve, 113,7; 115,6.14; 116,14; maintain, 136,35; *sôzesthai*, survive, 127,23.24

sperma, seed, 103,11; 201,24; sperm, 201,12

sphaira, sphere, 87,1; 100,6

sphairikos, spherical, 90,29

sphairoeidês, spherical, 86,25

spoudaios, good, good man, person, 108,7.26.28.35; 157,16; 172,26.27; 174,11.13; 184,1.3.4

spoudazein, be concerned, 157,11; be at pains, 191,12

stasis, standing, 106,25.27; 107,5.8.9.23; rest, 190,19

sterein, deprive, 175,6–20

sterêsis, privation, 111,5; 144,10.12.14, etc.

sterêtikos, privative, 180,13

stigmê, point, 90.9

stoikheion, element, 83,18; 122,20; 193,2.12; 201,27; letter, 193,6–24; 196,21

strephein, revolve, 111,18; go round in a circle, 111,18

strophê, revolution, 111,15

sullabê, syllable, 88,13.14.31; 89,9; 90,1; 193,6.15.17; 196,22

sullogismos, syllogism, 171,19; 177,19; 180,29

sumbainein, the result is, 97,13.17; 113,15; 118,20; follow, 109,2; incidentally apply, 116,7; may, 116,22; be accidental, 116,25; 149,19; occur, 118,22; 186,7; happen, 119,25; 157,6; 200,26; turn out, 126,15; come about, 155,7; take place, 180,20; correspond with, 200,6;

sumbebêkos, accident, 109,3.20; 115,3; 124,22–7; 126,15; 199,15; accidental, 115,25; 116,16.18.19; 171,3; *kata sumbebêkos*, derivatively, 92,8–26; 93,16; 98,29; 102,4; incidentally, 99,14; accidentally, 173,3.5.24.26; 174,1; accidental, 174,6

sumballein, help, 172,2; 174,22

sumbolê, engagement, 127,22

summetria, symmetry, 188,7–16; 191,4

summetros, appropriate, 190,26.27; *summetrôs*, consonant with, 160,9

sumperainein, draw conclusions, 129,5

sumperasma, conclusion, 156,7; 193,1

sumphtheiresthai, perish along with, 128,19; 136,5.8

sumplekein, combine (with), 108,19.21; 125,2.6.9.11.23.27; 163,17.18.19.21.23; 164,3.4; 185,12.26

sumplêrôtikos, constitutive, 147,12.13.14.22.24; 148,12. fig.; 160,28.30

sumplêroun, be constitutive, 147,15; contribute to, 171,6

sumplokê, combination, 163,4.7.9; 186,1.3.5.8.10.14; 189,6.9

sumptôma, symptom, 150,5.6; circumstance, 151,7; occurrence, 151,9

sunagein, bring together, 124,31; conclude, 126,21; derive, 131,4; obtain, 184,25

sunagôgê, collection, 173,15

sunaitios, being mutual causes, 179,13

sunakolouthein, follow upon, 119,19

sunanairein, also eliminate, eliminate as well, along with, 94,14.16; 117,7; 118,3; 120,1.6; 121,22.23.25; 122,7.8; 133,14; 169,10; 193,19; take away as well, also, 114,23.24

sunapollusthai, perish together, along with, 97,5; 126,28

sunapomarainein, fade away along with, 136,3.4

sunaptein, join, join together, 89,21.25.27.30; 90,1.9.11.15.17.24; 91,3.4.7.10.15.17.20; 95,25; 154,13

sunarithmein, count among, 87,21

sundein, bind, 122,26; link together, 191,13

sundesmos, conjunction, 168,5

sunêgorein, second, 179,16

sunêgoria, advocacy, 115,23

suneisagein, imply along with, also, 94,14.15; 97,6; 117,6; 122,8; 169,9

suneispherein, entail, 118,3.4; 169,9.13

sunekheia, continuity, 86,16; 89,28; 91,24; 184,12; coherence, 168,9

sunekhês, continuous, 83,6; 84,5.8; 86,11–34, etc.; *to sunekhes*, continuity, 87,7.13.15.29; 88,2; 91,25; 98,17; *sunekhôs*, continuously, 90,13

sunepinoein, think of as well, 117,8

sunêtheia, common practice, 85,23; normal, common, everyday usage, 113,15.20.21.29; 114,8; 157,10; 167,26; 191,25; 193,30; 195,17; parlance, 126,2

sunistanai (intransitive forms), be composed, 88,19.22; 91,27; exist, 88,24.26.28; 99,5.7; 110,23; 119,12; 190,4; coexist, 92,2; subsist, 108,14; 170,29; be constructed, 119,15; 120,25; be made up, 122,13; 124,26; occur, 125,1; consist of, 167,2

sunkeisthai, be composed, 152,15; 154,6.7; be made up, 153,5; be constructed, 155,19.20; 193,27; *ta ex hôn sunkeitai*, components

sunkhôrein, concede, 94,7.10; 96,23.24; agree, 193,14

sunkrinein, compare, 96,11

sunkrisis, comparison, 94,28

sunodos, approach, 118,15; conjunction, 128,4

sunoikein, live in wedlock with, 205,18

sunoikhesthai, disappear, 97,7

suntattein, count with, 85,15; class, classify (along) with, together, 91,28; 136,12.17.19

sunthesis, synthesis, 86,1

sunuphistasthai, coexist, 119,24

sustoikhos, corresponding, 107,27

suzugia, pairing, 124,30; 184,22.23.26; 185,2

tattein, place, 83,23; 84,1; 102,17.23; 103,26; 138,3; 169,4; order, 127,11; arrange, 128,12

tautomaton, the uncaused, 127,14; *ek tautomatou*, without cause, 127,12.18; uncaused, 127,13; 128,10.11; by accident, 127,23

tautotês, sameness, 190,18

taxis, place, 83,8.14.18; 139,3–22; 169,11.15.20; position, 103,28; 133,7.8.9.21; 187,21; order, 89,2–16; 134,12; 138,2; 168,17; 191,21; 192,18.20; 193,13–22; 196,21.23

tekhnê, procedure, 106,18; art, 113,21; 119,2.3.12; skill, 140,24; 141,1.22; *tekhnê grammatikê*, literacy, 123,14

tekhnêtos, artificial, 119,4.11.24; product of a craft, 127,30; 128,8

tekhnikos, artificially produced, 153,18; of art, 169,19

telein, fall, come, [under], 190,9.12; 191,6.8.9.10.12

teleios, fully, 123,14; perfect, 141,24; 142,2; 146,1; 166,8; 184,5.15; perfected, 166,11; completed, 157,10

teleiotês, perfection, 164,15.16; 190,24
teleiôtikos, perfective, 134,16-21; 135,20-33; 136,2-23; 137,19; 138, fig.; 148,12
teleioun, perfect, 164,18
teleutan, perish, 127,22; end, 166,20
telos, goal, 127,32; end-product, 166,29.31; end, 168,6
teretisma, twittering, 167,16
tetragônismos, squaring, 120,7; 121,4.8; 123,32
tetragônos, tetragonal, 120,22; rectangular, 155,30.31.33; *to tetragônon*, square, 120,9.25; 121,1; 152,12; 159,25; 202,8-203,18
thanatos, death, 184,14
theios, god-like, 121,1; divine, 149,1; 169,19; 184,18; *to theion*, divinity, 145,14; 146,1; 166,9
thelêma, will, 145,25
theôrein, see, 84,33; 85,5; 88,9; 89,30, etc.; consider, 88,9; 166,17.19; 201,14; 161,13; detect, 99,19; observe, 108,29; 121,30; 138, fig., etc.; attend to, 116,27; regard as, 165,4; 166,5.16; think of (as), 166,17.19; 188,27
theôrêma, topic, 142,22; theorem, 187,27.28; 188,20; 189,16; 190,8; 193,4.5.12
theôrêtikos, contemplative, 142,2.3
theôria, thought, 148,10
theos, god, 103,29; 127,7; 145,10.21.26; 171,2
therinos, summer, 128,6
thermainein, heat, 139,8; 145,8.9; 164,1.2.12; 200,19.27; 201,16
thermansis, heating, 200,17
thermasia, heat, 159,20
thermos, hot, 97,25; 133,15.27; 158,4; 168,26; 169,15; 170,25; 179,29; 181,25; 182,3; 183,21; 190,3; *to thermon*, heat, 88,5.7; 137,16; 182,1
thermotês, heat, 135,17.23; 138, fig.; 139,23.27; 142,9; 147,14; 148, fig.; 149,16; 159,17; 172,19.20; 174,5; 183,11.13.31.32
thesis, position, 88,19-89,18; 91,26-92,5, etc.; bearing, 179,23; *thesei*, positional, 100,13

thnêtos, mortal, 126,25.27; 128,23.25; *to thnêton*, mortality, 159,8
thrasutês, rashness, 188,14
tiktein, give birth to, 107,28.29; bear, 175,14; 182,16
timan, honour, 127,5
timiôteros, ranked higher, 102,20; 133,12; 139,2
tmêma, division, 124,29; section, 135,31; 136,1.21; 167,22.27; 168,3.6
topos, place, 83,20; 84,9; 86,12.15; 87,7-28, etc.; area, 85,10.13.22; space, 153,31; 201,29; 204,12; location, 200,9; *kata topon*, local, 201,15-33; 204,8.20
trakhus, rough, 152,20-156,3
trakhutês, roughness, 152,25; 154,30
trigônos, triangular, 120,22; *to trigônon*, triangle, 113,24; 120,22; 137,22; 152,12; 155,23; 158,2; 159,25.28.29; 161,1
trikhêi diastaton, to, the three-dimensional, 83,16; 84,2; 88,6; 95,27
tripêkhus, three cubits (long), 93,9; 94,2; 95,1.6.12.22; 96,16
tropê, solstice, 128,6; change, 135,28; 136,30; 137,14.18
tukhaios, chance, 127,13-30
tuphlos, blind, 169,18; 170,17; 175,14; 176,16; 180,22; 182,16.26; 183,2.8; 184,16.17; 186,13.18.21; 187,5.18
tuphlôsis, blindness, 144,13; 176,2.3; 178,8-179,36; 180,15.22; 183,23.24
tuphlotês, blindness, 168,27.28.29; 176,2-178,30; 179,17.20; 181,3; 185,9

xanthos, yellow, 172,25
xêros, dry, 188,6
xêrotês, dryness, 147,14
xestês, pint, 89,11
xestiaios, a pint, 153,28
xulon, log, 85,27; 86,32; 104,35; 109,5.18; 116,24.25; 137,23; 164,14; (piece of) wood, 139,15; 205,11

zêtêsis, investigation, 156,13
zôdiakos, zodiac, 86,21
zôê, life, 127,2; existence, 128,16
zôion, animal, 95, 15-19; 112,7.8; 113,2-11.31, etc.; organism, 103,28

Subject Index

Note: References are to the page and line numbers of the *CAG* edition of the Greek text (indicated in the margins of the translation).

acting (the category), *poiein*
    a combination of substance and quality, 163,23–164,2
    if the quality admits of contrariety and more and less, the instance of acting does, if not, not, 166,33–167,9
    not motions, 197,16–198,1
    two species: an agent acting on itself and one acting on something else, 164,10–12
    why acting and being-affected are separate categories and not relatives, 165,22–166,26
    why Aristotle used the section title *On Acting and Being-Affected* rather than *On Action* (*poiêsis*) and *Affection* (*pathêsis*), 166,26–33
actuality, *see under* potentiality and actuality
affective quality and affection, *pathêtikê poiotês* and *pathos*
    constitute the third species of quality, 134,9 ff.; 139,11–19; 147,7–9
    four types: present to a whole species and constitutive of it; present to a whole species and not constitutive of it; not present to the whole of a species and long-lived; not present to the whole of a species and short-lived, 147,9–148,6; the last type is classified as a quality if it doesn't easily give way, under 'being-affected' if it does, 136,32–137,7; 147,30–148,6; 150,11–12
    may be bodily or psychic, 148,8–149,5; 150,15–16
    relation between affective qualities and affections, 149,11–30

affection, *see under* affective quality and affection
affirmation and negation, *kataphasis* and *apophasis*; *see also under* oppositions
    distinguished from what is affirmed or denied, 177,3–12
Alcibiades, 195,21
angel, *angelos*, 159,8; 196,26
Archimedes, 121,2
argument types
    a fortiori, 115,5 ff.; 122,15 ff.
    reductio ad absurdum, 126,18 ff.
    reductio ad impossibile, 97,16 ff.
    second-figure syllogism, 171,19–24; 177,19–24; and cf. 180,29–181,4 and 183,20–25
Aristotle, 83,17; 84,4; 86,4.13.23; 92,13; 96,15; 104,13; 121,3; 145,3.27; 146,3; 148,5; 154,16.29; 156,3; 158,25; 164,6; 166,3; 167,13; 171,13; 179,10.16.35; 188,24; 190,20; 191,24; 202,10; as 'the philosopher', 84,13; 133,19; 141,23; 165,23; 175,19.24; 197,22
    criticism and correction of, 108,31 ff.; 114,13 ff.; 121,5 ff.; 125,30 ff.; 161,11–27; 178,7; 190,28–9; 193,13–27
    nature of his teaching: caters for beginners, 87,23–5; 153,18 ff.; 199,20–21; starts from what is clear, 130,29–31; 133,31–134,2; 139,31–140,5; restricts self to logical aspects of a subject, 199,21–4; 198,18–19; encourages self-motivation, 133,2–4; 156,8–10; 205,26; uses puzzles as a path to learning, 132,27–133,2; scholarly approach, 92,11 ff.

works cited by name: *History of Animals*, 112,15; *Metaphysics*, 104,14; *On Interpretation*, 145,2; *On the Soul*, 167,15; *Physics*, 84,13; 153,25; 166,3; 168,31; 197,14; 198,16; 199,11

being-affected (the category), *paskhein*
  a combination of substance and quality, 163,23–164,2
  if the quality involved admits of contrariety and more and less, the instance of being-affected does, if not, not, 166,33–167,9
  not motions, 197,16–198,1
  two species: a thing is either destroyed or brought to perfection, 164,13–18
  why acting and being-affected are separate categories and not relatives, 165,22–166,26
  why Aristotle used the section title *On Acting and Being-Affected* rather than *On Action* (*poiêsis*) and *Affection* (*pathêsis*), 166,26–33
being-positioned (the category), *keisthai*
  a combination of substance and relatives, 164,3–4
  relationship to position, a species of relatives, 106,27–107,31; *see also* position
  three species: lying, sitting, standing, 164,19–22
body, *sôma*; *see also under* quantity
  animal an ensouled body, 121,24
  moved by soul and nature, not vice versa, 103,29–31
  parts of the human body in a fixed relationship, 103,24–8
  'three-dimensional' part of definition, 84,2–3; cf. 83,14–18

capacity and incapacity, *dunamis* and *adunamia*; *see also* potentiality and actuality
  how it is that incapacity can be a quality, 143,28–144,14
  rational agencies need not exercise their capacities, non-rational ones must, 144,26 ff.; but divinity does not have unfulfilled capacities or show incapacity, 145,14 ff.
  three senses of capacity and incapacity, 144,18–147,2
  together constitute the second species of quality, 143,12–13
category, *katêgoria*
  Aristotle leaves it to us to work out the definitions, distinctive features, and division into species of the six compound categories, 164,6–10
  as most generic genera, cannot be defined, 93,17–25
  four of the categories, substance, quantity, relatives, and quality, are simple, the other six a combination of substance with one of the other three or with itself, 163,4–164,5; 83,20
  some claim that the categories are purely conceptual, 167,12–17
cause, *aition*, *aitia*
  a providential cause presides over the cosmos, 128,9 ff.
  cause and effect as relatives, 105,9
  prior to effect, 194,6–25; 196,9–17
  relatives cause one another, 179,13–14
chance and the accidental, 127,11–30
colour, *khrôma*
  are affective qualities, 150,3
  good in quality is having the appropriate colour, 190,27
  some are substantial qualities, 150,7–9
  supervene on other affections, 150,6–7
condition, *see under* state and condition
continuous, the, *see under* quantity
contraries, *enantia*; *see also under* acting, being-affected, motion, opposites, and the subdivision distinctive feature under quality, quantity, relatives
  are relatives, 188,27–9
  at war with one another, 96,31–2; 97,10–12
  belong to a subject either accidentally or per se, 173,3–19
  both of a pair need not be instantiated together, but qua contraries both always exist, 188,20–189,13

Subject Index 215

division of, 172,11–27
fall under same genus, or contrary
   genera, or are genera themselves,
   190.8 ff.; 158.10; but always under the
   same most generic genera, 191,5–14
occur in things generically, specifically, or
   numerically the same, 189,17–190,5
the contrary of a good thing is always a
   bad one, that of a bad one may be
   good or bad, 187,27–188,4
things that seem to have two contraries,
   188,4–17
corollary, definition of, 131,4
counter-objection, *see under* objection and
   counter-objection

definition
   and per se predicates, 173,3–19
   and things that admit of degrees,
      158,26–161,3
   definiendum not to be included in
      definiens, 130,23–4
   definition of most generic genera not
      possible, 93,18–19
   only substantial differentiae should be
      included in definitions, 147,17 ff.
Demosthenes, 98,16
destruction, *see* generation and destruction
differentia, *diaphora*, 147,12 ff.
   substantial differentiae, 147,19–22
distinctive feature (*idion*), *see under*
   category; quality and the qualified;
   quantity; relatives
divinity, the, *see under* god
division, *diairesis*; *see also under* category;
   contraries; motion; opposites; quality
   and qualified; relatives; true and false
   notional, 87,16–20
   of the *Categories* into three parts,
      167,22–168,3
   potential, 90,15–17; 91,8–9

Euclid, 152,14

figure and shape, *skhêma* and *morphê*
   figure applies to inanimate things and
      mental representations, shape to
      animate beings or natural things,
      137,20 ff.; 151,17–20

shapes also have figure but not vice
   versa, 151,14–17
together constitute the fourth species of
   quality, 151,13–14

generation and destruction, *genesis* and
   phthora
   is motion of substance in *Categories*,
      199,5; but in *Physics* is a species of
      change and opposed to motion,
      199,10 ff.
   paths between the potentially existent
      and the actually existent, 199,18–20
genus and species, *genos* and *eidos*; *see also
   under* many other headings
   definition of most generic genera is not
      possible, 93,18–19
   genera are more indefinite than their
      species, 95,14–15
   genera are prior to species, 197,5–8
   genera obtained from the same division
      are co-ordinate, 196,24 ff.
   good and bad are extra-categorial most
      generic genera, 190,15 ff.
   reason Aristotle talks of '[subaltern]
      genus' rather than 'species' under
      quality, 143,13–17
   some believe that Aristotle only
      recognizes conceptual genera,
      167,12–17
   to exist, a genus must have at least one
      species, 178,19–20
geometry and geometers, 84,9–86,10;
   113,23–6; 120,9–121,3; 131,3–5;
   141,2–20; 193,1–5; 202,7–203,17
god, *theos*
   cannot do evil, only good, 145,10–11
   deficient in no respect and so
      unchanging, 166,9–10
   good a substantial attribute of, 171,1–2
   goodness, knowledge, and providence,
      127,7–8
   has no need to deliberate or exercise
      choice, 145,25–146,2
   has no unactualized capacities,
      145,18–21
   is absolute wisdom, 146,1
   will and capacity in him coincide,
      145,14–24

good and bad
  are most generic genera, 190,11; but outside the categorial scheme, like Plato's five greatest kinds, 190,15–22
  god good essentially, 127,7; 171,2; can only do good, 145,10–11
  not opposed as contraries but as possession and privation, 190,28–191,5
  per se vs. accidental good, 170,3–171,15; former has no opposite, latter opposed to bad, 171,1–4
  their nature in each category, 190,24–8
  the opposite of a good thing is always a bad one, that of a bad one can be another bad one, 187,28–188,17
  the truly good person vs. the conventionally good person, 184,4–9

having, *ekhein*
  as a category, when it refers to the arrangement of one substance around another, 164,4–5; 165,17–19; 204,24–205,1
  other uses of *ekhein*, 205,2–23
Herodian, 180,20
Homer, 130,15; quotations, 126,5–7

incapacity, *see under* capacity and incapacity

knowledge, *epistêmê*
  as a genus is a relative but its species are qualities, 162,7–11.17–19
  contrary of ignorance, 108,6.24
  is well-grounded comprehension, 132,9–13
  knowable prior to knowledge, 117,16–20; 118,4–26; 120,3–6; 121,3–17; artificial things an exception, 118,32–119,25; and qua relatives they are simultaneous, 122,31–124,3
  knowledge and the knowable are relatives, 105,7; 117,16–17; nature of their reciprocation, 106,23–4
  knowledge and the knowledgeable person as relatives, 108,8.31 ff.

three types of: first philosophy; sciences with stable subject matter; practical knowledge, 140,23–141,23

language, *logos*
  a discrete quantity, 84,9; 88,11–15; 89,31–90,2
  does not have parts with relative position, 88,27–89,2; put parts do have a natural order, 89,7–9
  spoken vs. internal, 90,2 ff.; only former a quantity, latter a quality of the soul, 90,1–7

matter, *hulê*
  lowest of things, 132,11–12
  nature creates a sixth finger through a surplus of matter, 128,34
  prime matter, 83,14–15
  things are posterior to their matter, 122,21–2

motion, *kinêsis*
  a different division in the *Physics*, 199,9–24
  cannot take place in a void, 86,23–4
  fundamental to natural science, 197,12–15
  located in the patient rather than the agent, 166,3–15; but may be thought of as in both, 166,15–21
  measured by time, 86,17; 87,32–88,1; 92,28
  none of the motions reducible to another, 199,28–203,21
  oppositions between the various types of motion and between them and rest, 203,27–204,21
  paths to the categories, 197,25–198,1; from potentiality to actuality, 87,22–3; 166,5–6; 204,3–4
  six species of, 198, 21 ff.; demonstration of this by division, 198,26–199,9
  the movement (*kinêma*) is the extensionless principle of motion, 86,2–3

negation, *see under* affirmation and negation
now, the, *nun*
  the extensionless principal of time, 86,3 ff.

number, *arithmos*
    as a quantity, 83,21–84,3; 88,1; a discrete quantity, 84,9; 88,11.15–16; 89,23–31; 95,9 ff.
    has natural order, 89,9–10
    number in things that are counted has parts with position, in soul does not, 89,10–16
    on defining it, 173,11–16

objection and counter-objection, *enstasis* and *antiparastasis*, 94,8–98,4
opposites, *antikeimena*, 167,18–191,14
    belong to the same genus, 144,5 ff.; 158,10; and therefore same category, 158,8–10
    cannot be in the same thing in the same relation at the same time, 100,10
    constitutive qualities cannot be replaced by their opposites, 160,23 ff.
    division to show that there are only these four types, 168,16–169,2
    examples of, and distinctions between, the four types of opposites, 170,19–187,24
    opposed in four ways: as relatives, as contraries, as privation and state, as affirmation and negation, 168,13–15
    reason for order of presentation: moves from weakest to strongest opposition, 169,4–170,16

perception, *aisthêsis*
    divine and rational senses, 149,1
    perception and the perceptible are relatives, 105,6–7
    qualified things apprehended by the senses, qualities by mind, 133,27–8
    senses affected in perception, 149,13 ff.
    the perceptible is prior to perception, 118,26–9; 121,20–123,31
place, *topos*; *see also under* quantity; where
    a species of continuous quantity, 84,9; 106,30
    definition: the limit of the container by which the contents are contained, 87,7–8; 165,1–2
    gives rise to the category 'where' (*pou*), 107,29–31

Plato, 104,18; 109,27; 141,18; 171,9; 189,29; 190,17
Porphyry *Isagoge*, 93,20; 184,23
position, *thesis*
    a species of relatives, 106,27–107,6
    gives rise to the category 'being-positioned' (*keisthai*), 107,27–8
potentiality and actuality, *dunamis* and *energeia* (*see also* capacity and incapacity), 123,11–124,14
    an agent required to advance the potential to the actual, 126,12–14
    motion is the path from the potential to the actual, 87,22–3; 166,5–6; 204,3–4
prior, the, *to proteron*
    five senses of, 191,19–195,25
    the prior and the posterior are relatives and therefore have linked senses, 194,28–195,4
privation and state, *sterêsis* and *hexis*; *see also under* opposites
    conditions for correct use of terms, 175,3–16
    distinction between being deprived and privation and being in a state and the state, 175,19–176,27
Protagoras, 103,32; 104,20.22
puzzle, *aporia*
    raising puzzles a road to learning, 133,1–2

quality and the qualified, *poiotês* and *to poion*, 133,5–162,28 (*see also under* state and condition; capacity and incapacity; affective quality and affection; figure and shape)
    distinctive feature (*idion*) of quality: apparent, 157,23–161,3; actual, 161,6–27; Aristotle's formulation of the latter needs adjustment, 161,11–27
    explanation of the order of the four species, 138,2–139,22
    explanation of section heading, 133,21–134,7
    qualified thing (*poion*) vs. quality (*poiotês*), 133,23–8; 156,16 ff; but *to poion* can also be used of a quality, 134,2–7

qualities are universals grasped by the mind, qualified things are grasped by the senses, 133,24–8; 139,32; therefore qualified things are more familiar to us and placed first in the section title and in Aristotle's teaching, 133,31–134,2; 139,31–140,6
qualities in own right are unchanging; they only change when they enter a subject, 183,27–8
reasons it has fourth position among the categories, 133,9–21; 102,16–29
some qualities can be assigned to more than one species, 139,22–9
substantial or constitutive qualities, 88,4–8; 135,29–30; 147,12 ff.; and cf. 149,11 ff. and 150,7–8
there are four species of, 134,8–10; a division to demonstrate this, 134,10–138,2

quantity, *poson*, 83,5–102,9; *see also under* place, time
body as quantity vs. body as substance, 88,3–10
cannot be defined because quantity is a most generic genus, 93,15–24
composed of parts with position vs. not so composed, 88,18–89,18; 91,28–92,6
continuous (line, surface, body, place, time) vs. discrete (number, language), 84,5–9; 89,23–90,22
distinctive feature (*idion*): apparent, 93,25–101,26; actual, 101,27–102,9
nature of body, surface, and line, 84,10–86,10
place and time not continuous in own right, 86,12–87,20; 87,32–88,2; cf. 165,1–17
quantities in the strict sense vs. derivative quantities, 92,11–93,13
reasons it has second position among the categories, 83,7–84,4
substantial quantities, 88,4–10
why motion is not a quantity, 87,21–32

reciprocation (*antistrophê*)
ensuring reciprocation by correct specification of the correlative, 112,5–116,27
of implication of existence, 192,3–13; 194,10–25; 195,27–196,17; 197,5–8
of relatives, 105,19–29; 106,15–24; 111,12–26; could be called 'equiversion', 111,19 ff.

relatives, *ta pros ti*, 102,10–133,4
Aristotle first gives the inadequate definition of the ancients and exposes its shortcomings, 105,12 ff.; 106,2–3; 109,19 ff.; 124,17 ff.; those who say it was Plato's are wrong, 109,26–31
Aristotle's method of presentation, 105,12–18
Aristotle's own definition,129,24 ff.; does not include *definiendum* in *definiens*, 130,22–31; a corollary: to know one of a pair of relatives is to know the other, 131,3 ff.
distinctive feature (*idion*): apparent, 107,34–108,30; 110,4–111,8; actual, 111,12 ff.; 117,4 ff.
division of, 105,1–11
explanation of section heading, 102,29–103,17
reasons they have second position among the categories, 102,16–29; 133,9–21
status of relatives, 103,18–104,36; have real existence, 103,18–31; but not true that all things are relative, 103,31–104,25; the related items actually belong to other categories, 104,28–34; 108,10–12; cf. 106,14–15
the ways a relation can be expressed, 105,19–29; 106,8–11.15–24

senses, the, *see under* perception
shape, *see under* figure and shape
simultaneous, the, *to hama*
these opposed to senses of the prior, 195,10–14.18–24; 195,27–196,17; 196,20–2
three senses of, 195,14–18.25–7; 196,18–197,8

Socrates, 89,19, etc.
soul, *psukhê*
  a proof of its immortality, 126,24–128,21
  knows self, 164,11–12
  language in soul as opposed to spoken language, 90,3–7
  moves body, 103,29–30
  number in soul as opposed to that in things counted, 89,10–16
  qualities that affect the soul, 148,8 ff.; 150,15–16
  soul and angel are co-ordinate species, 196,26
state and condition, *hexis* and *diathesis*
  a state is lost with difficulty, a condition easily lost, 140,19 ff.
  are relatives as well as qualities, 106,21–4; 161,31–162,28
  states are also conditions but not vice versa, 140,20–21; 143,3–9
  together constitute the first species of quality, 140,18
substance, *ousia*
  a division of substance, 124,27–125,15
  are its parts relatives?, 114,7–29; 124,21–126,21; 129,10–133,4
  is receptive of contraries through quality, 157,27–8
  nature of good in substance, 190,24–6
  role in formation of the six composite categories, 163,15–164,5
substratum, *hupokeimenon*
  the three-dimensional (prime matter plus extension) is called the second substratum, 83,14–17
surface, *epiphaneia*; *see also under* quantity
  surface vs. plane, 90,25–9

Thales, 118,7.23; 123,21.23.27
time, *khronos, see also under* quantity; when
  a species of continuous quantity, 84,9; 106,30
  gives rise to the category 'when', 107,29–31
  the measure of motion, 86,16–17; 87,32–88,1; 92,28
true and false
  only an affirmation and its negation divide in every case into true and false, 185,5 ff.; 186,10 ff.
  only a statement with a subject and a verb can be true or false, 185,8–19

virtue, *aretê*
  grades of, 141,23–142,3
  nature of opposition between virtues and vices, 187,27–188,17
  virtue is symmetry, vice disproportion, 188,6 ff.
  wisdom the most perfect virtue, 146,1
void, *kenon*
  motion cannot take place in a void, 86,23 ff.

when (the category), *pote; see also under* time
  a combination of substance and time, 163,19–21
  covers indications of time and things that are in time, not time itself, 164,22–3; 107,31
  three species: present, past, future, 164,23
where (the category), *pou, see also* place
  a combination of substance and place, 163,21
  covers indications of place and things that are in place, not place itself, 164,23–4; 107,31
  six species: up, down, right, left, in front, behind, 164,24 ff.

www.ingramcontent.com/pod-product-compliance
Lightning Source LLC
Chambersburg PA
CBHW072233290426
44111CB00012B/2074